From Grammar to Politics

From Grammar to Politics

Linguistic Anthropology in a Western Samoan Village

Alessandro Duranti

UNIVERSITY OF CALIFORNIA PRESS

Berkeley / Los Angeles / London

University of California Press
Berkeley and Los Angeles, California

University of California Press Ltd.
London, England

Copyright © 1994 by
The Regents of the University of California

Library of Congress Cataloging-in-Publication Data
Duranti, Alessandro.
   From grammar to politics : linguistic anthropology in a Western
Samoan village / Alessandro Duranti.
      p.   cm.
   Includes bibliographical references and index.
   ISBN 0-520-08245-1 (cloth : alk. paper)
   ISBN 0-520-08385-7 (paper : alk. paper)
   1. Political anthropology—Western Samoa—Falefā.
2. Linguistic anthropology—Western Samoa—Falefā.
3. Samoans—Western Samoa—Falefā—Politics and government.
4. Samoans—Western Samoa—Falefā—Social conditions.
5. Samoan language—Grammar.   6. Samoan language—Political
aspects—Western Samoa—Falefā.   I. Title.
GN671.S2D87   1994
306.2′099614—dc20   93-18095
                                                                        CIP

Printed in the United States of America
   2   3   4   5   6   7   8   9

mo Elenoa

Contents

Acknowledgments

The work I present in this monograph would not have been possible or even imaginable without the help and cooperation of many people and organizations. The people of Falefā, in Western Samoa, from our first days in the village, welcomed our research team and allowed us to record public events as well as more private, often even intimate interactions. Without such generosity, often mixed with a genuine intellectual curiosity about our work, we would not have been able to get so much out of our experience both at a professional and at a personal level. Several families and individuals were particularly close to us in our work and our everyday affairs. Rev. Fa'atau'oloa Mauala, his wife, Sau'iluma, and their children were first generous hosts, then dear friends, and finally invaluable collaborators. Fa'atau'oloa's interest and sophistication in linguistic matters has been a continuous source of revelations for my understanding of Samoan grammar. The head carpenter Chief Tavō (now also orator Fulumu'a) Utulei and his wife, Sui, opened their house to us and were always available for advice and warm demonstrations of friendship. The late orators 'Alo Eti and Iuli Veni (Lua Veni at the time of our first fieldwork) shared with me their knowledge of Samoan speechmaking and tradition. Chief Savea Savelio and orator Tūla'i Tino spent many long hours with me in front of a transcript or listening to a tape, explaining the subtleties of Samoan government and etiquette. The two senior orators (Matua) Moe'ono Kolio and Iuli Sefo allowed me to sit in the fono and record the proceedings for as many hours as I wanted without exerting any control over the uses I would make of such material. I also learned a great deal from the younger people in our research team. In particular, from Sililo Tapui I learned about the world of Samoan male adolescents, some of their wishes, and some of their struggles. Outside of Falefā, on warm and quiet Sunday afternoons, we often enjoyed Italian conversation and a good cup of espresso with Ernesto and Maria Coter, artists and friends. In the winter of 1978–1979, during what might have been the most challenging three months of my life for trilingual translation and cross-cultural communication, my parents Ivio and Rossana Duranti visited us in the village and shared our meals and daily routines, including sitting cross-legged on Samoan mats and listening to many hours of exchanges they could not possibly follow. Since then, their adaptability to the most diverse situations has never stopped amazing me. Finally, the members of our team-family in 1978–1979, Elinor Ochs, Martha Platt, and David Ochs Keenan, created a loving and cooperative atmosphere that not only sustained our work in its more demanding moments but also made possible our integration in the life of the community we were studying. When Elinor and I returned to Falefā in 1981 (and then later in 1988), our son Marco added a new dimension of life and study as he helped us uncover further aspects of childhood and family life in a Samoan village.

Several grant agencies and institutions helped financially in the realization of the work that is at the basis of this monograph. The National Science Foundation sponsored the first fieldwork in 1978–1979 (Grant 53-482-2480) and three more years of research in 1986–1989, including an additional trip to Falefā in the summer of 1988 (Grant BNS-8608210). Special thanks go to Paul Chapin, Director of the Linguistics Section at NSF, who has been very helpful and supportive of our efforts to stretch the boundaries of traditional linguistic research to reach out toward anthropology. Our second trip, in the spring of 1981, was sponsored by the Department of Anthropology of the Research School of Pacific Studies, at the Australian National University, while Elinor Ochs and I enjoyed postdoctoral fellowships at that university. The discussions during the rest of that academic year with an impressive and original group of researchers, including Penelope Brown, John Haviland, Judith Irvine, Roger Keesing, Stephen Levinson, Bambi Schieffelin, Edward Schieffelin, Michael Silverstein, and Robert Van Valin, provided the foundations for much of my thinking about the place of grammar in social interaction.

In the last five years, at the Department of Anthropology of the

University of California at Los Angeles, I have enjoyed an ideal academic environment, where faculty, staff, and students have made my work and my transition into a new intellectual and administrative environment extremely easy. I am especially grateful to my colleagues in linguistic anthropology, Paul Kroskrity, Claudia Mitchell-Kernan, Michael Moerman, and Marcyliena Morgan, who have been a continuous source of inspiration for their intellectual vigor and commitment to a science of language that is not divorced from culture and society. After the first draft was completed, I was very fortunate to receive detailed comments and supportive criticism from several colleagues and friends, including Aaron Cicourel, Don Brenneis, Fred Myers, and Bambi Schieffelin. Francesca Bray, Ken Cook, Chuck Goodwin, and Elizabeth Keating read a second draft and provided further insights on how to improve its organization, content, and style. My copy editor Linda Benefield added clarity and consistency by enthusiastically entering the world of Samoan language and culture and providing countless valuable suggestions.

The research presented in this book would not have been possible without the loving support of my wife Elinor Ochs, from whom I have learned the blend of discipline and passion needed to pursue what seemed at first mere intellectual matters but always turned out to be more than that.

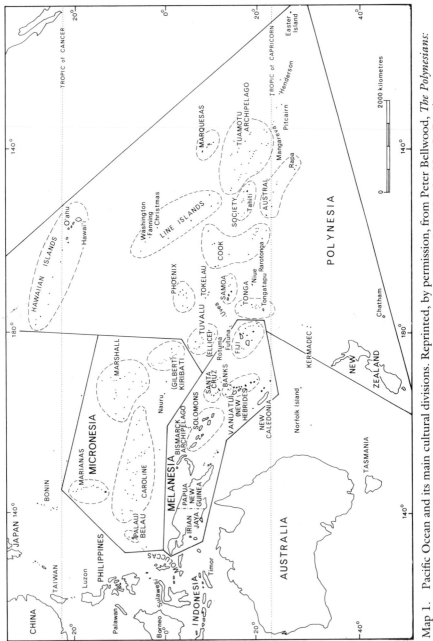

Map 1.   Pacific Ocean and its main cultural divisions. Reprinted, by permission, from Peter Bellwood, *The Polynesians: Prehistory of an Island People* (rev. ed., Thames and Hudson, 1987), 8–9. Map by Mrs. J. Goodrum.

1

Introduction

In the summer of 1978 I arrived in the village of Falefā, on the northeastern coast of 'Upolu, in Western Samoa. I was part of a research team sponsored by the National Science Foundation to document the process of language acquisition by six monolingual Samoan children. As I describe in more detail in chapter 2, when we started our project, my job was to collect and analyze the grammatical forms used by the adult population, whose speech constituted the "target" system for the young children growing up in the village. During the next thirteen months, however, I became deeply involved in a realm of verbal performance—oratory—and a domain of social action—politics—that were quite distant from the kind of phenomena I had planned to study as a linguist trained to describe grammatical patterns in discourse. Rather than collecting sentences from informants or selecting well-formed utterances out of recorded conversations, I found myself listening to people fighting to maintain political control over their constituency, defending their kin's or their own right to sit in the village council or live in the village. During this experience, my professional orientation changed in rather dramatic ways. Instead of collecting and analyzing grammatical forms, I became more and more interested in the poetical and rhetorical mechanisms through which speakers celebrate their past, make a point, win an argument, blame, apologize, accuse, invoke sentiments, and redefine their own and others' rights and duties. Through the experience of having to perform and understand political speechmaking, I came to look at grammatical patterns in political discourse from a different perspective. I saw grammar as embedded in and constitutive of political action. This book is my attempt to recapture that experience and use it as an analytical grid—or perhaps "plot"—to uncover the interrelationships among texts and the contexts of their use. The themes introduced in this chapter will be amplified and discussed in the rest of the book.

The Place of Grammar

At the start of our project in Falefā, I was interested in Samoan grammar as a set of patterns; I wanted to find out how often and under what conditions those patterns would be realized. My interest in traditional oratory, which, as I explain in chapter 2, developed out of my role in our research team (seen as an extended family), seemed at first completely disconnected from the grammar and in particular from the nominal case marking I had gone to study. At first I ventured into speechmaking thinking—and at times worrying—that it might just remain a parallel project, not necessarily associated with my doctoral research. While I was faced with the issue of how to get access to the orators' knowledge, which seemed distributed and tied to contexts difficult to re-create in interviews, I stumbled into the *fono,* the village council in which titleholders in the community discuss political and judiciary matters (see chaps. 2, 3, 4, and 5). Oratory then acquired a new dimension for me. I started to see it as intrinsically tied to social dramas, political confrontations, judiciary processes. I also became aware of the tremendous amount of variation exhibited by what appeared to be the "same" genre, the *lāuga* (ceremonial speech). I became attuned to the relationship between the features of the verbal performance and the type of social event in which it took place. While recording, transcribing, and interpreting the fono speeches, I realized that I was being exposed to a domain of discourse which was in between ceremonial oratory and everyday talk. As I later discovered, it even contained "narratives." In contrast to other places in Polynesia, for example, Tonga, where the fono are not real discussions but simply announcements of decisions taken elsewhere, in Samoa participants in a fono are expected to discuss and challenge contingent truths, although these may be embedded within the most elaborate and reassuring celebrations of eternal truths.

For quite some time, however, I did not closely connect the study of grammar with what had developed on my part into an interest in village politics. I still had two sets of lenses. I either thought of people as speakers who could provide good examples for grammatical analysis or thought of them as social actors who used language as a "form of life" (Wittgenstein 1953). Only later did I learn that in a fono certain kinds of utterances (those I will describe below as involving an "ergative Agent") were embedded within larger narratives about the events that caused a crisis to erupt or a violation to be committed. Such linguistic structures were powerful tools for the establishment and assignment of responsibility in the political arena. Only certain key actors in the community were powerful (or bold) enough to use those patterns and take advantage of their force. Others were confined to resisting definition of agency by proposing or alluding to alternative frames, in which connections of causality between people and events were less direct (viz., through different types of grammatical marking, as discussed in chap. 5). Furthermore, the discourse of conflict management that went on in a fono was itself embedded within larger interactions and in opposition to other forms of exchange and communication among the same people. As I will discuss in chapter 4, political discourse existed as a parasite genre, which was both in opposition to and based upon a different mode of verbal interaction, namely, the ceremonial speaking represented by the canonical forms of the lāuga. An understanding of the structure, content, and functions of the lāuga became crucial to an appreciation of how powerful figures in the community can come to confront each other in the context of a fono.

The Political and Moral Dimensions of Grammatical Choices

In an event such as the fono, which is largely defined by and through verbal performance (by professional speechmakers), the political struggle takes, to a large extent, the form of a linguistic problem. That is, much of the negotiation process is about how to tell or, in some cases, *not* to tell a story, how to mention or *not* to mention a given event or its agent(s). Thus, the struggle between prosecution and defense is often centered on the ability to frame the reason for the meeting as involving or not involving certain key social actors. A careful examination of the ways participants retell and work out the background knowledge that brought them together suggests that the search for a solution to the crisis is often a search for an acceptable definition of the reason(s) for the meeting. For the participants, "Why are we here today?" is not a routine rhetorical question. It is *the* question of the event. The grammatical framing used to answer this question reflects the stance a speaker takes vis-à-vis current issues or accusations. In this context, there is no neutral reconstruction or reporting of past events. As argued by Lamont Lindstrom (1992) for verbal disputes on Tanna Island, Vanuatu, the construction of what counts as "true" is but an instrument of power, which must be negotiated through the matching of appropriate domains of discourse with expected rights, duties, and responsibilities. Similarly, in the Samoan fono, there is no storytelling for the sake of storytelling. There are accusations to be made or avoided, there is blame or mitigation, there are willful agents or ignorant victims. As I show in chapter 5, each grammatical choice made by a speaker can be politically relevant. It presents certain events as valuable or damaging for the community. It introduces social actors as characters whose deeds need to be assessed. As I discuss in chapter 6, these properties of grammatical forms are not unique to the political arenas. They can be found in everyday conversation, while people tell stories about the latest fight or while children compete for a piece of food. We discover then that the explicit mentioning of certain referents as agents is not only dependent on what Wallace Chafe (1979) has called the *information flow* of discourse (e.g., whether or not the referent has been mentioned in the prior discourse) but also on what I call the *moral flow*. Transitive clauses with fully expressed agents enter in the constitution of what amounts to *a grammar of praising and blaming*, that is, a linguistically constituted moral world, in which stories are told not just because they are new information but because they can be used to assess the participants' stance with respect to important social values in the community.

Getting to the "Facts"

This book shares with phenomenologically and sociohistorically oriented approaches to social action the assumption that reality is routinely negotiated by participants in an interaction and that "facts" are constituted differently according to the points of view of the actors involved, the norms evoked, and the processes activated within specific institutional settings (e.g., legal, medical, educational). This view does not imply that there is no reality outside of talk or that all interpretations are equally acceptable, but rather it holds that in institutional as well as in mundane settings various versions of reality are proposed, sustained, or challenged precisely by the language that describes and sustains them and that such negotiations are not irrelevant linguistic games but potentially important social acts. Oral history, like the written one, is constantly being updated and negotiated. Linguistic choices play an important part in this process of shaping collective memory. Particular attention must be paid to the linguistic techniques or discourse devices used within legal and political arenas to frame the events, assign responsibility, and look for "solutions." The awareness of the strict linkage between language and sociopolitical processes has inspired anthropologists and sociologists to be more attentive to conversational interaction and discourse processes (see Brenneis 1988 for a review). To use actual "texts" produced in the course of arguments, disputes, or courtroom interactions has become more and more common (see Atkinson and Drew 1979; Goldman 1983; Goodwin 1980, 1982a, 1982b; Grimshaw 1990; Moerman 1988; Philips 1984; Watson-Gegeo and White 1990). We should continue along this road and pay close attention to the syntactic and semantic encoding of participant roles in the utterances produced within legal and political arenas as well as in more mundane contexts.

Intertextuality and Heteroglossia

The grammatical interconnection between different speech events and speech activities is one of the aspects of Samoan discourse that exhibit what literary critics called *intertextuality* (Kristeva 1986, 448) and semiotically minded anthropologists called *interpenetration* of codes (Leach 1972). The idea is simply this: even the apparently most homogeneous or self-contained text exhibits, at a close analysis, elements that link it to other texts, with different contexts, different norms, and different voices. Furthermore, what is said in one code may be echoed or even contradicted in another code. The autonomy of speech from its surrounding context and from other codes is more likely the product of analytical limitations or programmatic positions than an objective property of human communication. In all kinds of social situations, verbal and kinesic conventions interpenetrate one another to form complex messages, with multiple points of view and different voices. The intercontextual connections between genres and expressive forms help create what Mikhail Bakhtin (1981) called *heteroglossia*, namely, the simultaneous existence of multiple norms and forms. The differentiated access to such norms and forms—the ability to know them and use them—can be a crucial component of power relations in any given community. Ethnographic studies such as this one complement literary studies of heteroglossia by identifying the social roots of linguistic variation. What we learn from looking at the words produced by Samoan chiefs and orators across contexts is that variability and multiplicity of norms are not simply due to the messy nature of linguistic performance—as opposed to the orderliness of underlying, abstract models that give it meaning. Rather, the diversity of codes, genres, registers, contents, and forms—Bakhtin's "centrifugal" forces—within what is often considered the same "language" or the same (homogeneous) speech community is an outcome of the diversity of "forms of life" (Wittgenstein 1953) in which humans engage as social beings, as members of a community. The notion of *communicative competence*, originally introduced by Dell Hymes (1972a), now acquires a different meaning that goes beyond the cognitive connotations inherited from Noam Chomsky's (1965) notion of competence. To be a competent member of a given speech community means to be an active consumer and producer of texts that exploit heteroglossia and at the same time reproduce at least the appearance of an overall encompassing system.

An aspect of intertextuality that has continued to intrigue me has been the interplay between verbal and kinesic behavior. In particular, as discussed in chapter 2, spatial distinctions seem to reverberate claims and rights assigned through linguistic means such as the ceremonial address or the right to speak at a certain time.[1] But the right of certain names to be mentioned and the right of certain people to sit in a given place offer only incomplete models of the social order. Participants, in their various roles, are busy producing orders and oppositions that can be assessed and played against legitimate expectations. Intertextuality—across channels and material resources (viz., sounds vs. physical bodies)—asserts common goals, namely, support of a particular social order, while also hinting at possible variations. Thus, the different channels—body position and body motions versus address forms and rights to speak—enter the economy of both centripetal (by reconfirming similar orders) and centrifugal (by offering slight variations or violations) forces in the semiotically constructed political economy of the community.

Representations of the Social Order

The ethnography of Samoan political discourse presented in the chapters to follow supports a view of social structure as extremely dynamic or, more precisely, as a joint achievement produced by a number of individuals and institutions, tied by specific collective activities. It is within such an ever-evolving structure that communication can have the crucial role that I claim for it in this monograph. As I suggest in chapter 3, many principles and considerations can enter the representation of power relations. Thus, the person who is in charge of assigning kava at a Samoan fono has access to a number of criteria for choosing one order over another—conversely, members of the audience have potentially similar but not necessarily identical sets of interpretive principles. At the same time, the choices made at any given time can give legitimacy to established orders as well as to new political configurations. In this process, in other words, the social actor is never alone. Others, copresent, will let the server know whether the choices made are acceptable or not. This I have encountered again and again in my Samoan experience and have tried to represent here in analytical-descriptive terms. Whether the issue is the place where one decides to sit or the point at which one decides to take the floor, others will have the option of opposing choices that seem violative, sometimes by framing them as "not fitting."

The joint nature of representations and interpretations, however, does not entail equal power by all members. In fact, communication in the political arena of the fono continuously reasserts differentiation, without denying an institutional commitment to negotiation. Hierarchical relations and differential access to resources are always represented at many levels. Such multilayer representations allow for different actors to appropriate or affect the process in their own terms and with their own individual (however limited) authority and expertise. No one knows whether a small change performed today will be remembered next week or next year. But the possibility of such longitudinal effects makes participation more engaging, makes socially constructed collectivity potentially susceptible to individual agency.

As discussed in chapter 3, the fono house itself can be seen as a "station" (in Hägerstrand's sense) and a "locale" (in Giddens's sense) that defines the participants as part of a privileged body of persons in the community, that is, a group of people who have direct access to political decision making. Not only is the right to be inside the fono house significant for someone's status and prestige in the community, but the specific place where he or she sits is also important. The cultural organization of space within the fono house, with its "front" and "back" regions, for instance, represents a powerful resource for that interplay between background assumptions and emergent patterns that enters into what Anthony Giddens (1979, 1984) calls the "duality of structure." The organization of space in the fono house is itself both resource for and outcome of the established social order (Pader 1988). It is a resource because it presents itself as part of a more general patterning of positions which can be expected to be at work in any social encounter in Samoa. In other words, it assumes a general model, with traditional distinctions and complementary relations between chiefs and orators, between high-ranking and lower-ranking titled individuals, between politically active members and those who are witness to their actions. Some of the same distinctions relevant in a fono are thus also relevant in other contexts, for instance in a Sunday meal (to'ona'i) with the pastor and the deacons. The organization of space in a fono or a Sunday meal is however also an outcome, an emergent structure that can never be completely predicted. A clear case of this is represented in chapter 3 by the decision of orator Tafili[2] Sofa'i to sit in the front row despite the fact that an orator from her subvillage is already there. She thus asserts her status, namely, her right to be sitting in the front, and at the same time her determination to be an active participant in the forthcoming discussion. As we shall see, the reactions to her decision illustrate the dynamic nature of the Samoan political system: her active participation is first recognized in the kava ceremony and later during the discussion.

Change

As any ethnographic account of Samoan society suggests (see Mead 1930), the fono is seen by the participants themselves as a faithful map of the political structure of the unit it embodies (subvillage,

village, extended village, district, etc.). Such a unit is always given an internal hierarchical organization, whether it is instantiated in the seating plan or in the ceremonial address (*fa'alupega*) discussed in chapter 3.

The study of discourse and other semiotic resources employed in a fono can be an invaluable tool for assessing ongoing or future changes in the hierarchical social structure of a village. In particular, the detailed study of communication in face-to-face encounters makes the ethnographer less dependent on members' characterizations of their own social system and hence less dependent on group idealizations or individual interests.

As has been discussed by other ethnographers who studied Samoan society, ceremonial addresses change over time. Certain names are dropped and others are added. The analysis of the actual discourse produced by the people gathered in a fono presented in chapter 5 gives us important hints on the likely direction of future changes. More importantly, however, it gives us an alternative map of the power structure in the community. The fact that explicit assertions of agency, for instance, are made more often by certain parties than by others and that certain members of the fono tend to avoid direct commitment to claims of responsibility are important hints about the political direction of the community and any emerging leaders. This is particularly important in the context of twentieth-century Samoa, where the traditional *matai* system—in which a few titled people (matai), typically older men, are in total control of the material and human resources of their families and communities—is partly under attack from external and internal forces. As pointed out by a high chief in one of his concluding speeches, there are now in Samoa two orders: the traditional structure at the village and district level, with its emphasis on hierarchy, public debate, and search for consensus, and the new order of the central government, with its implied and imported notions of equality, free elections, and secret ballot. A close examination of the fono proceedings can give us important clues about the position of a particular polity and its leaders vis-à-vis pressing Western values and institutions (see Duranti 1990a).

Talk and Conflict: The Relevance of Genre Distinctions

We learned from a number of detailed studies of conflict management in different cultures (see the articles in Bloch 1975b; Brenneis and Myers 1984; Watson-Gegeo and White 1990) that the mere possibility of communication among parties with competing interests is a first important step in the necessary negotiations for any resolution or containment of conflict. Getting the matai to sit down and talk is that very first step. It signifies a willingness on their part to maintain or reproduce some kind of order. In the Samoan case such order implies hierarchies, predetermined dependencies, and complementary oppositions. We need, however, much more than the general category "talk" to understand how a diverse audience can reach a state of cooperation that will generate acceptable definitions of the "problem" and some of its possible solutions. Even hierarchical Samoa limits the ability of a powerful party to impose a solution on a less powerful one. A Samoan proverb says that no matai prepares the oven for another matai, meaning that once someone has a matai title, that person has some sovereignty over his or her own actions. Such sovereignty is in fact secured by the matai's right to sit in a fono. Any charge against a matai must be presented to the assembly, which must approve by consensus any redressing action. The rhetorical devices used in such an arena must be both flexible and constraining. How is talk in the fono shaped to represent diverse interests and agreed-upon compromises? How does talk, in turn, help shape the interaction and the solutions arrived at? The mechanisms for controlling the length and content of a speech, as discussed in chapter 3, are an example of the ways in which one person's linguistic contributions are actively shaped by the other participants' acts. The use of different styles and genres, such as the "corruption" of the ceremonial *lāuga* to fit the needs of contingent problems and contemporary issues, is an example of the ways in which different linguistic forms and patterns are conducive to different kinds of actions: reassuring and celebrating in the opening speech as opposed to argumentative and persuasive in the later discussion (*talanoaga*).[3]

As shown in chapter 4, different kinds of speech events also allow for different types of contributions by coparticipants. The interruptions within the fono, although structurally similar to the interruptions in ceremonial settings, must be understood in a different "key," namely, as more serious and more dangerous acts.

My analysis includes attention to patterns of use, including overall organizations of events and their parts, boundaries of activities, and native categorizations of the elements invoked by the participants. I underscore the processual, co-constructed nature of discourse units. The choices that are made during the performance of a speech must be supported by the recipients. One's ability to carry through, to make it to the end, is only partly guaranteed by one's status (e.g., chief vs. orator) or rank (high vs. low). As we will see in chapter 3, for instance, even a high chief might be unable to break the first round of speakers and quickly end the meeting by admitting his fault. He may be asked to wait his turn and let lower-status orators finish their round of speeches.

What Kind of Pragmatics Is This?

To the extent to which the study of Samoan discourse presented here relates patterns of speaking to other dimensions of interaction, it falls within the domain of study called "pragmatics." At the same time, the nature of the phenomena studied and the methods for their analysis differ in some important ways from pragmatics as usually practiced within linguistics and the philosophy of language tradition. In these disciplines, the term *pragmatics* is used for the study of the relationship between linguistic expressions and certain aspects of the context of their use, including speaker, hearer(s), social situation, and spatial and temporal coordinates (Carnap 1942; Morris 1938; Levinson 1983). Such a broad definition would seem to naturally comprise cultural practices, including the empirical study of speaking as a form of political action or as an instrument of artistic performance. Instead, somewhat predictably, pragmatic studies within linguistics and philosophy are strongly influenced by the theoretical and methodological concerns of those disciplines, which have very little interest or expertise in the study of culture. The kind of pragmatics presented in this book, however, is informed by analytical concerns developed within sociocultural anthropology and, in particular, within approaches to the study of verbal performance which are ethnographically grounded. I like to refer to such an approach as *ethnopragmatics*, by which I mean a study of language use which relies on ethnography to illuminate the ways in which speech is both constituted by and constitutive of social interaction (see chap. 7). Thus, drawing from a number of descriptive and analytical traditions, including the ethnography of speaking, conversation analysis, and literary studies, I will present here a picture of Samoan discourse as always embedded within socioculturally organized activities and as constituted by a heterogeneity of codes, genres, and grammatical forms. Furthermore, rather than systematically hiding the persona of the linguist-ethnographer engaged in linguistic analysis, I will at times try to make my experience of Samoan discourse part of the data in need of description.

A Speech Event Approach

The accounts and analyses presented in the following chapters represent a small part of a larger project that is meant to provide an ethnography of everyday speaking in a traditional Samoan village. It continues and elaborates the discussion presented in my *The Samoan Fono* and Elinor Och's *Culture and Language Development* and in a number of articles and book chapters by the same authors (see References).

In this case, I have mostly concentrated on one particular social event, the fono, seen as a *speech event* (Hymes 1972b), that is, as a bounded strip of social actions that are mostly, but not exclusively, constituted through linguistic performance. The meaning of the language of such events can be more fully appreciated only if we are prepared to look beyond speaking and beyond one specific event. For these reasons, in chapter 3 I will illustrate the use of spatial and temporal relations in a fono. Through such a discussion, we will be in a better position to appreciate the role of language in the midst of other sophisticated semiotic resources. Speech, it will be shown, is only one of the available codes, possibly the most powerful in this context but not necessarily the independent one. I will in fact suggest that the simultaneous use of a variety of codes is crucial to the constitution of a dynamic social system, which allows for multiple and socially distributed representations of the local hierarchies. A variety of codes easily translates into a variety of interpretive keys for the constitution of a stratified access to political decisions and economic resources.

The cross-contextual perspective characteristic of the ethnography of communication approach will be especially put to use in chapters 4, 5, and 6.

In chapter 4, I compare the speech of matai in a fono with their speech in other public events where aesthetic canons play a major role. The differences between various implementations of what is essentially one stock of poetic and rhetorical devices—the lāuga genre in the general sense—point toward a variety of roles of speechmaking, depending on the nature of the social event, and toward the emergent creation of a hybrid genre that displays some of the very characteristics of linguistic heteroglossia predicted in M. Bakhtin's (1981) dialogical approach to the uses of language in the novel.

In chapter 5, I examine the role of grammar in the constitution of agency and hence responsibility in political discourse. My main point will be that, if much of the confrontation in a fono takes the shape of talk—and consensus is indeed established through linguistic coordination around a common problem—it is linguistic forms that we must study in order to understand the assumptions as well as the outcomes of such a political event. We will then learn that there is a place for grammar in the study of political struggle and juridical negotiations. The very same grammatical morphemes and constructions that seemed so rare in the early stages of my fieldwork experience turn out to be part of the very essence of one of the major aspects of Samoan social life, namely, the political process.

In chapter 6, I extend the study of the constitution of agency to everyday settings to show that rather than separate and largely irrelevant to each other, as often presented in the common wisdom of ethnographic studies and programmatic statements (see Bloch 1975b), formal or institutional talk and everyday talk can illuminate each other. The understanding of the role and force of ergative case marking gained from the analysis of political speeches helps us understand the dynamics of interactions that characterize family politics and a wide range of social relations in a Samoan community. The presence or absence of a particular grammatical construction should not then remain the exclusive concern of linguistic anthropologists interested in discourse patterns and language use but should become a common research ground for any social scientist interested in the dynamic construction of power and responsibility across all kinds of social situations.

2

Methods as Forms of Life

The ability to understand linguistic texts in the context of the sociocultural activities in which they originated is an essential part of any attempt to explicate speech as a cultural phenomenon. At the same time, a century of attention to language as a formal system has shown that linguistic expressions can also be removed from their original contexts of use and analyzed as autonomous, independent objects whose structures have a logic of their own, not necessarily isomorphic with their functions in acts of speaking. In other words, just as air *affords* breathing and hard soil *affords* walking (Gibson 1986), *language is a medium that affords formal description and manipulation*. Words and sentences can be decomposed, substituted, and reassembled in new orders and with what seems to be only a small price in meaning depreciation. Such metalinguistic activities are themselves fascinating and in many respects rewarding for the dedicated specialist. As any student of linguistics knows, time flies when one starts to manipulate linguistic expressions in search of generalizations about their paraphrasability and sequential constraints. Time also flies when one gets busy writing logical proofs using linguistic propositions. It is easy to assume that the symbols we are studying can be freely manipulated once we separate them from the forms of life and social activities they presuppose. To the analyst, it might appear that there are no limits to how far one can go in abstracting from the contexts of speech, just as there seem to be no limits to how far one can go in contextualizing speech and evoking new layers of meaning.

Such a freedom, however, is but an illusion. Categorizations, abstractions, and argumentations, like any other form of human thinking, are always embedded in cultural practices. And for this reason what may seem obvious in the world of Western science that we inhabit and sustain through our actions and writings can become strange or absurd in other contexts, with different participants and cultural traditions. Our assumptions about what constitutes appropriate levels of linguistic description encounter unforeseen obstacles when we change the context of our inquiry. For linguists this experience may take place when they move from one subdiscipline to another, as, for instance, when grammarians become fascinated by sociolinguistic variation and try to discuss language use with the same line of reasoning they were using when working on sentences in isolation and native speakers' acceptability judgments. They soon discover that in the world of language in context one cannot apply the same type of methods and argumentation that form the backbone of grammatical description (see Labov 1972a, 1972b). An even more dramatic experience may be awaiting those students of language who leave the familiar grounds of academic institutions and actually venture into "the field." In these cases, two alternative ways of working are possible.[1] I will refer to them as *field linguistics* and *ethnographic linguistics*.

Field Linguistics

In this paradigm of field research, the linguists take only relative advantage of being in the community where the language they want to study is spoken. Rather than recording and analyzing the language native speakers use *with one another* in the course of their daily lives, researchers in this tradition identify a few key speakers who can provide them with the information needed to construct grammatical descriptions of the language.

What makes a good informant? The basic prerequisite is that the informant be an intelligent person with a good linguistic intuition. This means someone who is sensitive to the workings of language and who can convey to the linguist what nuances of meaning are, someone who likes his/her language and is proud of it, and someone who enjoys discovering together with the field worker its mechanisms, laws, and exceptions. (Craig 1979, 10)

Being on site is considered a better way of having access to such "good informants," that is, native speakers who are willing to be trained, as well as an opportunity for the linguist to hear the language spoken in a natural environment, but it is not necessarily a way of understanding the language through people's actions. Very much in the paradigm of "autonomous syntax" proposed by American structuralists in the first part of this century and more recently upgraded to "cognitive science" by the writings of Chomsky, the linguists in this tradition—regardless of their own theoretical preferences—need to create contexts in which they can systematically separate the native speakers from the flow of social life they are normally part of in order to instruct them in the ways of linguistico-analytical techniques necessary for grammatical descriptions. Rather than seeing the native speakers as teachers of the language, field grammarians often see them as potential students, that is, sensitive natives who can learn to apply the linguist's methods to their own native intuitions.

Ideally, good informants should be considered and treated as potential linguists; they should be taught linguistics and encouraged to investigate their own language, for they have the native intuition on which all good linguistic analysis must rely. (Craig 1979, 13)

For everyone but the person who has already served as a linguistic informant, the first weeks or months will be a time of training. Even the best candidates will have failings which must be corrected. . . .
   The ultimate goal is to get the informant to think about language as the investigator does, that is, in terms of broad generalizations based on what is actually said or could be said. (Samarin 1967, 41)

Linguistic data are thus collected by eliciting sentences from a few "good" (usually bilingual) informants and, in some cases, by eliciting a few "texts." Such texts are either written down by the native speakers or narrated into a tape recorder. Since they must be told by one person into a tape recorder, these texts must by definition be monologic:

The topics of the texts collected may vary from traditional or mythological tales retold, most often, by older people to narratives recounting remarkable events in the life of the community—weddings, fiestas, and accidents—or routine activities such as how to grow corn, make tortillas, make soap, or build a house. (Craig 1979, 21)

Such methods keep the linguist in control of the linguistic products. They guarantee that the native speakers do not impose their own agendas on the researcher. It is the latter who decides whose language should be recorded and which genres are appropriate for extracting grammatical forms and inferring grammatical rules.

Ethnographic Linguistics

By contrast, in ethnographic linguistics, which is practiced by most but not all linguistic anthropologists (or anthropological linguists),[2] the researcher's goal is to understand linguistic forms as constitutive elements of cultural practices. Ethnographic linguistics is an emergent method of linguistic investigation that uses participant-observation and recording of spontaneous indigenous interactions as the starting points of any analytical discussion of the forms and contents of language as a social activity. It is influenced by but not necessarily identifiable with several approaches, including the ethnography of communication (see Bauman and Sherzer 1974, 1975; Gumperz and Hymes 1964, 1972), sociolinguistic studies of urban speech communities (see Labov 1972a, 1972b), and recent attempts to blend ethnography and conversation analysis (see Goodwin 1990; Moerman 1988).

In this approach, ethnography as the documentation of local ways of interacting and interpreting the world is extended to the analysis of talk. Native speakers are seen not as *informants* but as *social actors*. Rather than spending most of their time eliciting examples and acceptability judgments from native speakers, ethnographically oriented field linguists must be able to participate in, record, and analyze *locally meaningful speech events,* that is, situations in which language is used for ends other than the linguist's need to collect examples (see Hymes 1972a; Duranti 1985). In this perspective, grammatical description of sentences or morphemes is only one part of the research agenda, and typically it is in a subordinate role to descriptions of higher-level units such as, for example, speech genres (Bauman 1992; Duranti 1981b, 1983; Kuipers 1990; Sherzer 1983). For those who are interested in language as a social activity, grammatical forms must be routinely connected to speech acts, speech acts to speech activities, speech activities to events and larger institutional settings (Cicourel 1992).

Maintaining this complex level of analysis, however, presents several challenges. The most difficult one is the special type of relationship de facto existing between language and culture. Such a relationship is best illustrated through a drawing that I am borrowing from Gestalt psychology (see fig. 1), the famous vase/faces picture. Language and culture stand with respect to one another very much like the vase and the faces. They are interdependent, that is, they mutually constitute one another. There is no vase without the faces and there are no faces without the vase. The same can be said about language and culture. One cannot exist without the other. When researchers concentrate on seeing one of the images (the *figure*), however, the other one disappears (or becomes the *ground*). Similarly, every time researchers concentrate on either language or culture, they easily lose track of the other.

Once researchers become interested in social life, it is difficult for them to go back to sentences and morphemes and even harder to maintain a dialogue with those students of language who are mostly interested in its formal properties (Duranti 1985). The exclusive focus on language as a formal system is easier to maintain as long as we stick to forms and try to keep the contents of speaking out of the way. As soon as we venture into the real world of speech exchanges as social encounters, with their negotiations, challenges, and material as well as ideational consequences, linguistic forms become *invisible*,[3] that is, they acquire the same *unobtrusiveness* that Martin Heidegger characterized as typical of tools and other familiar objects we use in our daily life:[4]

The beings we encounter in the everyday commerce have in a preeminent way the character of *unobtrusiveness*. We do not always and continually have explicit perception of the things surrounding us in a familiar environment, certainly not in such a way that we would be aware of them expressly as handy. It is precisely because an explicit awareness and assurance of their being at hand does not occur that we have them around us in a peculiar way, just as they are in themselves. In the indifferent imperturbability of our customary commerce with them, they become accessible precisely with regard to their unobtrusive presence. (Heidegger 1988, 309)

In taking language for granted, researchers in various fields, social and cultural anthropology included, go along with the *natural* attitude of not being able to see the workings of language, that is, those specific features that make it a ready-to-use object (they see the faces but cannot see the vase). Ethnographic linguists, by stressing the importance of ethnography as a research practice, are concerned precisely with the exposure of the unobtrusiveness of language as a particular type of cultural artifact (see Whorf 1956).

Figure 1. Figure-Ground relation

In Search of a Method

If we become concerned with establishing a balance between the readiness-to-use properties of language and its formal attributes, a method must be found (or agreed upon) for such an enterprise. For such a reunion of different perspectives to take place, linguist-ethnographers must immerse themselves in different projects at different times. For the same reason for which it is impossible to see both the vase and the faces at the same time, it might in fact be impossible to be simultaneously a participant and observer and a field linguist interested in grammatical patterns. Those two personae must be distinct in time and place, even though such times and places may not be too far from one another—that is, separated by only a few hours or a few yards. This is true for language just as it is true for culture. The recent criticism of ethnographic methods (see Clifford and Marcus 1986; Clifford 1988, 1990) must take the need of such a spatiotemporal separation into consideration. We cannot write about what we have seen *while* we are seeing it. And we cannot write without a language and a writing instrument (e.g., a pencil, a typewriter). That these instruments count is no news. The problem is how to display their *counting*, how to show what has been produced by the different ways not only of describing our subjects but also of interacting with them. Despite the wave of insightful criticism of ethnography as a cultural practice, we still haven't learned to say what we gain by choosing one form of representation over another (e.g., a photograph over a tape recording, a three-by-five-

inch index card over a computer file, a videotape over a written description of what we can remember a few hours or sometimes a few years
later). That such discussions are often not admissible or not reputed to
be interesting in the context of academic writing is indicative of a widespread methodological deprivation complex, that is, the fear of waking
up without having a method and, hence, without having a science.

In the next few sections I will briefly discuss my own methodological
transformation in the field, as I moved from one type of interest and
expertise, field linguistics, to another type, ethnographic linguistics. The
path followed in such an intellectual journey coincides more with the
experience of living up to people's expectations about my role and prerogatives than with my own predetermined methodological preferences.
One of the messages I tried to include in the pages that follow is that
methods are not always (or perhaps never) completely predetermined.
They are not only brought in the field, they are also found. More often,
they are the product of a dialogue between radically different traditions.
It is of such a product, in its developmental dimension, that we should
be ready to tell our colleagues so that they might judge not only the
results of our research but the path through which such results were
made possible. It is of such a path that I now tell.

The NSF Project

In the summer of 1978 I went to Western Samoa as a
graduate student in a research team directed by Elinor Ochs, then professor of linguistics at the University of Southern California. Ochs had
received a grant from the National Science Foundation to study the
acquisition of a non-Indo-European language like Samoan (an Austronesian language). She pointed out that most of the putative universals
of language acquisition up to then were based on a restricted number
of languages (e.g., English, Italian) with a relatively homogeneous set
of grammatical features. Samoan morphology and syntax could offer a
much-needed test case for some of those universals. To collect a comparable set of data, Ochs and another graduate student, Martha Platt,
were to transfer the longitudinal study techniques adopted in collecting
linguistic corpora in American and European white middle-class homes
to the study of the language of Samoan households. Their plan was to
follow the development of six young children from six different families

in the same Western Samoan village over a period of approximately twelve months. The interactions of the children with the other members of their families would be audiotaped at regular intervals and (once a month for half an hour) videotaped in the children's natural habitats, while surrounded by or interacting with their caregivers or peers.

Like any child language acquisition project, Ochs's also needed to rely on a good description of the "target" language, that is, the adults' linguistic system that the child was expected to acquire. Before arriving in Samoa, we suspected that the Samoan grammar described in the existing literature was but a pale image of what was spoken in everyday interaction in the village. Even Andrew Pawley's (1966) careful study of Samoan morpho-syntax and George Milner's (1966) excellent dictionary had an aura of "proper" speaking that to us was a limitation. We wanted to become familiar with the range of phonological, morphological, syntactic, semantic, and pragmatic structures used both inside and outside the household by native Samoan speakers in the course of their daily lives. We wanted to have a clear idea of the *communicative competence* (Hymes 1972a) that a Samoan child, whether boy or girl, was expected to master as part of his or her socialization process. Such information was only scantily available in the literature. We needed a firsthand look.

I was hired as a consultant to compare grammatical descriptions of proper or elicited Samoan with the patterns inferable from recordings of adults talking with one another in a variety of settings. I had been trained by Larry Hyman to work with native speakers of Bantu languages and produce syntactic and morphological descriptions. I had also collaborated with Ochs on a research project on Italian syntax based on conversational data. I was still completing articles on pronouns in Bantu languages and Italian conversations at the beginning of my stay in Samoa. For my doctoral thesis, the range of phenomena I had in mind did not go beyond syntactic analysis of spontaneous discourse.

One feature of Samoan that prompted a professional interest in its language acquisition is a particular type of grammatical marking called *ergativity,* a property of languages in which the subject of transitive clauses (e.g., *the boy* in *the boy broke the ball*)—also called *agent*—is treated differently from the subject of intransitive clauses (e.g., *the ball* in *the ball broke*) (see next section and chap. 5). This typological characteristic of Samoan, which is shared by many other languages in the world but not by English and other well-known European languages, raised a number of interesting questions for child language acquisition:

how do children acquire such a system? What is the interplay between word order and case marking in such a language? What kinds of (over)generalizations would children make when faced with a system that seems to favor semantic factors over syntactic ones?

For my thesis, I envisioned myself examining, in the adult language, the interplay between grammatical marking and discourse features such as word order and pronominalization. I wanted to stretch the boundaries of field linguistics to include texts of a different nature from the usual ones and for this reason I was planning to record conversations. But I did not see myself as someone interested in verbal art and even less did I consider myself an ethnographer.

Research Agendas and Acquired Social Identities

On July 25, 1978, after exactly three weeks spent in a hotel in the Western Samoan capital, Apia, we moved to Falefā, a relatively large village of about twelve hundred people along the northeastern coast of 'Upolu. Our integration into village life was rather smooth. With the help of the village pastor, Fa'atau'oloa Mauala, and his wife, Sau'iluma, we easily found several people willing to help us with our project. We soon encountered, however, a typical problem of fieldwork. Our roles in the community could not be simply defined by professional affiliation or expertise. We needed to fit into the local logic of kinship relations. I was the only adult male of our group. This had several consequences. First of all, it meant that Elinor Ochs's status as a professor and principal investigator in the project and my status as a graduate student hired as "consultant" became irrelevant. These were terms that had meanings for the world of granting agencies and Western academic institutions but were not locally relevant categories. It also didn't matter that Martha Platt and I thought of each other as fellow students and friends. What mattered instead was that Elinor and I were a couple (*ulugāli'i*) and that even before her seven-year-old son David arrived, two months later, we were a family. Martha was also part of our family. The first day we arrived in the village of Falefā, while Elinor and I were explaining our project to the Samoan pastor and his wife, Martha was asked by the children who hung around the pastor's house how old her father was. Before answering, she had time to turn and see that the children were looking at me. There are three or four years difference between the two of us. At that moment we were being introduced into the Polynesian logic of kinship and social relations.

"Father" (Samoan *tamā*) is any adult male who provides for you, protects you, and is concerned with your public behavior (see Hogbin 1934). In our small "family," I was the only possible candidate. From that moment on, women would praise Martha in front of me, adult males would joke about when I was going to get her a husband, and children would continually come to report to me about Martha's doings so that I could assess whether she was behaving as was expected of her.

The combination of being the father of the family (*tamā o le 'āiga*) and being seen as someone in control of substantial financial resources (I was the one who paid our research assistants at the end of the week) gave me both the authority and the responsibility that in Samoa are ascribed to the titled person of the family, that is, the *matai*. Like a Samoan matai, I would be seen as the one representing my family in making decisions, granting permissions, requesting labor, and providing food and economic resources for those working for us and, in some cases, for their relatives. Some of the young people who worked for us were often seen as part of our extended family (*'āiga*). Thus, for instance, when I took one of them, Sililo Tapui, to the district hospital to be treated for an infection, the nurse asked me what was wrong with my "son" (*atali'i*).

The next important consequence of being seen and treated as the matai of the family was that I was expected to speak on public occasions on behalf of the family. Despite the fact that my social status in the community would make me more likely to be seen as a "chief" (*ali'i*) than as an "orator" (*tulāfale*), being the only adult male of the group meant that I had to perform both roles[5]—part of my socialization to Samoan life-style involved learning how to switch from one role to the other.

The fact that my fluency in Samoan was very limited when we first arrived in the village did not stop people from expecting me to perform verbally. To the extent to which they immediately accepted and facilitated our goal of understanding the Samoan way of life (*fa'aSāmoa*), the people in Falefā could not but expect me to comply equally readily with the social status they were willing to grant me for the success of our project. The ability to speak in public arenas was one of the fundamental aspects of my social persona. After only a few weeks in the village, once our two houses—one for Elinor, me, and (later) David and

the other for Martha—were completed, I was expected to give a ceremonial speech (lāuga) on behalf of our "family" at the big feast where
the carpenters were paid and the people of the village thanked for accepting us into their community.

It was around that time that my interest in traditional oratory began
or, rather, was stimulated by the events. Once I realized that giving
speeches was perceived as one of my duties, I decided to learn a bit
more about Samoan oratory.

I should point out that at this point (after a few weeks in the village)
the acquisition project was well under way. Elinor and Martha had already identified the six children (in six different families) they were going to study and had begun recording at regular intervals. They had
also started to train some of the young people in the village to transcribe
for them. On my part, I had also started to work on grammatical patterns with a couple of young bilingual people in the village and had
begun to make a few recordings of conversational interactions which
were also being transcribed.

In a few more weeks, I started to develop a sense of unease about
what I perceived as a radical difference between the type of data that I
was able to elicit from bilingual speakers and the utterances recorded
during interactions among Samoans themselves.

One of the most striking findings in my own work, also supported
by the recordings made by Elinor and Martha during household interactions, was what at first seemed a relatively rare use of ergativity in
spoken discourse. That the pattern existed and was alive and well was
confirmed by the ease with which it could be elicited. Asked to translate
English sentences like the two given below, Samoan bilingual speakers
would promptly[6] produce the classic ergative pattern, with the subject
of the transitive clause marked differently—with the preposition e—
from the subject of the intransitive clause—with no preposition—(see
Appendix for the abbreviations used in the interlinear glosses of Samoan
examples and chap. 5 for a discussion of the ergative pattern):

(a) *The boy* caught the fish in the net.
(b) *The boy* went to Apia.

(a) *na   pu'e   e   le   tama   le   i'a   i   le   'upega.*
    PST catch ERG ART boy ART fish in ART   net
    The boy caught the fish in the net.

(b) *na alu le tama 'i Apia.*
    PST go ART boy to Apia
    The boy went to Apia.

In other words, Samoan grammar distinguishes between a human actor (e.g., the boy in [a]) whose actions have consequences for another entity (e.g., the fish in [a]) and an actor (e.g., the boy in [b]) whose actions have consequences only for himself. It is the first type of subject or "Agent" that is distinctively marked in ergative languages.

In spontaneous linguistic interaction, however, such sentences seemed rare. In fact, in the first transcript I worked on, during an intense fifteen-minute conversation mostly between two people, only one case of ergative Agent could be found. This one case is reproduced below in example (1) (see the discussion at the end of this chapter for transcription conventions of Samoan examples taken from transcripts of spontaneous interactions):

(1) Pastor and Deacon.

    A; 'ae ga fai mai ā e lākou
    but PST do DX EMP ERG they
    But they did (it) (for us)

In addition, such an example was not a "canonical" one, in the sense that (i) only the agent was present (that is, no object noun phrase was expressed), (ii) the agent was expressed by a pronoun rather than by a full noun, and (iii) it had an emphatic connotation provided by the emphatic particle *ā* after the verb and by the very presence of the pronoun, which is relatively rare in spoken discourse (see Duranti 1981a; Duranti and Ochs 1990; Ochs 1988).[7]

Although in subsequent transcripts, depending on the type of interaction among participants, the number of utterances with ergative markers increased, our research team continued to be puzzled by these frequencies and the apparent discrepancy between elicited forms and utterances in spoken discourse.

It is in this context that my initial interest in speechmaking should be framed. It provided an alternative to a type of work which was becoming increasingly difficult to make sense of and organize. I felt disappointed by the kind of data I was obtaining by elicitation, but at the same time I did not quite know where to go next with the conversational data. I was discovering some of the problems of mixing methodologies. There are reasons—many of them left implicit—for field researchers not to go beyond elicited texts (i.e., stay within the boundaries of field linguistics as previously defined), and there are also reasons for ethnographic linguists to shy away from grammar and concentrate on verbal art. I had broken the boundaries of the methodological genre without having a clear idea about how to operate with these new types of hybrid data and how to integrate them with traditional analytical descriptions of linguistic structures.

Interviews, Metalinguistic Awareness, and Native Taxonomies

To learn more about speechmaking, I decided to ask a few knowledgeable members of the community some basic questions about speechmaking. I had learned that the word for "formal or cere-monial speech" was *lāuga* and, with the help of a couple of bilingual people in the village, I made up a list of questions to ask "experts," mainly speechmakers (*failāuga*) in the village. At first I concentrated on questions of order; in particular, I almost immediately started to focus on the internal sequential organization of formal speeches. I know now that what I was doing then was extending field linguistics methods from grammatical forms to speech genres. The problems I encountered were then due to the fact that units larger than sentences do not readily afford the same kind of analysis that sentences do.

I should mention here that people were very eager to talk about speechmaking. Not only was it a permissible topic, but it was also some-thing that everyone felt proud of. There was no question that for me to spend time with adult men asking questions about traditional oratory seemed a perfectly legitimate and worthwhile activity to everyone in the village. This was so for at least two reasons. First, speechmaking is rightly felt to be one of the most important aspects of Samoan cultural tradition—something for which Samoans would like, and in my opinion deserve, to be known to the rest of the world. Second, it seemed ap-propriate to everyone that I would try to learn traditional speechmak-ing: it would make me into a better member of the community. Thus my curiosity was not only justifiable but routinely encouraged and even praised.

This reaction was quite different from the response at first given to the interest exhibited by the other two members of our research team for spending time around toddlers and observing them babble, cry, fight, curse, sleep, and be fed. In contrast to my inquiring about an old and honorable tradition like oratory, Elinor Ochs's and Martha Platt's curiosity about babies, siblings, and mothers made little sense to our Samoan hosts, as manifested by the fact that their activities were initially reframed by the people in the village: Elinor's and Martha's observation and recording of children's behavior in the household was at first re-labeled as "doing school" (*fai le a'oga*), despite their repeated attempts to explain that not only did they not want to teach anything to the children but they did not wish to attract any special attention or be treated with any particular respect (see Ochs 1988, 1–2).

At first I enjoyed doing something that was not only acceptable but meaningful to the people in the village (or at least to those who knew what I was doing). I discovered that there are different types of lāuga. Speechmakers told me that there are "Monday speeches," speeches for the artist-carpenter (*tufuga*), speeches for the affines (*paolo*), speeches for the exchange of fine mats (*'ie toga*), speeches for the installation of a new title (*saofa'i*), and so on. At the time, most of these terms didn't have more than a dictionary meaning for me.

When I asked about the structure of a lāuga, I learned that there were parts (*vāega*) and that they could be named. I also found a variety of answers concerning the number of parts: some people would say three, others four, and one young but reputedly knowledgeable orator went up to seven. The seemingly variable knowledge displayed by the orators in the community could be a form of distributed knowledge (different people had access to different bodies of knowledge) or the effect of a faulty methodology. In the latter case, at least two possibilities came to mind: either I wasn't asking the question in the right way or I shouldn't ask it at all. I decided to stop asking questions and instead invite a few orators to show me what a real speech sounded like. After having transcribed the speech, I would ask them to identify the different parts.

The result of this other method was not very satisfying either. I col-lected long speeches, short ones, some with three parts, some with four or five. In one case, I succeeded in getting the maximum number of parts (seven) and clear boundaries between each of them—I asked the orator to stop before a new part began. While going over the transcript of the speech, the same speechmaker realized that he had "mixed" parts from speeches for different occasions (Duranti 1983). Simply talking with people did not reveal the criteria for one combination over another, although there were some parts, for instance, the Thanksgiving part (*fa'afetai*) (see chap. 4), that seemed to be always present.

I became convinced that knowledge of these matters is very context bound, but not in the sense that people would not be able to abstract and talk at a metalinguistic level. On the contrary, people seemed very comfortable with talking about what they said in a lāuga. In fact, they seemed eager to display their competence. Knowledge of the context however was needed to decide how many parts were going to be performed and what their actual content should be. It became clear that real speeches had to be recorded during spontaneous and locally meaningful activities.[8] I began asking about any ceremony or event at which speechmaking would take place. In the meantime, I began keeping notes on my encounters and discussions with various members of the community who seemed willing to help me learn about speeches.

Discovering the Fono

I often talked to an orator named Tūla'i Tino. In addition to speaking very good English, Tūla'i was friendly, enjoyed talking with me, and knew a lot about what was going on in the village. Soon my journal was filling with things he told me. For example, on January 9, 1979, for the first time Tūla'i volunteered information about the current political situation in the village. He started explaining to me some recent developments in the campaign for the forthcoming elections for the national Parliament. He told me that the holder of one of the two senior orator titles in the village, Iuli Sefo, had just returned from New Zealand and had manifested a strong interest in running for the Parliament. Unfortunately, Tūla'i added, Iuli was late. Only one week earlier the village council had decided to reconfirm the incumbent M.P. from the nearby village of Lufilufi. This procedure, as Tūla'i explained, represented a "traditional" solution to the "new" politico-legal order; it was a way of avoiding the elections—a "Western" practice—by having the matai from the different villages in the district agree on one candidate through public discussion—a "Samoan" solution. Apparently unaffected by these events, however, Iuli was still determined to request the support of the matai from the district. In a few days there was going to be a fono, that is, a meeting of the village matai. Tūla'i suggested that I attend. It would be a way of getting some good recordings of traditional speechmaking: "If you want to know about lāuga," he said, "you better go and sit in a fono. That's the best place."

Only much later did I learn that this was a peculiar statement, given that, as I will discuss in chapter 4, most of the lāuga in the fono are seen not as prototypical ceremonial speeches but rather as mixed or hybrid compositions. At that point, however, I was becoming intrigued by the political scene in the village and was anxious to see the matai in action with my own eyes. Without knowing it, I was turning into an ethnographer. It was the political drama that really attracted me, even more than the logic of speechmaking.

MY FIRST FONO

On January 11, Tūla'i took me to the fono. When we arrived at the large Western-style house where the matai were gathered, I saw many people sitting on mats around the periphery of the large rectangular room that was reserved for the meeting. Tūla'i took off his shirt, moved the kava bowl that was on the floor closer to him, sat down, and indicated to me to sit next to him. He then started to mix some already pounded kava roots with water. This was not the first time I witnessed the preparation of kava, a nonalcoholic drink with soporific or numbing effects made out of pounded dry roots of a pepper plant (see chap. 3), but this was the first time I saw kava being prepared and served for such a large number of matai. After sitting down, I noticed that no one had greeted us. Then a man who was sitting next to me told me to move to his left. Someone else was going to sit there. After a few minutes, while everybody was talking, the senior orator Moe'ono Kolio, who was sitting across from where we were, about twenty-five feet away, asked me something I could not quite understand. Tūla'i translated for me: "He wants to know how your car is." A few days earlier I had been involved in a minor accident on the road that goes through the village. I quickly answered that the car was fine, hoping the conversation would end there. Moe'ono's following words seemed addressed to others. I heard him say the words *pati* (clap) and *lima* (hands). A man began shouting and all the matai in the house started to clap their hands, slowly, asynchronously. Kava was served, clearly following a protocol, with each cup presented with a loud chanting.

I drew maps of the seating arrangements inside the fono house and made lists of the order of kava distribution. When I tried to match my notes with what Tūla'i later told me, I faced a problem. Tūla'i said that

Moe'ono had been served first, but my notes showed that there had been three other people served before Moe'ono. Was Tūla'i wrong? Did he forget? Or did I miss something? I later learned that the people who drank before Moe'ono were guests (*mālō*) and therefore didn't seem to count in terms of the reportable order of distribution for that particular occasion. "Moe'ono was first" meant that he had been served first "among the people from the village" or that he had been served "before Iuli," the other senior orator. As I was to learn in the subsequent months, it was the tension and conflict between the two senior orators Iuli and Moe'ono that occupied the minds of the community leaders. Tūla'i was also concerned on that occasion about the conflict and contextualized his reply accordingly.

Interpreting the Texts

Over the next few months (January–April 1979), I was able to record seven fono. I initially asked a Samoan teenager to transcribe the fono tapes, but I soon found out that he was not able to either hear or understand parts of what was on the tape. Many of the metaphors were new to him and his guesses about what was being said were not always accurate. I decided then to hire one of the best orators in the village, a young matai in his early thirties, Lua Veni, who transcribed most of the fono tapes and then went through them with me to check for inconsistencies or unclear passages. Using the transcripts as a point of reference, I would also discuss with Lua the organization of speeches in the fono and the uses of certain rhetorical devices.

In addition to Lua, with whom I spoke only Samoan, I worked with Tūla'i, who, thanks to his fluency in English, could provide a rough English translation of the fono transcripts made by Lua. Another matai in the village, Chief Savea Savelio, was also an important source of information about tradition as well as the latest events in the village political arena. Since his English was not as good as Tūla'i's, I would alternate between Samoan and English, depending on the subject matter or the nature of the question. These three knowledgeable members of the fono, each with a different social identity, expertise, rank, and with different family interests—their titles were from three different descent groups and they lived in different parts of the village—provided me with a good range of interpretations and background facts on which to base my own ethnographic and linguistic analysis of the events discussed in the meetings. Occasionally, I would also discuss specific matters with other members of the fono. Thus, for instance, I consulted with various orators about kava ceremonies and with the senior orator Iuli about his role in the political arena and his relationship with other matai (Moe'ono in particular) in the village. In a few cases, I talked to people outside our village to get a sense of the generality of what I had observed or learned in one particular community. I thus learned that there was a considerable amount of variation in protocol from one village to another, although most of the basic interpretative principles seemed to apply across villages and districts. Following a standard practice within the ethnography of communication paradigm, I also participated in and often recorded several other kinds of events where oratory was performed, including an exchange of dowry and bride wealth, an installation of new matai titles (*saofa'i*), Sunday meals with invited preachers (*to'ona'i*), funerals (*maliu*), and visits of traveling parties (*malaga*). Finally, throughout my stay (and in later visits) I continued to record and transcribe ordinary conversations among friends, kin, and members of various groups in the village (see chap. 6 for an analysis of conversational material). In all of these cases, I tried to collect as much information as possible about the topics that were being discussed in the conversations. I found that even people in the same village would misinterpret utterances when removed from their immediate context and the fact of speaking the same language or living in the same community was no guarantee of the accuracy of transcription and interpretation. I often needed to go back to the participants in the interaction I recorded or to their close kin. The situatedness of talk became even more dramatically apparent when I returned to the United States and tried to work on some of those transcripts with Samoans who lived in urban America. In many instances, linguistic expressions and passages that had seemed semantically transparent in Falefā became obscure or terribly ambiguous in Los Angeles. Many Samoan sentences seemed even more ambiguous away from the place where they had been uttered. The elliptical nature of Samoan syntax, where a single verb might do what in English might need at least a verb and a pronoun, became a real problem in decoding the texts. Whatever ethnographic information I had been able to collect while still in the village became very precious. The linguist in me could do his work only to the extent to which the ethnographer had done his much earlier on.

To decode the speeches in the fono I needed to be familiar with the social structure of the village. Long before I started to understand it through the transcription and translation of the fono speeches, I was exposed to the political and mythical structure of Falefā through its *fa'alupega* or ceremonial address. In the next section, I will discuss such fa'alupega as an introduction to the idealized version of Falefā's hierarchy and as an example of the type of background work that was necessary on my part to be able to decode the fono speeches discussed in the next chapters.

The *Fa'alupega* or Ceremonial Address of Falefā

The village *fa'alupega* is a series of names that refer to the village's most important titles and descent groups. Its basic form is a list, and it can be inserted in a wide range of discourse contexts, including formal greetings as well as those parts of a formal speech in which a speaker wishes to refer to the community as a whole or to recognize explicitly its various components. A fa'alupega provides a basic outline of the village hierarchy (Mead 1930). Thus, the order in which the various titles and names of historical sites are mentioned is usually relevant. At the same time, as I discuss in chapter 3, it should not be taken too literally. Fa'alupega change over time and from one occasion to another, although only some of these changes come to be incorporated in the more standard versions that are known throughout the country by competent speechmakers.

At the time of my fieldwork, the basic structure of Falefā's fa'alupega, in its most reduced version, was composed of three parts, with the third allowing several possible variations:[9]

(a) ... *'Āiga*[10] *ma aloali'i*
    ... the chiefs (lit. 'Families') and the son-chiefs

(b) *lā'ua*[11] *matua*[12] *Iuli ma Moe'ono*[13]
    the two of them the senior orators Iuli and Moe'ono

(c) *ma le putuputu o tagata o le Tuiatua*[14]
    and the gathering of the people of the King-of-Atua
    (or)
    ma le tofi fa'asolo i le tagata o le Tuiatua
    and the various appointments of the people of the King-of-Atua

(or)

ma le 'a'ai o Fonotī
and the village of Fonotī

(or)

ma le 'a'ai o le tupu
and the village of the king

The first term in the first phrase literally refers to the descent groups ('āiga) in the village, as identified by the names of their respective ancestors. Thus, for instance, an important descent group in Falefā is Sā-Fenu'unu'uivao, that is, the total number of extended families and their titles that claim Fenu'unu'uivao, daughter of the high chief Leutele, as their common ancestor (see Krämer 1902, vol. 1, 300). However, in the context of the ceremonial address, the term *'Āiga* refers, more specifically, to all the chiefly titles. The *aloali'i* 'son chiefs' Muagututi'a and Luafalemana are also included here.[15] Despite their prominence in the fa'alupega, at the time of my study of the Falefā fono, the holders of these two titles did not have an important role in the village politics. In some contexts, the specific names of the various "families," or descent groups, are spelled out, as for instance in the first speech in a fono, but otherwise, only the words *'Āiga* 'families' and *aloali'i* 'son chiefs' are used.

The second part of the fa'alupega refers to the two senior orators, Iuli and Moe'ono, who are considered the spokespersons for the high chiefs Salanoa and Leutele respectively[16] (see fig. 2). I have elsewhere translated *matua* as 'senior orators' to convey the fact that they are the highest-ranking orators in the village. Not only are they associated with the two highest chiefly titles in the village, they are also a real and effective political force in the community. They are the ones who call a fono and direct its proceedings. Although nominal power rests with the chiefs, in my experience it was the two senior orators who dictated the agenda of the fono and did the necessary work for carrying out a particular political or judiciary campaign. The two of them did most of the talking in a fono and often alternated at playing different roles. Moe'ono usually acted as the official chairman and prosecutor, but if Iuli was bringing a charge against someone, then Moe'ono might act as a defender. In some cases, especially when things seemed in danger of getting out of control, they would unite their forces to intimidate a powerful party or restrain a defiant and emotional speaker (see examples of these strategies in chaps. 3 and 4). As the orator Tūla'i once told me,

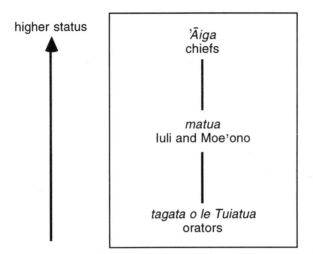

Figure 2. Mediating role of senior orators Iuli and Moe'ono

the two matua can be thought of as standing between the chiefs on the one side and the orators on the other (see fig. 2).

As is not unusual with political mediators, in Iuli and Moe'ono's case, their power often seemed to extend quite beyond the mere function of facilitator or community organizer.[17] This becomes more apparent in their authority to scold other members of the fono and especially high chiefs. Furthermore, as discussed in chapter 5, Moe'ono was certainly the most outspoken of the matai participating in the fono.

The third part of the fa'alupega refers to the whole body of orators (*tulāfale* or *failāuga*) in the village. They are seen as having less authority than the chiefs or the matua and as merely an advisory board. The orators are divided according to the descent group to which their title belongs. In Falefā this means an association between a main descent line and a particular subvillage (*pitonu'u*). Each of the four most important families has an official spokesperson for the entire subvillage who bears the highest orator title. The rest of the orators are ranked accordingly, after the two matua. In table 1 is a list, in hierarchical order, of the most important orator titles for the four subvillages and their respective high chiefs.

Despite these affiliations, on whose behalf a given orator is going to act is not always predictable. In a fono, the orators have conflicting allegiances. They may act on behalf of their respective subvillages, their

Table 1 *Titles of Falefā's Four Highest-Ranking Chiefs and Their Respective Orators*

Subvillage	Highest Chief	Highest Orator
Sagapolu	Leutele	Moe'ono (senior orator)[b]
Saleapaga	Salanoa[a]	Iuli (senior orator)[b]
Gaga'emalae	Alai'a-sā	Fa'aonu'u
Sanonu	Suluvave	Leuta

[a]"Salanoa," which is the name used by people on most occasions and also the one found in Krämer (1902/3, 277), is in fact a shortened form for "Lealaisalanoa." The longer form would be used only in ceremonial or political contexts, not in everyday conversation.

[b]Moe'ono and Iuli, in addition to being the highest orators of their respective subvillages, are also the two senior orators for the entire village.

descent group, a particular section of their extended family, or even for their own personal gain (sometimes to be defined on financial grounds). It is in the unpredictable role of the orators in any given discussion that one can recognize the ambivalent nature of the Samoan fono as both an association of titleholders representing the interests of specific descent groups and an independent political body that might act somewhat autonomously from its "elective" constituency (this is one of the features of the Samoan political system that was used by Irving Goldman [1970] to classify Samoa as an "open" system). In fact, at different times during the fono proceedings, the same orator may speak on behalf of his subvillage, his descent group, his chief, or simply on behalf of himself. As I will discuss in chapter 3, in a relatively flexible system of this sort, the spatial and temporal characteristics of a speech (e.g., where is the speaker sitting? At what point in the proceedings is a particular speech delivered?) become particularly important for allowing the audience to assess which "voice" is speaking on a given occasion.

Some of the phrases of the fa'alupega contain references to past events that are important in defining claims to certain prerogatives in the ritual and political arena. Thus, the alternative phrases *le 'a'ai o Fonotī* 'the village of Fonotī' and *le 'a'ai o le tupu* 'the village of the king' are two different versions of the special title given by the King Fonotī to the village of Falefā as a reward for fighting on his side against the rebels Toleafoa and Samalaulu (Henry 1979). As I show in the discussion of interrupted speeches in chapter 4, the shared knowledge embedded in such collectively remembered events is usually expected to remain implicit. When it is brought up and recounted in some detail, it can become the source of interactional trouble.

In addition to the village fa'alupega, each matai title has its own ceremonial address (often referred to as *fa'alagiga*) that can be used when that person is being greeted or spoken of. Thus, for instance, the high chief Leutele may be greeted as *le tinā o Tupua* 'the mother of Tupua,' because his daughter Fenu'unu'uivao, wife of the King Mu-agututi'a, acted as mother of Muagututi'a's adoptive son, Tupua. For similar reasons, high chief Salanoa may be identified as *le tei o Tupua* 'the brother of Tupua' or as *le tama o malili e fā* 'the boy of the four (high) *malili* trees.' The use of these more detailed ceremonial phrases is not only a sign of the speaker's ceremonial expertise, it also shows appreciation for the tradition and respect for the title and its holder. I was always praised when I displayed knowledge of specific ceremonial phrases associated with particular titles. I soon became accustomed to identifying people through their fa'alupega, and the fa'alupega phrases acquired with time a different reality. The more I felt comfortable using them in public encounters the less I was perceived as an outsider (as compared to other foreigners who did not know or had not bothered to learn these aspects of Samoan tradition).

What's in a Transcript?

In the second part of my fieldwork (January–July 1979), the fono became the main focus of my research. I often asked myself what made the fono so interesting to me. Only later, over the years, did I realize how unconventional my choice had been. As I mentioned above, when field linguists collect "texts," they tend to choose tradi-tional stories. When cultural anthropologists collect texts, they tend to favor songs, poems, myths, spells, curing formulas (Malinowski 1935). The fono speeches do not quite fit in any of these categories. They have "stories" in them, but the stories are constructed in unusual ways (see chap. 5). They refer to myths and make use of traditional metaphors and proverbs, but they are not just about the past and they do not always employ the beautiful language of lāuga discussed in chapter 4. Political and legal anthropologists, of course, participate in and sometimes re-cord what is said in political and judiciary arenas. But they rarely analyze the texts so collected beyond their referential content. In some cases, metaphors are considered important vehicles for "explaining" or justifying the system from what Malinowski called the "natives' point of view," but the grammar of political rhetoric is rarely discussed with the sophistication expected for cultural or strictly economic analyses of political processes. However, if so much of the political processes that are being studied take the form of a linguistically mediated search for a consensus, the specific linguistic resources available to the social actors and their ability to utilize them effectively in decision-making arenas must be an important factor in the collective shaping of the community's future.

With this working hypothesis in mind, I have tried to demonstrate in the following chapters that one can unite detailed linguistic (in some cases even strictly grammatical) analysis of political "texts" with ethnographic investigation of the political scenes implied or constituted by those texts. The result is the production of what we might call *ethnopragmatic accounts,* that is, descriptions of the ways in which the politics of representation within a particular sociohistorically defined community is actively constituted through linguistic choices. Such choices, in turn, acquire their meaning and, ultimately, their effectiveness by means of the ability that social actors have to revise, negotiate, or improvise upon certain aspects of their representation of reality while holding other aspects constant. The tension between what we might have once called "form and content" and more recently, with Giddens (1979, 1984), what we call "duality of structure" needs a complementarity of methods requiring intellectual and institutional efforts that go much beyond the limited goals and results of this study. The enterprise is certainly not new. Old and new metaphors in the social sciences and the humanities seem to be trying to capture the same dialectics, namely, the contrast between the need for individuals to rely on some predetermined system of coordination—a system of rules, forms, expectations, or, simply, a "structure"—and the need to adapt those already available and tested forms to new and often unpredictable contents— subjective and social, conscious and unconscious, individual and collective. In this tension, the role as well as the internal complexity of humanly produced symbolic resources should never be underestimated. At the same time, an exclusive interest in the formal-aesthetic dimensions of such resources, their grammar, their internal coherence, would blind us to our responsibility—and the often more compelling responsibility of the subjects of our study—as historical, social, and moral beings. It is the assumption of this book that grammar and politics can be reunited, with ethnography playing the role of the mediator in this process, because politics and grammar are in fact never separated in the world of human praxis, in the everyday struggle of human conflict. The transformations my interest underwent in the field should then be seen as a process of becoming what might be necessary for this story to have a happy ending (although the word "ending" seems inappropriate when referring to real life events). Becoming interested in speechmaking and political discourse meant not only that I was being exposed to speaking as a social and important activity in the community but also that my questions about Samoan language were being recast in local terms. As I will discuss in chapter 5, the patterns of occurrence of fully expressed Agents in Samoan discourse[18] started to make sense to me only when I eventually managed to link the marking of grammatical roles (subjects of transitive clauses) with the constitution of political roles in the fono. Grammatical forms became interesting again and in a different way when I realized that they were being used as linguistic resources for local politics. In a fono, I discovered, *grammatical* agents were powerful rhetorical instruments through which *social* agents were being constituted.

The detailed study of such linguistic resources can be a powerful method for arriving at complementary if not alternative understandings of the local hierarchy so statically represented in the village ceremonial greeting discussed above or in normative statements collected in talking to members of the community. As I show in chapter 5, when we examine the types of referents that are portrayed as Agents as well as the specific speakers who use transitive constructions with fully expressed Agents in the fono discourse, we gain access to a social system that only partially coincides with the one celebrated in the ceremonial greeting of the village.

The community emerging from the fono discourse is very much a territory of controversy, struggle, and probing, in which participants question one another about what it means to be a Samoan, what is needed to hold on to the tradition, and what is the price to pay for change as well as for continuity. The social actors who emerge from these data are also complex characters who must endure conflicting interests and make difficult choices. In order to capture the subtleties of such complex dynamics, it is mandatory to take the process of *transcription* very seriously.

Writing Interaction

Cultural anthropologists have lately become particularly aware of the implications and consequences of their reliance on writing in their work (see Clifford 1988; Clifford and Marcus 1986; Sanjek 1990). To postmodern anthropologists, the interpretive proposal of culture as text (Geertz 1973) seems just as ambiguous as the concept of participant-observation. Important distinctions have thus been drawn between different types of writing practices and the kinds of information they are more likely to capture or overlook (Clifford 1990). Linguistic anthropologists bring to these discussions their experience in recording, transcribing, and interpreting linguistic data, tasks that are still a great part of an ethnographer's corpus and field experience—an important component of participant-observation consists of listening to what people say and engaging in dialogues with the natives (Tedlock 1983). Inspired by the careful work of transcribing natural speech practiced by child language researchers and conversation analysts, linguistic anthropologists have refined their skills at recording and then transcribing the words (and more recently, with the improvement of video technology, some other actions) of the people whose linguistic practices they want to study. However imperfect, transcription of natives talking to one another is one of the best antidotes to "selective forgetting" and other biased uses of specialized information collected by modern ethnographers (Johnson and Johnson 1990). The practice followed in this book of making transcripts of the interactions studied available to readers is also another important principle of contemporary linguistic anthropological research. However selective and skewed by an author's specific arguments, the display of what was said by the social actors at a particular time opens the door to potential refutations and interpretive criticism. The lack of such records in a researcher's published writing simply increases the privileged access he or she has on the material collected and later compiled for the study.

Among many methodological differences, we find evidence for a common characteristic of linguistic anthropologists: a tremendous trust in their linguistic data and in the technologies available for collecting and analyzing them. They are confident that in the midst of all kinds of historical, personal, and institutional changes, something remains the same (or at least close enough for most practical purposes): the words recorded on a magnetic tape. The very process of linguistic transcription in this case then hides a professional tension between two different, often conflictual interests. On the one side, there is the professional commitment to the very process of interpretation; there is, in other words, a seemingly rational acceptance of what is in fact a nonrational, that is, endless, largely meticulous, but fundamentally creative process that shapes data and conclusions moment by moment, that is, text by text, utterance by utterance, morpheme by morpheme, segment by segment. It is in this context that the notion of "transcription as theory" should be evaluated (see Ochs 1979): we become aware of the fact that what we decide—consciously and unconsciously, explicitly or implicitly—to first hear and then transcribe is the product of systems of choices due to a mixture of conventional orthographic systems and theoretical assumptions about what constitutes relevant data. Timed pauses, interruptions, and overlaps, for instance, are important for some analysts and uninteresting to others (Moerman 1988). On the other side, there is an interest in finite, time- and space-bound objects of inquiry. This means that even the most dialogically oriented anthropological linguists hide somewhere inside a positivist homunculus, a little heir of Durkheim and Bloomfield, who believes that there are "facts" (speeches, words, sounds, and silences) and that science is done by finding appropriate—that is, communal and debatable—ways of representing those facts. And this is not by simply challenging their ontological status, in the tradition of critical theory. To be a linguistic anthropologist means to share the view that capturing the natives' point of view must involve hundreds if not thousands of hours of listening and transcribing audiotapes or, more recently, videotapes, followed by the construction of paradigmatic oppositions and classifications that take advantage of the segmentation of talk produced on a page or, more often nowadays, on a computer screen. The order that can be reconstructed, inferred, and predicted on the basis of studying and analyzing transcripts becomes a source of confidence that often makes linguistic anthropologists—and their colleagues in related, partly overlapping fields—less tentative in their analysis, although not always daring in their conclusions.

The dialectics between these two sides of the discipline drove much of the work I did on the audiotapes of the interactions that constitute the basis of this study.

TRANSCRIPTION CONVENTIONS

In the transcripts of actual talk, I have borrowed several of the transcription conventions developed by Gail Jefferson for the

METHODS AS FORMS OF LIFE   41

analysis of conversational turns in English conversation (see Sacks, Schegloff, and Jefferson 1974 or Schenkein 1978). I have done so despite the fact that most of the examples in this book (with the exceptions of those discussed in chap. 6) are not from conversational interaction, but from speech events in which speakers' turns are rather long although often punctuated by short, partly predictable responses from the audience (e.g., *mālie!* 'well said!').

(1) Title	The name next to the number of an example is the title of the transcript of a recording of spontaneous interaction, for example, "Fono of April 7, 1979" or "Women eating." The few examples without title were created by the author for expository reasons.
Iuli;	Speakers' names are separated from their utterances by semicolons, followed by a few blank spaces. I have usually used the actual titles of the speakers in public arenas such as the fono and ceremonial settings, but I have used pseudonyms for those conversing in more informal settings such as conversations (see chap. 6).
?;	A question mark instead of a name or initial indicates that no good guess could be made as to the identity of the speaker.
??;	Multiple question marks followed by semicolon indicate that the speaker's identity is not clear but there are reasons to believe that it is someone other than the last unidentified speaker.
?Iuli;	A question mark before the name of the speaker stands for a probable but not safe guess regarding the identity of the speaker.
(2.5)	Numbers between parentheses indicate length of pauses in seconds and tenths of seconds.
. . .	Three dots indicate an untimed pause.
[. . .]	Three dots between square brackets indicate that some material of the original transcript or example has been omitted.

=	Equal signs indicate "latching," that is, no interval between two adjacent utterances.
e ke:le aso	A colon indicates the lengthening of the sound it follows.
'o lea- 'ua-	A hyphen stands for an abrupt interruption.
[	A square bracket between turns indicates the point at which overlap by another speaker starts.
//	An alternative symbol indicating point of overlap.
'ua alu le kama	Underlining is used for my expository emphasis and does not signal special emphasis or contrast in the speaker's talk.
(e leai)	Words between parentheses in the Samoan transcripts represents the best guess about a stretch of talk that was difficult to hear.
(village of)	Words between parentheses in the English translation represent either information that is understood by native speakers but is not easily traceable to specific morphemes in the Samoan text or the meaning of those portions of the Samoan text that are also between parentheses in the prior line.
(? ?)	Blank spaces inside parentheses with occasional question marks indicate uncertain or unclear talk; the length of the blank spaces between parentheses gives a rough indication of the amount of unclear speech.
k(h)e(h)l(h)ē	Audible aspirations typical of laughter are inserted as they occur in the word.
-hh	Audible inhalations.
((LG))	Laughter.
→	An arrow next to a line of transcript is occasionally used to help readers identify the portion of the interaction that is being analyzed.
((sits down))	Material between double parentheses provides extralinguistic information, such as descriptions of bodily movements.

All the original transcripts used in this study were done by hand while still in Western Samoa. The transfer to computer disk of some of them was facilitated by a program ("SCAN") written and generously shared by John B. Haviland. Among other things, SCAN inserts line numbers, marks overlaps, and allows for interlinear glosses.

Transcripts, like translations, are never perfect and never final. I have returned to the same segments of tapes many times over the last thirteen years to revise earlier transcripts and translations; I am sure that more revisions can be expected in the future. I am also very aware that the bits and pieces of Samoan speech transcribed here are mere approximations of the sounds often so eloquently or so passionately produced by Samoan speakers at the time of the recordings. Our writing conventions are indeed still very inadequate to capture the richness of sounds and even less the complexities of human interaction. Nevertheless, I feel about these transcripts the way most people feel about their folk theories: no matter how inadequate they may be, they are better than no transcripts at all.

A NOTE ON SAMOAN PHONOLOGICAL REGISTERS

In reproducing examples of actual speech, I have tried to be as faithful as possible to the way in which Samoan was actually spoken by the people whose speech I recorded. Without attempting a detailed phonetic transcription, which would have impaired comprehension for readers not familiar with phonetic conventions, I adapted traditional Samoan orthography to the needs of linguistic transcription. This means that, contrary to what is practiced by many other students of Samoan language and culture, I have not changed people's pronunciation to fit the style that is felt appropriate for written Samoan. My methodological and theoretical orientation have prevented me from fitting my data to the wishes of those speakers who might feel uncomfortable seeing in print what is considered appropriate only in spoken language. Of this choice, I assume full responsibility. At the same time, it should be kept in mind that my examples are *not* examples of written Samoan, but examples of spoken Samoan. As I discuss below, I have taken measures to help the reader distinguish between canonical forms and actual (spoken) forms.

This chapter on methods cannot end without a note on Samoan phonological variation and the conventions used in my transcriptions.

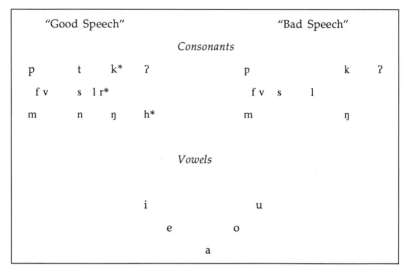

Figure 3. Phonemic inventories of "good speech" and "bad speech" (sounds marked by an asterisk are found only in loanwords)

"GOOD SPEECH" AND "BAD SPEECH": NOT A FEATURE OF "FORMALITY"

Samoan has two phonological registers, which are called by Samoans themselves *tautala lelei* 'good speech' and *tautala leaga* 'bad speech'. The first is always used in writing and most of the time in speaking during Western-inspired activities such as school events, radio shows, church services, and other church-related activities. The second, bad speech, is characteristic of both casual everyday interaction and traditional formal events such as the fono discussed in this book and ritual encounters of all kinds in which speechmaking is used (see Duranti 1981a, 1990b; Duranti and Ochs 1986; Hovdhaugen 1986; Shore 1977, 1982). Although the choice of one variety over another is very much activity bound—thus, people would typically switch from bad speech to good speech in starting a prayer before eating—it is not unusual to hear a fair amount of code switching from one register to the other during all kinds of interactions, especially when there are foreigners around, such as fieldworkers, with whom many Samoans feel it is appropriate to speak only in good speech (see Duranti 1990b for some examples of switching within the same conversation).

Contrary to what was stated by several authors in the past (see Cook

Table 2 *Pairs of Words that Differ Only in One Sound in "Good Speech" and Become Identical in "Bad Speech"*

"Good Speech"	"Bad Speech"
/ t / vs. / k /	/ k /
lota 'my' vs. *loka* 'lock' (from English)	*loka* 'my' or 'lock'
/ n / vs. / ŋ /	/ ŋ /
fana 'gun' vs. *faga* ([faŋa]) 'bay'	*faga* ([faŋa]) 'gun' or 'bay'
/ l / vs. / r / (no minimal pairs)	/ l /
taliga ([taliŋa]) 'ear'	*kaliga* ([kaliŋa])
rosa 'rose'	*losa*
Mareta 'Martha'	*Maleka*

1988, 55; Milner 1966, xv–xvi), good speech is *not* the "formal pronunciation," at least not in any of the usual meanings of the term "formal" (cf. Irvine 1979), and bad speech is not "colloquial pronunciation" either.[19] With the exception of a few words or phrases, the great majority of fono discourse recorded in 1978–1979 in Falefā was in bad speech. When asked about it, participants told me that they felt bad speech was the appropriate style for speaking in a fono. In the words of an old orator, "in a fono, bad speech is good."

Figure 3 shows the complete phonological inventory in the two registers. In bad speech the sounds /t/ and /n/ disappear and in their place /k/ and /ŋ/ (written "g" in Samoan orthography) are used. This means that whereas in good speech there are a few minimal pairs with the t/k and the n/g alternation, in bad speech, these minimal pairs are neutralized (see table 2).

Thus, the word that is written *lota* 'my' (inalienable) is pronounced [lota] (or [lot:a]) in good speech and [loka] (or [lok:a]) in bad speech. The word *fana* is pronounced [fana] in good speech and [faŋa] in bad speech. Loanwords with /r/ in good speech are pronounced with /l/ in bad speech (e.g., rosa → [losa], Mareta → [Maleka]). In this book, I have used good speech when I mention words out of a particular speaking context, but I have left the bad speech pronunciation any time it occurred in my recordings of actual talk. To distinguish between the two, when discussing specific examples, I used obliques to mark words or phrases taken out of transcripts, that is, words actually used by native speakers in interaction. The same word may thus be found in two different versions depending on whether it is given in its citation form or in the way in which it was pronounced by Samoan speakers on a particular occasion: thus, the readers will encounter both *le Atua* and /le Akua/ 'the Lord, God' and both *fono* and /fogo/ ([foŋo]) 'meeting, council'.

In the version of traditional Samoan orthography used here, the letter *g* represents a velar nasal (ŋ) and the apostrophe (') represents a glottal stop (ʔ). Long vowels are here represented with a macron: ā, ē, ī, ō, ū. This is a departure from my earlier choice (e.g., Duranti 1981a, 1988; Duranti and Ochs 1986) to represent long vowels with two identical vowels, namely, in their phonemic form. What I used to write *aa* is now ā. This solution renders my transcription easier to use for native speakers of Samoan and others who are already familiar with Samoan orthography.

3

Hierarchies in the Making: Space, Time, and Speaking in a Fono

As I recounted in chapter 2, my encounter with Samoan politics was somewhat accidental. I went to my first meeting of the village fono thinking of it simply as an occasion for collecting examples of live performances of traditional speeches. Little did I know that I was being introduced to a realm of language use which would reshape some of my methodological and theoretical assumptions about how to study grammar and discourse. I was prepared for some of the difficulties of studying linguistic performance, but I was not ready for the interpenetration of codes typical of sociopolitical arenas like the fono. My idea of Samoan social structure was also still very much based on written records and limited encounters with titled people in the village. When I entered the house where the fono was taking place I was faced with Samoan hierarchies in a new and dramatic way. Even before I could start working on the audiotapes of what was being said in the fono, I was perceiving nuances that at first I was not sure how to describe. Earlier literature was helpful only in too abstract terms.

Earlier sociohistorical accounts of Polynesian social systems did not offer many clues on how specific linguistic strategies and other communicative behaviors can have a role in the constitution of the polity as an emergent and ever-evolving system. I felt that I was seeing the dynamic nature of ancient Polynesian social structure discussed by I. Goldman (1970) in action. But I did not have the instruments for describing it. Even Felix Keesing and Mary Keesing's (1956) description of what they called "elite communication" in Samoa seemed artificial and removed from the atmosphere I was experiencing. Bradd Shore's dissertation (1977), which we had taken with us to Samoa, was the best source of insights into local concepts of authority and status negotiation, but it did not get into the details of everyday encounters that interested me. I was thus left with the task of finding my own way of talking about what I was experiencing. Not only did I need a metalanguage to express the linguistic and ethnographic experience I was undergoing, I also needed a way of identifying which communicative resources were being used as instruments for the constitution of those distinctions that make Samoa a hierarchical (or stratified) society. I kept thinking about one main question: How important was speech? And how was it related to other kinds of communicative resources available to and exploited by the participants?

In the following pages, I discuss how I came to have a sense of the specific nature of Samoan society as a hierarchical and yet extremely fluid social system through an examination of the role played by different semiotic codes in face-to-face encounters. It is in the context of such a highly structured and yet dynamic communicative system that words acquire the important role I ascribe to them in the subsequent chapters.

A Love for Order and Its Permutations

By sitting in on the fono, observing what was happening and recording what was being said, I started to develop an appreciation for the multifarious ways in which Samoan social actors display a love for hierarchies, their permutations, and their violations. I learned that the inherently sequential nature of human interactions and communicative exchanges is routinely exploited in Samoa for constructing a local, that is, context-specific and at the same time context-transcending, sense of order. Such an order encompasses the local political structure to include an aesthetics of variations upon variations, where nuances of small increments, gains, and losses are measured and evaluated against a grid of possible and impossible alternative moves. The knowledge necessary to be part of such transactions is highly valued. One needs only a few days, sometimes only a few hours, in a village to be told where it is appropriate to sit, when it is appropriate to talk, and what is appropriate to say to whoever is present. "Alesana, you sit here," hosts would tell me when I walked in their house. "Alesana, you must let him finish and then you will reply," a matai sitting next to me would tell me while another one was delivering a welcoming speech. "Alesana, you should learn the fa'alupega[1] of the village we are going to visit. They will be very impressed," the passenger in my pickup truck would tell me while I was driving to the site of a ceremony a few miles down the road. "Alesana, he gave you a box of biscuits, you give him a few dollars," someone would suggest in the middle of a ceremonial exchange. I never lacked teachers in Samoa. I was constantly taught to look, to listen, to speak, and eventually to "feel" like a Samoan matai. Even when I didn't want to think about the hierarchies, the differences in status and rank, someone would be there to remind me, to check whether I had learned something from the past experiences and whether I was now prepared to face the next challenge.

I had forgotten about this process when, in 1988, I returned to Falefā, ten years after our first visit. A friend came to visit from the United States. After only one day in the village, he began asking me where he should sit when we went for the evening prayer. The same night, back in our house, he raised questions about the order of servings during the meal. "I noticed," he said, "that tonight I was served first, but yesterday you were served before me." For a moment I froze, my mouth dropped. How could it be that in less than forty-eight hours he had already become so conscious of status differentiations and social hierarchy? Or was it simply that he too was being transformed into an ethnographer?

From my first experience in a fono, every time I went to a gathering where I knew that speechmaking was likely to take place I brought a tape recorder with me.[2] My entering the realm of politics and my attempts at keeping an ethnographic record of what was happening in the political arena in the village were thus characterized from the beginning by a professional preoccupation with speech. But as soon as I left the domain of grammar to adventure in the domain of social action, I realized there was a lot more than speech to keep track of. Before speeches could be exchanged or a linguistic sound produced, there were conventional acts performed by human bodies. And before human bodies, there was space, not just empty space, but culturally meaningful space, that is, space always ready to be occupied by social personae engaged in specific activities.

In my attempts to describe what was going on in the fono house, I became preoccupied with deciding how to capture the movements of the bodies in space, their collocation vis-à-vis one another, their role in contextualizing the words just exchanged and those to be said next.

In 1978–1979 we had no film with us, only a very heavy reel-to-reel Sony portapack video recorder with a battery that would last the full thirty minutes on a good day and only during the first few weeks. The village had no electricity at the time and getting to a generator to re-charge the battery pack meant so many complicated negotiations and possible implications for future reciprocity that, with a few exceptions, we limited the use of the video deck to one session a month with each of the six families that were part of the child language acquisition study. I also felt at the time that it was too imposing to attempt a visual re-cording of a fono.[3] I was becoming more and more aware of the po-tential problems of my presence in the fono house, and I was doing my best to be less "on stage" during the meetings; I had also developed a sensitivity to the seriousness of the matters being discussed which stopped me from imposing yet another element of intrusion in the midst of the heated debates. I resorted then to drawings and notes, which I would later use as starting points for questioning some of the partici-pants on the procedures used during the meeting (see fig. 4).

But the limitations were not only methodological or technical. Cer-tainly, a visual record would have helped (see Duranti 1992b). But it was not just a question of finding the right tool. What seemed more compelling at the time was the question of how to handle the variety of inputs, how to navigate in the sea of principles, exceptions, and ex-amples that I kept collecting or simply witnessing by the very fact of living in the village and participating in village affairs. How were all these different semiotic behaviors organized? Which ones should one pay more attention to? What were their functions? How did they con-nect to one another? Where to start? Was there an overall organizing principle?

One obvious place to start was the fa'alupega (see chap. 2). The address forms referring to the various titles in the village were indeed considered a mirror of the local hierarchy by the people in the com-munity. Speechmakers referred to those names and epithets during any kind of public speaking and in the informal discussions I had with them. It is not surprising then that A. Krämer's (1902/3) comprehensive ac-count of Samoan history and social organization was very dependent on fa'alupega, which he very much interpreted as historical records. However, more recent ethnographic accounts have shown that fa'alupega change both over time and across social contexts (Pitt 1969;

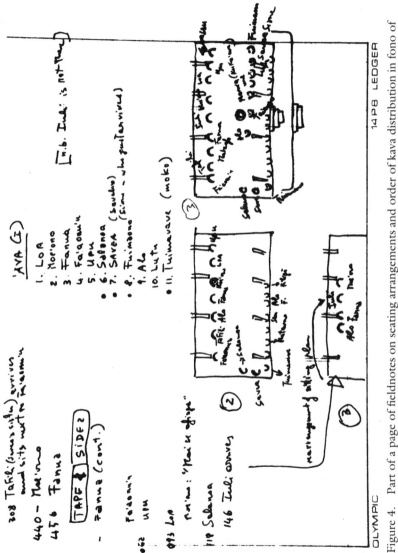

OLYMPIC   14P8 LEDGER

Figure 4. Part of a page of fieldnotes on seating arrangements and order of kava distribution in fono of April 7, 1979 (the numbers on the left refer to the counter in the tape recorder)

Shore 1977, 1982).[4] Perhaps, as suggested by Mead, it would seem more appropriate to think of fa'alupega as *ideal* versions of the local hierarchy:

Fa'alupega is the arrangement of phrases of ceremonial recognition to the fono itself, and to special names, or special categories in which numbers of names are arranged, which must be recited at the opening of any fono, large or small. . . . [T]hese phrases serve as a convenient mnemonic framework for recording an ideal situation which never occurs in practice. (Mead 1930, 10)

Such an ideal version of the local organization of matai titles and their ranked relations could be used to interpret rather than determine various other ceremonial arrangements, including the seating positions in a public gathering, the order of distribution of kava, the sequential right to the speaking floor (see fig. 5).

Such a top-down hierarchy of these different procedures is however misleading. When we look at their interaction in real social situations, we find that such procedures—in some cases prototypical "ritual" activities—are being interactively exploited, across social actors, media, genres, and activities, to form a general yet context-specific model that is constantly updated, executed, tested, mended, and interpreted so as to constitute what might be considered an emergent collective memory, dialogically based on a variety of media, channels, codes, characters, and audiences. The resources of such collective, intersubjective remembering can be any subset of a number of prerogatives, which include: who is greeted with which phrases, who sits where, who gets served kava and when, who speaks when and about what. Thus, such resources for the constitution of the local hierarchy include language but go beyond our usual concept of language.

After a few months spent in the village, I became convinced that there were distinctive elements "out there" and that they were ready to be inscribed and described by the ethnographer-linguist. But one needed to approach them with a variety of methods, with a range of sensitivities and methodological inventions. In a fono, the elements included the complex linguistic repertoire that made speechmaking such a prestigious skill in the community (see chap. 4), but they also encompassed nonverbal (kinesic, but not only kinesic) semiotic dimensions, such as: (i) the seating arrangement in the house, with its nuances of "next to," "opposite to," and "closer than"; (ii) the temporal ordering of any kind of material distribution (kava, food, gifts); and (iii) the right to speak at a given time, as appropriate to the occasion.

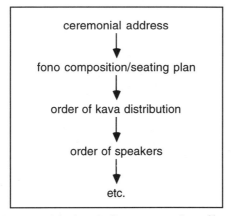

Figure 5. Top-down model of symbolic representation of local hierarchies (the vertical arrows should be interpreted as "is predictor of")

Since all of these elements fed into one another, it seemed misguided to favor one system of signification over another or to look for the "basic principles"—for instance, the true or original fa'alupega—that might explain all the others. In fact, precisely because, as Maurice Bloch (1975a, 1989), Giddens (1979, 1984), and others have taught us, each semiotic system is part of the political resources that help produce and legitimize the socioeconomic system, it was important to maintain a multitude of possibilities. Various interpretive schemata were played against one another, in some cases to progressively and chorally build a common understanding of the existing social order, in other cases to allow for the symbolic representation of social breaches or structural ambiguities in the power structure. To try to grasp such richness of messages and possible interpretations meant for me that I had to momentarily put aside my linguistic preoccupations—and with them the sense of confidence that came with my linguistic training—and concentrate on what I could make of the other codes and dimensions to which I was being exposed.

Space

It has been more than thirteen years since that morning on January 11, 1979, when I walked into chief Tuimavave Sefo's big house (see photo insert) and sat down, feeling at the same time shy and fortunate, intrusive and proud. "This is a *fono*," I said to myself, but all I could see were about two dozen mature men, many of them in their fifties or older, sitting cross-legged at the periphery of a large room, silently listening to one man speaking in a slow, deep voice. The sounds of the speech were as unfamiliar as most of the faces in the room. The process of familiarization with those faces over the following months and with their voices over the following years has diminished my ability to accurately describe my first reactions to an event that has become so much a part of my intellectual life and has served as a root metaphor for my understanding of our own decision-making events. I do remember, however, that while walking into my first direct encounter with Samoan politics in the making, I had the sense of having entered another "space." This feeling was not simply due to my realization of having violated the boundaries of an activity that is usually hidden from foreigners. It was more than that. It was an awareness of moving or placing oneself within a dimension of human interaction in which the location of the actors, the proximity of their bodies, their most minimal physical reactions meant more than I could understand. When I sat down to write about this experience, I looked for analytic notions that could help me explicate for others as well as for myself the meanings of those bodies in space.

SETTINGS AND FRAMES

I found two sources of inspiration: Erving Goffman's work, especially his discussion of boundaries in *Frame Analysis* (1974), and the ethnography of communication (see Gumperz and Hymes 1964, 1972), a research program that has often emphasized the importance of the spatiotemporal coordinates of any speech event. Thus, for instance, Hymes's (1972b) grid for analyzing speech events in different societies, the so-called SPEAKING model, started with the "setting"—the "S" of the SPEAKING mnemonic—that is, the spatial and temporal coordinates of the event. Where and when a given interaction takes place was recognized by Hymes as constitutive of the event as a type of social encounter.

For Hymes and other anthropological linguists, an ethnographically oriented analysis of language use could not, a priori, keep the *acts* of speaking separate from the other components of the speech event. Thus, one could not assume that talk was separable from the *ends* or goals of the interaction or that the *norms* for speaking could be discussed without taking into consideration the *genre* used by the *participants* and the *key* in which talk should be interpreted (e.g., whether serious or frivolous, sacred or profane, formal or mundane). Of all the components of the speech event discussed by Hymes, the setting seemed to me the aspect that was first attended to by the Samoan matai as they gathered in a fono.

SPATIAL BOUNDARIES

Since exploring his earlier interest in the individual acting with his body in a social space, Goffman had been particularly attuned to the spatial and temporal framing of human social activities. In *Frame Analysis*, he provided a fuller discussion of the interface between spatiotemporal dimensions of situations and the keying devices necessary for making those dimensions relevant for the participants:

Activity framed in a particular way—especially collectively organized social activity—is often marked off from the ongoing flow of surrounding events by a special set of boundary markers or brackets of a conventionalized kind. These occur before and after the activity in time and may be circumscriptive in space; in brief, there are temporal and spatial brackets. (Goffman 1974, 251–252)

Like Goffman, I also began seeing the spatial organization within social events as a way of defining their boundaries, as a collectively orchestrated resource to which participants would key their own performance and gain insights into others' potential and actual contributions.

I thus became convinced that to understand a fono required an understanding of the way participants themselves would "see" the space in which they operated. Such an understanding could not be limited to the fono. My ethnographic experience in the village told me that, however unique and specific, space within a fono was in some ways related to other spaces. This knowledge came from participating in other events in which the same people would get together among themselves or with other members of their community.

More recently, Giddens's attempts to integrate Torsten Hägerstrand's time geography with Goffman's intuitions about face-to-face encounters has uncovered further areas of relevance of spatial organization to structuration, that is, the process whereby social structure is presupposed and at the same time reproduced. In Hägerstrand's (1975) framework, social actors appropriate different time-space zones in the reproduction of everyday life. This is what Hägerstrand calls "region-alization," the use and significance of different time-space "regions" in social life. In this framework, we can distinguish actors from one an-other in at least two ways: (i) in terms of their movement in time-space across a variety of "stations," and (ii) in terms of their relative presence-availability within each "station" (what Giddens calls a "locale"). A member of a household, for instance, is distinguished from other mem-bers, among other things, (i) in terms of his or her movements from the house to other stations like the local stores, the public market, the school, the workplace, public buildings, other private houses, and so on, and (ii) in terms of his or her access to specific areas of the house such as the kitchen, the bedroom, the dining area, the head of the table. Similar considerations can be made about the Samoan matai in the fono house. By virtue of the fact that they have a title, the matai can be inside the fono house. At the same time, different titleholders have access to different regions of the fono house and, as I will show, they have dif-ferential access to the floor in the proceedings.

It should not be too difficult to see the potential integration between time geography and the microsociology of everyday encounters. Goff-man's activity boundaries become one of the features (the "form" for Giddens [1984, 121]) of Hägerstrand's regionalization. By paying at-tention to the internal spatial organization of the locale "fono," its internal regionalization and division into "front" and "back" regions, we have a chance to see Samoan social structure and cultural distinctions displayed and reproduced through dimensions that have culture-specific relevance. Such distinctions, however, have both universal and cross-contextual validity to the extent to which they are shown to be at work in a variety of settings.

"FRONT" AND "BACK" ACROSS CONTEXTS

Seeing matai place themselves inside the fono house was certainly not my first experience with the relevance of the relative po-sition of people inside a Samoan house. From our very first days in the village, we had been made aware of the importance of where one sits (see Ochs 1988, 1). During the to'ona'i, the Sunday communal meal with the pastor's family and the matai and their families who are mem-bers of the local *ekalesia* (church organization), for instance, we were always invited to sit along one side of the pastor's house. It was the part referred to as the "front" (*luma*). Some matai (all of them male deacons

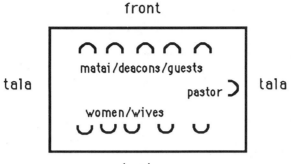

Figure 6. Seating arrangement in a formal Sunday meal (*to'ona'i*)

in the church organization) also sat there. Their wives would sit on the side facing us, the "back" (*tua*).[5] The pastor would be in the center of one of the short sides, called *tala* (see fig. 6).

After the first few weeks, first Martha and then Elinor moved back with the other women and with the lower-ranking male members of the congregation (who would sit at the edge of the back row). This was a conscious decision on Martha's and Elinor's part not to alienate the other women in the congregation and to partially remove their for-eigner-guest-outsider status. Their decision was easily accepted by those who attended the to'ona'i. Rather than feeling sorry for Martha and Elinor or embarrassed by our implicit acceptance of the usual gender discrimination, I felt abandoned and often envied them. I saw them as having more freedom of action. Their place in the back allowed them to be less "on stage." True, they were served food later, after the best portions had gone to the pastor and the people in the front, but as if to compensate for that, they had less social pressure on them. Thus, for instance, they could whisper to one another and make side comments a bit more freely. They could even get up and leave without their ab-sence being as noticeable as mine would have been. Most importantly from my point of view, they were not expected to perform verbally. I, instead, could be called upon to give a speech or react to a new cere-monial challenge at any moment. Rather than simply enjoying my food, I spent my time worrying about when to make a remark, start a new topic, stop eating, offer some of my food to someone else, pull out some money for a collection. I also had to make the decision about when it was appropriate for our group to leave the rest of the company and retire to our houses for the midday Sunday siesta (*malōlō*). These remarks should not be taken to mean that the matai at the to'ona'i were never relaxed or that there would not be a good dose of storytelling and jokes. On the contrary, most of the interaction was quite casual and most of the talk exchanged would not seem very different from talk at a dinner party in our own society. What differed was the potential that the situation could suddenly turn into a formal one, in which bodies would stiffen and highly formal speech would be used. Instead of "he" or "you," the people present would then be referred to with phrases like "The Honorable So-and-so" or "Your Highness." Instead of short, conversational turns, speakers would engage in long-winded speeches, full of metaphors and proverbs, to which members of the audience (again, usually those in the front, but not the women in the back) would rhythmically reply *mālie!* 'nicely said!' or 'sweet (to the ear)!'

One time I decided to test the system. I wanted to see whether in fact it was the place that mattered more or the person. It was hard for me to give up the Western idea that no matter *where* you are, you are *the same person*. If I was a high-status member of the community, deserving respect and good food on public occasions, what difference would it make if I sat in the front or in the back? One Sunday I decided to sit in the back, with the women and with the lower-ranking male members of the congregation. Against everyone's better judgment ("Alesana! What are you doing? Come and sit in the front!", the several matai insisted), I located myself in the back and toward the center, in the place that I judged in that context to be the lowest-status position.[6] Then I waited for the food to arrive. The first tray went by, directed as usual to the pastor, then the second tray, for the highest chief present, then came the trays for the other chiefs and the orators sitting in the front, for the pastor's wife, and for Elinor and Martha, who were all sitting at my right, closer to the pastor's side. And me? I was served last! By the time one of the young boys who was carrying the trays of food got to me there was no fish left. I only had taro and *palusami* (coconut cream). Even more surprisingly, no one seemed to care—at least for a while. After a minute or two, my friend chief Tavō Utulei seemed to suddenly wake up and realize what happened. "Alesana has no fish!", he exclaimed, lifted a large portion of the baked bonito that was on his tray, and told one of the boys to take it to me. Upon seeing this, the pastor did the same with parts of his meal. My experiment was over. I had been able to show the relevance of the locally defined spatial distinctions (front vs. back region) for establishing the status of a participant in a public event. At the same time, I had proven to myself that the system was flexible. Different "parts," namely the servers versus the matai, or the kids versus my adult friends, were acting on different premises. For the kids who brought in the trays with the food and for the untitled adults who were preparing the portions, it was safer to follow the basic spatial distinctions. They had no way of knowing the details about who was doing what on a particular occasion. The spatial arrangement in the house constituted a first key to know how to operate with a minimum assurance of appropriateness. As far as the young, untitled members of the gatherings knew, there might have been reasons for me to act "low" that day and stay out of the action. It would have been too presumptuous on their part to compensate my own personal choice by acting in a way that would have reminded everyone what my status usually was on other occasions. In a society like Samoa, which allows great variation in the distribution of tasks and may see the highest of chiefs act very humbly if necessary, the safest way of making sure that things are done appropriately, especially when there is no time for rehearsal, is to start with a basic plan and then correct it on the way if necessary.

In most cases, the seating plan works very efficiently to convey a first sense of order. Whether or not that order conforms to the relative statuses of the participants as displayed on other occasions is not something that low-status people must be concerned with. Their socialization teaches them that any hierarchy must adapt to contingencies, must fit the task. Their theatrical sense of social interaction transmitted through continuous challenges to perform in public at the earliest age also teaches them that, as Margaret Mead pointed out over fifty years ago, "the play" counts more than "the players" (Mead 1937), and the play must go on at any cost. Hesitation, unless appropriately calculated, should be avoided. With a quick glance at the seating arrangement for the day, the people who are in charge of preparing or carrying ritually significant objects—such as food or gifts—can give a first estimate of "who is in charge" that day or "whose show it is." It is up to the more knowledgeable members in the gathering to complement or rectify the reading provided by the bare layout of the human bodies in space. In the case discussed above, it was Tavō's duty to repair the kids' first, intuitive judgment. This interplay, sometimes harmonious, sometimes conflictual, between different parts of the social body characterizes much of Samoan social life and gives it an aura of both systematicity and improvisation that sustains a much-felt tension in the social structure, which is only apparently predetermined and fixed. The distribution of knowledge about how to act on any given situation is thus functional to the distribution of power within the community. On the one hand, the lower-status people act on more general and hence more easily amendable models, that is, models that need additional information in order to operate appropriately. Higher-status people, on the other hand, not only have access to more specific information about the nature of the activity and the expected and expectable actions, they also control this more specific knowledge by putting it to use when they choose to do so. In particular, the orators, who are the true masters of any ceremony in Samoa, are those who routinely exploit their knowledge and their authority to their advantage and in the interest of those whom they represent.

THE IDEAL SEATING ARRANGEMENT

Samoans can easily provide an outsider with information about seating arrangements, which can be used to draw an ideal seating plan (see fig. 7). When matched with actual situations, this ideal seating plan shows characteristics of what cognitive psychologists call a "schema":

A schema is a knowledge representation that provides an organized set of expectations about a given situation, including the relations of the parts to the whole and to each other. Events, scenes, and stories are types of schematically organized knowledge. Schematic structures are held to be automatically activated in familiar situations and guide comprehension, action and later recall. (Slackman and Nelson 1984, 329)

Like other schemas discussed in the cognitive psychology literature, the one drawn in figure 7 allows for predictions that can be easily adapted to a great variety of situations. When further analyzed, the same figure can be shown to contain a number of important oppositions, the most important of which, as alluded to above, is the one between the front and back region. This opposition is not equivalent to the one between "seaward" and "landward" which has been said to be relevant in other Pacific cultures: for instance, in Fijian (see Sahlins 1976) and Tikopian houses (see Firth 1936, 1970). Instead, as illustrated in map 2, which is a simplified map of a section of the village, the front is the part of the house which faces and is the closest to the main road or the village *malae* 'ceremonial ground', and the back is the opposite side,

front

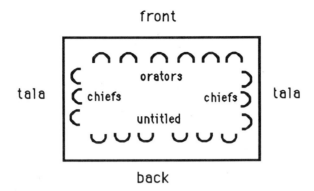

back

Figure 7. An ideal seating plan

which in some cases coincides with the side facing the back of the village or the *vao* 'bush', but in other cases may be the part of the house which is closest to the sea—for this reason, Shore's (1982) identification of "back" with "landward" is empirically questionable.

The front is the more public side, reserved for guests or orators of high rank. Not only does front/back translate into high/low status, it is also necessary for determining the other two sides of the house, the tala. As discussed in Duranti (1981a), in a rectangular house, the tala are the two shorter sides, while in a rectangular house with rounded shorter sides, the tala are the two rounded sides (see fig. 8), and in a circular house, the tala are simply those portions of the perimeter that are *not* front or back (fig. 9). In any given situation, the tala is occupied by people of higher rank; thus, if there are chiefs and orators, the chiefs sit in the tala; if there are deacons and pastors or invited preachers (*tofi*), it is the latter who sit in the tala.

Another important distinction is the one between "center" and "periphery" (Shore 1982). In both the front and the tala, the center part (or the center posts, in a traditional house with wooden posts instead of walls) is reserved for the highest-ranking persons: the highest-ranking chiefs (*tamāli'i*) sit at the center posts in the tala (one chief at center of each tala) and the highest-ranking orators sit in the center part of the front side (Shore 1982, 79–80).

Usually only matai are present in the fono house, although some untitled men usually hang around either outside or in a nearby smaller house, waiting to be called for duty. Occasionally, an untitled man may be present to prepare kava (see "Temporal Boundaries" section below).

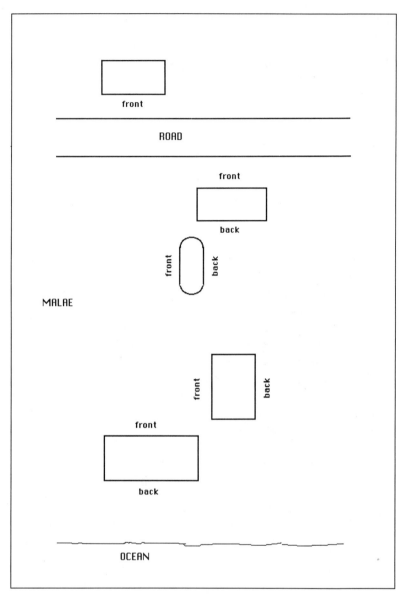

Map 2.   Schematic (not to scale) of section of Falefā

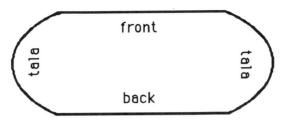

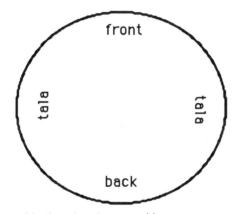

Figure 8. Front and back regions in a rectangular house with rounded shorter sides

Figure 9. Front and back regions in a round house

This means that the distinction between orators in the front and untitled in the back does not hold in a fono. Instead, the status difference is translated into a rank difference, with the orators of lower rank sitting in the back row (see fig. 10). In a Falefā fono, the holders of the four major chiefly titles are expected to sit in the center part of the two tala, facing each other, whereas the chiefs of lesser rank sit toward the periphery of each tala. The higher-ranking orators, which include the two matua Iuli and Moe'ono, sit in the front. The lower-ranking orators sit in the back, including those who are in charge of the kava ceremony, namely, the kava mixer (*palu'ava*) and the kava announcer (*tufa'ava*) (see "Temporal Boundaries," pp. 72ff.).

All of this, however, I learned much later. The first time I entered the fono house, I only saw people sitting around the edges of the house and noticed that some portions were unoccupied whereas other portions seemed crammed with people. I started to draw maps and ask the

front

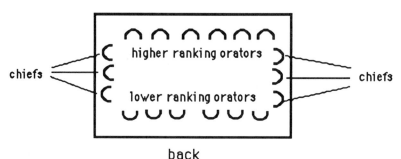

back

Figure 10. The ideal seating arrangement in a Falefā fono

matai who were sitting next to me to help me with the titles of the people who were present. Later, when I matched those maps with what I knew about what had been said and accomplished in the meetings, I realized that the spatial configuration at the beginning of a fono can provide relevant information about the political agenda of the day.

READING THE MAP OF THE DAY

During the time of my first stay (1978–1979), usually only one of the four highest-ranking chiefs in the village would participate in the fono: Salanoa Aukusitino.[7] For this reason the rest of the tala sides were usually left empty. On one occasion in which the holder of one of the other high titles, high chief Alai'a-Sā, was present, he sat in the opposite tala, diagonally with respect to Salanoa's position. Since the highest chief present acts as the representative of the chiefly titles from the four major families ('āiga) in the village (see chap. 2), sitting slightly "off" the center even when no other high chief is present shows that one is not advocating total or exclusive sovereignty over the role and status represented by that particular location in the house; it implies not only humbleness but also a sharing of authority with absent others. In addition to the two senior orators Iuli and Moe'ono, who would always sit next to each other and slightly off the center,[8] a predictable number of other orators would sit in the front, usually one for each of the subvillages represented in the meeting, which, in addition to the four subvillages of Falefā, might include the village of Falevao and the villages of Sauano and Saletele, in Fagaloa Bay (see map 3).

The range of participants was encoded in the name of the type of fono, which played on the metaphorical use of the word *fale* 'house' to stand for 'village' (*nu'u*) or 'subvillage' (*pitonu'u*). Thus, a *fono falefā* was restricted to the four (*fā*) subvillages in Falefā—which itself means 'four houses/subvillages'—a *fono falelima* (meeting of the five [*lima*] houses) included Falevao, and a *fono falefitu* (meeting of the seven [*fitu*] houses) included Falevao and the two villages from Fagaloa Bay (see fig. 11).

By matching the ideal plan for a particular occasion with the actual titleholders who occupied various positions in the house, one could obtain a first reading of the political situation and make a few predictions about the way in which the discussion might unfold. Thus, according to the kind of fono that was being held, a particular set of orators would be expected to sit in the front row. In such a system, every slight variation from what is considered the ideal plan is potentially significant. For this reason, as suggested above, the ideal plan acts as a cognitive schema that provides a key for the participants to interpret the contingencies of the day. The relationship between the ideal seating arrangement and the actual one gives a first approximation of the potential conflicts, tensions, and issues of the day. Let me give an example. At the beginning of the fono of April 7, 1979, the high chief Salanoa, the second-ranking chief in the village (see table 1 in chap. 2), sits in his usual spot in one of the tala and the other chiefs present sit at the edges of the two tala (see fig. 12, which uses only the relevant details from a drawing reproduced in fig. 4). The chief Tuimavave sits farther back at the edge of what will eventually be a second back row, probably to signify his low demeanor on this particular occasion, when the assembly of matai is about to discuss an issue concerning a chief from his descent group, Savea Sione. Savea Sione himself is also sitting in the back, but since he has no orators to his right (in fact the more senior chief Fuimaono Etuale is sitting there), his position is ambiguous. It could in fact be seen as part of the tala or as an extension of it. This is made clearer if we mentally transpose the rectangular plan represented in figure 12 onto the floor plan of a house with rounded tala (see fig. 13).

The contrast between the physical shape of the house and the positions chosen by the participants demonstrate that the definition of the different parts of the house (as front, back, tala) is a combination of physical dimensions and practical choices. Thus, for instance, the chiefs

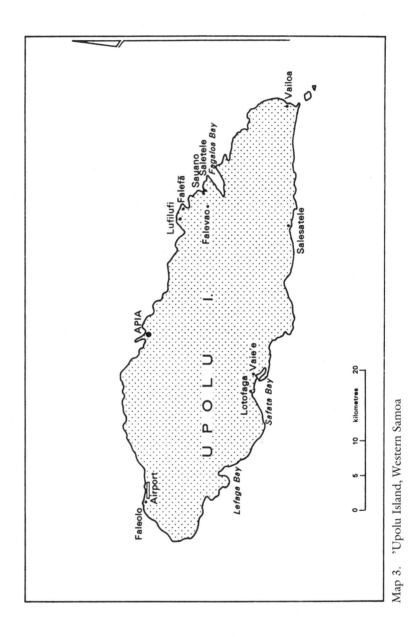

Map 3. 'Upolu Island, Western Samoa

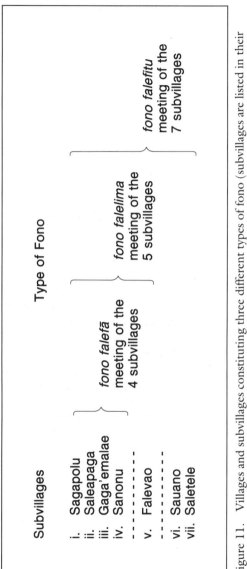

Figure 11. Villages and subvillages constituting three different types of fono (subvillages are listed in their hierarchical order)

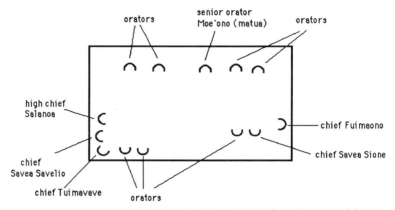

Figure 12. Seating arrangement on April 7, 1979, before the start of the
meeting

can virtually extend the tala by claiming parts of either the front or the
back. Samoans are in this respect true masters of spatial finesse, as dem-
onstrated by the position occupied by the matai who shares the title
with Savea Sione, namely, Savea Savelio.[9] He sits in a position that is
similar to Savea Sione's, but slightly "farther back." This he explained
to me as a sign of restraint: He should not take a foregrounded role in
the fono proceedings given that the actions of the one we might call
his alter ego, Savea Sione, were under severe scrutiny by members of
the assembly.

The examination of the transcript of the ensuing discussion confirms
the strategic alignments suggested by the seating arrangement. Tuimavave and Savea Savelio did not take the floor during the meeting and
Savea Sione presented himself as a humble and minor player in the grand
scheme of district politics and as someone who had not forgotten the
respect due to seniority.

(2) Fono of April 7, 1990. Savea Sione's first speech.

> *Savea;*   Since on this day the agenda and the meeting of the assembly
> concerns me, . . . well, oh chiefs (*'Āiga*), no, don't think about
> me . . . (as if) I didn't respect you very much . . .
>
> *Others;*   Well said!
>
> *Savea;*   The admonition and the word whispered to my ears . . . (have
> always been) the respect and the humbleness . . . those are the
> most important points I am weighing . . . that is also what my
> weak person is trying (to do) . . . Moe'ono, thank you for your
> honorable speech today, . . . you have spoken as a true parent.

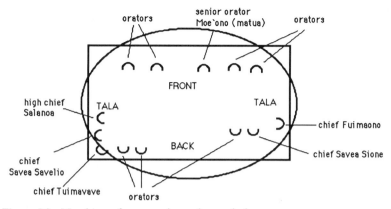

Figure 13. Matching of rectangular and round plans

Others; Well said!

Savea; You are upset and you scold me . . . but now I apologize to the dignity of the chiefs and . . . to the two supporting senior orators, and the son chiefs, and (the rest of) our village. . . .

In addition to Moe'ono, four more orators are sitting in the front. Each is from a different subvillage. This lining up follows the principle that each subvillage should be represented by the highest-ranking orator present, with Moe'ono's and Iuli's subvillages being represented twice, a custom that gives the two senior orators not only the chance to act as chairs but also the option of assuming positions and expressing opinions that might differ from those of other people in their respective descent group or subvillage. At the moment represented by the diagram in figure 12, Iuli is not present. He will arrive late and will go to sit, as expected, next to Moe'ono. Whether or not Iuli's late arrival is particularly meaningful in this case is difficult to say. Everyone knows that he is at church (this is what Moe'ono has been told when he asked about Iuli's whereabouts before starting the meeting), and this justifies his delay. That Iuli's absence is however noticeable is shown by the fact that when he finally arrives (during the third speech of the day) the discussion is interrupted to properly greet him, an honor that would not have been given to orators of lesser rank.

If we look at the seating arrangement a little later in the day, when the meeting has just started (but Iuli hasn't arrived yet) (see fig. 14, which is a more detailed version of a drawing reproduced in fig. 4), we also get a better sense of how important the positions in the house can

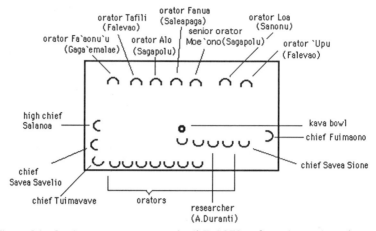

Figure 14. Seating arrangement on April 7, 1979, a few minutes into the
meeting

be for getting a sense of the political tension among participants. On
this day the subvillage of Falevao (see fig. 11) is represented by two
orators, 'Upu and Tafili, in the front row.

   This is unusual. What is even more unusual is that one of the representatives from Falevao, Tafili, is a woman.[10] She is in fact the only
female orator I have ever seen attend a fono of this kind. Although
women can hold matai titles in Samoa, they rarely do. Even more rarely
do they participate in male-dominated village politics. Women have
their own very active associations and committees (Shore 1982) and, as
is generally the case in traditional Polynesia (see Gailey 1987), control
the production of the most valuable cultural goods, namely, fine mats
(*'ie toga,* ritually referred to as *mea sina*). It is partly through the production of an item so central to the traditional economic system that
women acquire in Samoa a central role in all kinds of ritual transactions
(marriages, bestowals of matai titles, funerals, group visits, inaugura-
tions of buildings, etc.). Although the introduction of certain elements
of capitalist economy, namely, a heavy influx of cash from relatives who
migrated to New Zealand or the United States, has partly altered the
traditional importance of women in the local economy, their role is still
routinely recognized in a variety of ritual transactions and in decision
making in the extended family (*'āiga potopoto*). The routine adminis-
tration of justice and the management of political conflicts that take the
form of fono discussions are however usually left to male matai. It is for

these reasons that the presence of a female matai in a fono and in the space reserved for the more active speakers in the assembly requires some interpretive work that goes beyond the routine understanding of what Goffman (1974) called "primary framework." Tafili's presence is unusual and induces a search for explanatory statements. The most obvious explanation in this case is kinship. Tafili is chief Savea Sione's older sister. As the transcript of the discussion shows, she has come to speak out in defense of her brother and in open conflict with the opinion of the powerful senior orator Moe'ono. In her speech, her condemnation of Moe'ono's behavior during the political campaign for district M.P. will be only slightly veiled by ancient metaphors. She will in fact be the only one in the entire assembly who will dare to publicly confront the senior orator by accusing him of being the cause of the current crisis.

(3) Fono of April 7, 1979. Tafili's first speech.

> *Tafili;*   (. . .) Let me say that things like these are not done between brothers or within a family.[11] My explanation of these very things, Moe'ono and Iuli, will refer back. No.[12] I will get to the question of where all of this is taking. No. We think and believe. No. The water is not muddy without any reason. The water is muddy because the cause of all of this is Your Honor the senior orator. The opinion of the chiefs had already been delivered. What happened to it? No, things are bad because of whom? No. (The boat) really leaks because of Your Honor the senior orator. That is the real reason of the prolonging of this matter.

Although she will later choose to speak about Savea as "chief" rather than as "brother,"[13] Tafili is in fact relying on the right of an older sister to protect the actions of her *tei*, or young sibling, a right that she has gained in endless socialization routines that have taught her to protect and show compassion for her little brother, even when he, as in this case, might have misbehaved.[14]

Strong-minded and irreverent as he often is, Moe'ono will be savvy enough to avoid a direct confrontation with a concerned sister. He will reply to her accusations by involving the other senior orator, Iuli, and by presenting a picture of the situation in which he was a victim of the circumstances. Rather than sounding paternalistic or intimidating, as he often does, when he responds to Tafili, Moe'ono turns almost apologetic, such as when he reminds her that he stepped into the election race only after Iuli had already done so. Finally, he tries to brush the elections issue aside, reminding everyone that this is not part of the agenda. There are other things to worry about: above all, the relationship (*vā*) with the nearby village of Lufilufi and with its newly reelected M.P.

An understanding of the locally engendered meaning of the seating arrangement for the day suggests that Moe'ono, as well as the other matai in the fono house, had ways of expecting, ahead of time, Tafili's attack and her role in the meeting. If she is present *and* has chosen to sit in the front row, the place reserved for the more active members of the assembly, everyone knows that Tafili has come ready to speak and, most likely, to argue. Thus, even before a word is exchanged, Tafili's spatial claim provided Moe'ono with clues about the forthcoming discussion and gave him some time to prepare himself for it. In this case, the regionalization of the interactional space available to participants can communicate just as much as words.

Temporal Boundaries

There is a close relationship between the spatial organization in a fono and the temporal organization of the event. The kava ceremony is the first episode within the fono event that clearly exploits sequential structure and hence complements the political map of the day drawn on the house floor with the seating arrangement. As with other kinds of boundary markers, various aspects of the kava ceremony index some of the qualities of the ensuing activity and act as both reminders and cues for participants to the kind of interaction they are likely to have, the expectations they should legitimately hold, and the kind of power structure assumed for the occasion, even though in a fono such structure might be momentarily questioned during the ongoing crisis.

THE KAVA CEREMONY

Although not all fono need to start with it, for the kind of *ad hoc* fono I discuss here a kava ceremony usually acts as an opening boundary marker. In a fono, the kava ceremony is typically less elaborate than in other formal events,[15] but there are still strict rules of etiquette that regulate the ritual distribution of the beverage. One of the matai in the center of the back row acts as the the palu'ava, the one who mixes water with kava (*'ava*)—the pulverized dry roots of *piper methysticum*—

in a special wooden bowl (*tānoa*). Next to the palu'ava sits the tufa'ava, the one who names, one at a time, the matai who are to be served kava.[16] At a high volume and in a characteristic high-pitched melodic contour that drops very low toward the end of his call, the tufa'ava cries out the title or, in some cases, the special cup name, of the matai who should be served kava next. His chanting serves as an instruction for the cup bearer (*solitū*), usually one of the young untitled males who hang around the fono house, who stands in the middle of the circle of matai and carries the cup full of kava and graciously hands it to the named matai. The tufa'ava has an important and difficult job: he must competently recite the appropriate *solo*, or poetic lines, mixed with ceremonial phrases about the village ceremonial ground (*malae*), the most important titles in the district, and so on; he must remember and use the special cup names (*igoa ipu*) of the chiefs present and the drinking names (*igoa 'ava*) of the senior orators; and finally and most importantly, he must decide the order of precedence in the serving. Although most of what he does is highly predictable, he does have some leeway and might use it to different ends: to win the favor of a high chief or guest, to suggest a given alternative interpretation of the setting, to ridicule a matai who seems too confident of his status (*fiamaualuga*), to distance himself from a matai that he is related to.

When I asked matai in Falefā about the order of distribution of kava, they would first tell me that "chiefs drink first." In the fono I observed, however, it was orators who drank first. This apparent contradiction between theory and practice can be explained by the fact that, when asked out of context, matai tend to think of ceremonial occasions rather than of political events as the prototypical situations (as we shall see in chap. 4, this is also at work in the characterization of a typical formal speech). It took me some time to learn to be very specific in my questioning. If I left things vague, I would get stereotypical answers. If I explained myself in some detail, people would be challenged to match my knowledge with a more sophisticated competence. Accordingly, their normative statements would become more accurate, more context specific.

THE ORDER OF KAVA DISTRIBUTION IN A FONO

In a fono,[17] the matai who sit in the front are served kava first. This principle can be verified by matching the ordered list of titles

Table 3 *Order of Kava Distribution on April 7, 1979 (First Ceremony)*

Title[a]	Status	Subvillage
1. Loa	Orator	Sanonu
2. Moe'ono	Orator	Sagapolu
3. Fanua	Orator	Saleapaga
4. Fa'aonu'u	Orator	Gaga'emalae
5. 'Upu	Orator	Falevao
6. Salanoa	Chief	Saleapaga
7. Savea	Chief	Gaga'emalae (Savelio and Sione are both served)
8. Fuimaono	Chief	Sagapolu
9. 'Alo	Orator	Sagapolu
10. Lutu	Orator	Sagapolu
11. Tuimavave	Orator	Gaga'emalae (last cup: *moto*[b])

[a]Some of these names are shortened forms of the title: Loa stands for "Taofiuailoa," Moe'ono for "Moe'ono'ono," Fanua for "Fanualelei," and Salanoa for "Lealaisalanoa."
[b]The actual last cup may not be the official last cup, which must be especially announced by the tufa'ava with the words *moto le agatonu* 'bring the kava (agatonu) to an end'. Such an "ending cup" is usually given to an important chief. In the fono I observed, the ending cup was often given to Muagututi'a, one of the aloali'i.

of the matai who were served kava during the first kava ceremony on April 7 (table 3) with the diagram of the seating arrangement (fig. 15).

This distribution of kava, which is not unusual for this kind of fono, shows the following characteristics: orators drink first; but, with the exception of Lutu (see below), only those orators who sit in the front of the house are served; whereas all chiefs present are served.

The order of the first rounds of kava distribution was very consistent in the fono I observed. It was based on subvillages rather than on individual titles. The highest-ranking orator present from each subvillage would be served according to the order given in figure 16—thus, Loa drinks first because the orator Leuta is not present. After an orator from each of the represented subvillages was served, the next cup would go to the highest-ranking chief (Salanoa on April 7; see table 3).

In a fono of the five subvillages (fono falelima), an orator from Falevao would be served fifth, and in a fono falefitu, when the two subvillages of Fagaloa were also summoned, an orator from Sauano and one from Saletele would occupy sixth and seventh position, respectively. In the case summarized in table 3, the orator Fanua, from Saleapaga, drinks after Moe'ono because the senior orator Iuli, who is the highest-

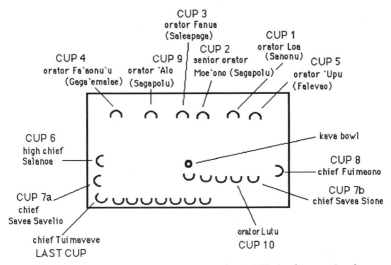

Figure 15. Distribution of kava cups on April 7, 1979, in the opening kava
ceremony

ranking orator from Saleapaga, has not arrived yet. The highest chief
present is served after one orator for each subvillage has already drunk.
As I mentioned earlier, compared to other occasions when kava is
drunk, this order is unusual. In fact, to my knowledge, this is the only
consistent exception to the principle "chief drinks before orator." Even
more exceptional is the fact that the first one to be served is an orator
from Sanonu, which is the lowest-ranking subvillage in Falefā. This
apparent "inversion" (lowest is first) seems linked to the "upside-
down" nature of the polity at the moment of the special fono discussed
here. This order is not unusual, however, within the fono itself: it is in
fact parallel to the order of speakers in the meeting (see below). In both
cases, what we have is the semiotic exploitation of the sequential nature
of serving drinks and taking turns at talk to evoke an inverse "order of
things," in which the highest-ranking titles must wait for others of lesser
rank to go first. This inversion has a historical explanation. Sanonu is
the subvillage that used to go first in times of war. "Sanonu would go
first, to make sure the way was clear and the king (Tuiatua) could pass
safely," a matai told me. Sanonu was the vanguard (*muā'au*). In a fono,
Sanonu still acts as the vanguard, to "clear the way" before other, more
powerful parties can present themselves and venture into the dispute.
It is also a matai from Sanonu who distributes kava. This is another

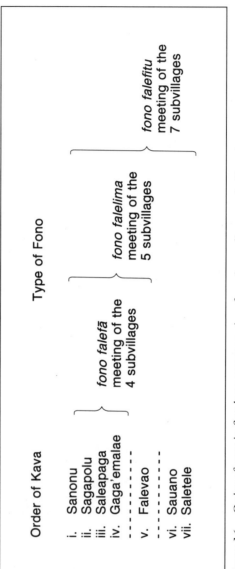

Figure 16. Order of cups in first kava ceremony in a fono (according to subvillages)

right that Sanonu has acquired for its people's courage in the wars. Anytime there are goods to be shared, it is a matai from Sanonu who decides how to divide things among those present.

As for the old orator Lutu, who is the only one in the back who is served in the ceremony, there are several possible explanations, the most likely of which is that he is from the powerful subvillage of Sagapolu and is related to the highest chief in the village, Leutele. It is probably in honor of the absent Leutele that he is served.[18]

Speaking

Before the meeting starts, matai gathered in the fono house chat with one another about varied topics that might cover national politics as well as the latest village gossip. Talk is exchanged in a conversational style that is not very different from what has been described for Western settings by conversation analysts (see Sacks et al. 1974). More than one conversation might be going on at the same time, people do not use ceremonial speech, turns at talk are relatively short, and there are occasional overlaps between speakers. The atmosphere before the meeting is almost comparable to the atmosphere in the West before any kind of formal gathering, when people who are familiar with one another occupy their waiting period with talk that is often purposely different from what will be exchanged during the formal meeting. The only noticeable difference in the Samoan case is the interruption of such pre-meeting informality by the greeting of new arrivals. When a person arrives and sits down, some of the people already in the house welcome him by addressing him with his title and sometimes with parts of the fa'alupega of his descent group. The newcomer, in turn, responds by addressing the people present with their titles and ceremonial address. Contrary to what Derek Freeman has stated (1983, 122), in my experience, not all chiefs are greeted, but only those who go to sit in the tala. Similarly, only the orators who sit in the front are formally greeted.[19] After the greeting is exchanged, informal conversation is resumed until the next matai arrives and is greeted.

Since not everyone is greeted and there are different ways of greeting and responding to a greeting, this kind of verbal exchange is yet another way of constituting locally relevant hierarchies while activating statuses and roles potentially relevant in the forthcoming event. The new arrival's response to the assembly also indexes the nature of the occasion. Thus, for instance, if the fono is a *fono o le pulenu'u* 'a meeting with the pulen-u'u' (a village matai who acts as a kind of mayor or government repre-sentative), the response to the greeting includes reference to the pulen-u'u. On other occasions, such as the *ad hoc* meetings discussed here,[20] the pulenu'u might not be mentioned at all, and the response is more likely to coincide with the basic fa'alupega of the village (see chap. 2).

Another way the greeting exchanges symbolically anticipate the forthcoming meeting is in the frequent episodes of eye contact aversion (Duranti 1992b). The same avoidance of eye contact can be found during the fono, when a speaker usually avoids looking at any one spe-cific member of the audience (even when he is talking about or to that person) and the members of the audience, in turn, tend not to stare at the speaker. When I asked Samoan matai about this kind of behavior, they described it not as a form of respect but rather as a practical matter. As they put it, "a person listens with the ears and not with the eyes."

THE ORDER OF SPEAKERS

Once the meeting starts, the talk exchanged is radically different from informal conversation. Thus, for instance, vocabulary terms of respect, metaphors, and proverbs are consistently used in the production of a specific ceremonial verbal genre called *lāuga* (see chap. 4). Furthermore, the rules for the allocation of the floor change. Rather than short turns, frequent change of speakers, and occasional overlaps, the general norm becomes "one person speaks at a time and for an extended period." To capture the difference between a turn in conver-sation and a turn in a fono discussion, I introduced (Duranti 1981a) the notion of a *macro turn,* by which I roughly meant a turn that co-incides with what could be thought of as an entire speech. One char-acteristic of a macro turn is that it gives speakers the right to the floor for a considerable number of utterances and for a large number of what, in a conversational sense, might be seen as separate turns. The macro turn, by way of conventions, establishes different rules for change of speakers and hence for what conversation analysts call "transition rel-evant point." What might be a possible point of intervention in con-versation is not necessarily so for a speech in a fono. In fact, as I will discuss in chapter 4, a claim to the floor before the current speaker has explicitly marked his speech as finished is considered an "interruption."

In many ways, the assignment of the floor in a Samoan fono is not very different from political debates or juridicial settings in the West. As in other kinds of similar events around the world, in a fono there is a strict protocol as to when it is appropriate for a given party to speak up and make his opinion known. This is particularly true at the beginning of the meeting, when matters of precedence seem to be stricter and more emblematic than later on in the discussion, when things follow less predictable schemes.

The preallocated right to speak at the beginning of the meeting can override high status and seniority. Thus, for instance, even a high chief might have to wait his turn until other speakers of lower status finish their speeches. In example (4), for instance, the high chief Alai'a-Sā tried to take the floor after the first speaker, instead of waiting for the orators to finish the first round of speeches[21]:

(4) Fono of March 17, 1979. The first speaker, the orator Loa, has just finished his speech and the high chief Alai'a-Sā[22] takes the floor instead of the orator 'Alo, from the subvillage of Sagapolu.[23]

Loa;	((finishing)) Good luck to the assembly and the fono.
?;	Well done!
?;	Good luck!
Alai'a-Sā;	Well, thank you-
'Alo;	May rest-
Alai'a-Sā;	your highness announced the topics.
	Well. (I am) not going to sit here heedlessly.
	I have to-
	because this one knows [i.e., I know]
	that it is this one who caused the trouble.
	Therefore now I ask you with humbleness.
	No one is perfect in this world.
	If there is some mistake, it's due to this old man (i.e., me)
	and the whole thing.
	No one can test this world.
	That's the thing for which I politely ask you,
	in front of the whole village
	((truck goes by, sound unclear))
	It's no use to be sitting and waiting for a long time.
	So there is something.
	I am just giving you humbleness.
	If this is what you all desire,
	then I just tell you that
	my words will not take too long.
	They will be short.
	It will be straight talk.

Others;	Very true.
	Well done!
Alai'a-Sā;	So, it's then finished-
Iuli;	Alai'as- Alai'a-Sā!
	Thanks for the honorable speaking from Your Highness.
	Yes, there will be a time to say this,
	but until- . . .
	now our subvillages have not finished.
	As there are also (other) positions and- (there is)
	(the) assembly of our village.
	So. This is my reply to your- (to the) honorable speaking
	from Your Highness Alai'a-Sā.
?;	Thanks.
'Alo;	So may the speech and the words of Alai'a-Sā rest (for now)
	in the chiefly house. . . .

In this case, the expected order of speakers is used to control the potential prevarication of a high-status individual. The two senior orators Iuli and Moe'ono have sufficient authority to stop a high chief from downplaying the importance of the proceedings and mocking the necessary etiquette. The fono is indeed an arena where respect for rank and protocol go hand in hand. Before taking the floor again, even the high chief Alai'a-Sā will have to wait until at least one orator from each of the subvillages represented in the fono has spoken and until the case has been formally presented by Moe'ono and discussed by the assembly.

Conclusions

In this chapter I have shown that in a fono social actors show a considerable ability to adapt what are perceived and presented as ideal models of the social order to the contingencies of any given situation and in fact to use apparent violations of normative principles— "chiefs drink kava first" is for instance routinely violated in the fono described here—as ways of symbolically reinforcing the specificity of the occasion. Despite the continuous reference to an eternal and immutable order of things (this is for instance the way the hierarchy is portrayed in the ceremonial lāuga; see chap. 4), the rituals of everyday life, including several included in the fono proceedings, refer to or imply an order that is only made to appear "the same," but in fact contains continual mutations. It is here that we encounter a symbolic paradox: in order for the system to stay the same, it must continuously change, adapt. Such changes and adaptations are sometimes very temporary (the space of an event or cycle of events, or someone's lifespan), other times more long lasting.

On a synchronic level, when we encounter variations of the canonical or ideal order, such variations are explained by members through some features of the interaction. Such explanations contain important clues as to the significance of the ongoing activity for the institutions it is embedded in and for the actors who participate in it. In this sense, spatial arrangements, temporal orders, and rights to speak at a given moment not only are essential parts of Samoan etiquette but also provide a continuous update on people's status within the community. In the very interplay of different systems of reference (spatial vs. temporal or drinking vs. talking) one can find confirmation of certain expected status or rank differentiations or the offer of alternative orders that in some cases may be occasional and exceptional and in other cases may forecast new arrangements, new alignments, or unexpected priorities that may survive the trial of time and thus be canonized into a new, acceptable ideal order (it is in this context that the changes in the fa'alupega should be judged). With respect to the social structure of the community, then, the different procedures I illustrated in this chapter can be seen as adding up to a heteroglossia of status symbols. That is, they are an interaction of languages, codes, media, activities whereby status and social hierarchies are represented for what they are, namely, a moment in the temporal succession of life experiences and life expectations. Whether or not a certain configuation of the various symbols used will survive and become part of history is highly but never completely predictable.

The amount of knowledge required to make sense of every subtle variation is considerable. Such knowledge is also variable. The reasons given for justifying one order over another may vary from one person to another or from one moment to another. People in another village may not know about a specific convention or an expected inversion. This fact supports the view that rituals help constitute group solidarity without requiring a uniform set of beliefs or interpretive procedures (Kertzer 1988). The relationship between status and knowledge is always constitutive. Someone's status may be used to explain how much that person knows or how many rationales for certain ritual choices he or she can find. At the same time, the complexity of that person's knowledge and explanations is but part of what constitutes that person's status within the community.

This dialectical, mutually constitutive relationship between knowledge and status also applied to my experience. There was nothing more impressive to my Samoan hosts than my display of ritual knowledge. The use of a few esoteric phrases learned from my audiotapes of fono and other social events would typically trigger an offer of a title by the matai present.[24] The inference at work was obvious: if I made use of such knowledge, I should be a matai.

The ceremonial address provides an important key for interpreting the various orders and arrangements performed throughout innumerable daily rituals. Thus, the performance of the extended ceremonial address (fa'atulouga) in the first lāuga in a fono lists, in hierarchical order, the names of the most important families and titles in the village (Duranti 1981a). We can use that order and those titles to make sense of other orders in the ongoing interactions. Many variations and violations can be explained by starting from the ceremonial address and then adding constraints due to the particular circumstances of the encounter (e.g., depending on the reason for the gathering, whether or not guests are present, the seriousness of the occasion). But each time a new reason for its violation is added, the predictive power of the ceremonial address for a specific situation is in fact reduced. Given that, as I mentioned earlier, the ceremonial addresses are themselves subject to variation and modification over time, we cannot rely on them as the final explanation of everything. If we took the fa'alupega to be the sacred text out of which all behaviors must be explained, we would have a hard time explaining how the text can change at all. Instead, there is a dialogical relation between the fa'alupega and the rituals that exploit it or simply hint at its existence.

Let us take as an example the order of kava drinking. We know that the kava announcer has a number of resources for making his choices and justifying them in case he needs to. They include, in addition to the ceremonial address, the setting (e.g., the house where the ceremony takes place), the type of event (e.g., fono vs. ceremony), the activity the ceremony embodies or foreshadows (e.g., opening vs. closing of event), the statuses and rank relations of the participants, and the ways in which they have seated themselves on that particular occasion (see fig. 17).

The choice made at each point, taking the various factors into consideration, partly conditions the next choice, but no one factor can be

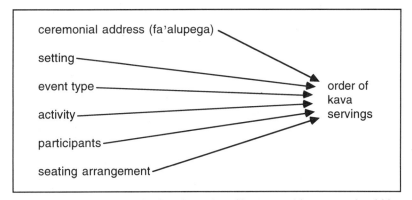

Figure 17.   Elements involved in the order of kava cups (the arrows should be interpreted as "informs")

said to be a "determining factor" or a feature by necessity more important than others. Thus, for instance, if the setting, the participants, and the activity warrant "first chiefs, then orators," after the first two cups to the two highest-ranking chiefs, the next two cups would go to their respective orators. If orators drink first, as in the fono discussed here, then the cup to the highest-ranking chief present would be the first cup after one orator for each of the groups (e.g., subvillages, descent groups) present had been served. However, if there are some visiting chiefs who have not been convened for the fono but just happen to be around when the fono is starting, they might be served first as a sign of "respect" (*fa'aaloalo*) to guests. In this case, the order "orators first" would have to be violated. None of these sequences would be determined by the factors involved but any might be justified by them. Ultimately, it is up to the tufa'ava to decide. Some of the matai in the assembly might complain, but the cup bearer would always execute the directive given by the tufa'ava's cry.

This means that, from the point of view of its ideological representation (symbolic acts included), the hierarchy itself is an example of what Wittgenstein (1953) called "family resemblances." That is, there is no core set of principles to be applied in all situations. Even what seems the most general and recurrent representation of local social distinctions, namely, the ceremonial address, can be used to explain a particular practice in the society—for example, kava distribution—only with several amendments. In fact, the ceremonial address may not in any way be more "general" than other (often less direct or transparent) kinds of symbolic representations. When we look at what is actually accomplished on a given day by the people who represent and physically embody the society's stratification, we find a number of only partly overlapping or partly connected principles, each emergent from specific, context-sensitive and at the same time context-creating practices. From the point of view of such diverse practices, what we might call a "chiefdom" is, at least at its symbolic or ideological level, an abstraction out of a number of those very same practices that might have been seen as instrumental to its existence (see Earle 1992). This means that, in the world of everyday practice, the distinction between rites used to represent a particular social system and rites used to sustain such a system is in fact a difficult one to make. The blurring of such a distinction is itself praxis producing. For one thing, it makes stratified societies like the Samoan society discussed here look much more fluid than one might think at first on the basis of normative statements taken out of context. The multiplicity of interpretive practices found in an event like the fono allows for a dynamic social system in which it is not always obvious who will be able to have access to goods or to decision-making processes. The ability of certain actors to control the system and its resources is not guaranteed by the system once and for all. Rather, it depends on their ability, and the ability of their supporters or vassals, to justify the logic that would give them—as opposed to others—the rights necessary for maintaining authority in some specific situations. Such authority, however, must be built, sustained, recalled, fought for. In chapter 4, I will start to discuss the ways in which such authority depends on verbal skills. To be able to enter the political arena and influence the decision-making process, a speaker must exploit traditional hierarchies and values while at the same time breaking out of them to face the deeds of mortals who err as a way of being. This is done in what I see as a struggle of genres and voices, a struggle that is reminiscent of what Bakhtin called "heteroglossia"—namely, the multitude of language varieties and human voices that inhabit any act of language use. It is within this struggle that we will finally encounter those very same grammatical patterns (namely, transitive clauses with fully expressed agents) I was looking for when I first arrived in the field.

Alessandro Duranti, at center, with head carpenter chief Tāvō (now orator Fulumu'a) Utulei, first on the left, and the rest of his crew in front of Martha Platt's newly finished house (August 1978). Back, third from left, orator Lua Veni.

Members of the research team during a break from transcription work. From left, Elinor Ochs, Alessandro Duranti (in the front), Sililo Tapui (in the back), Kasairina Vailalo, and David Ochs Keenan.

Alessandro Duranti with orator Lua Veni (subsequently appointed to the title of senior orator Iuli), discussing the *fa'alupega* of the different sub-villages represented in the *fono*.

Elinor Ochs listening to a tape and checking a transcript with research assistant Kasairina Vailalo (1978).

View of a section of Falefā from the ocean (1979). The white build-ing on the right is the church of the Congregational Christian Church of Samoa (demolished and rebuilt in 1988). Author's house is on the left, hidden behind the banana trees, next to the pastor's western-style building.

Chief Tuimavave Sefo's large western-style house, where most of the *fono* recorded in 1979 took place.

From left, high chief Salanoa Aukusitino, chief Savea Savelio, and chief Tuimavave Sefo.

Senior orators Iuli Sefo (looking at camera) and Moe'ono (with head down) while waiting for *matai* from another village to visit the *fono*.

At a *saofa'i*, young untitled men wait to be called to exhibit food offerings.

Kava roots for sale at the market.

An orator cleans the kava bowl (*tānoa*), while another one pounds the kava roots on a rock.

Two orators mix water and kava for an early morning gathering.

Women from the extended family (*'āiga potopoto*) listening to a speech during the discussion before a *saofa'i*.

The fine mats (*'ie toga*) are shown outside while someone cries out their number and qualities for everyone in the village to hear.

At a *saofa'i*, Alessandro Duranti and Martha Platt get ready to record the kava ceremony and the speeches that consecrate the acceptance of the new *matai* by the village.

Orator Lua Veni, holding an orator's stick (*to'oto'o*) and with a fly-whisk (*fue*) on his shoulder, gets ready to deliver a ceremonial speech (*lāuga*) on behalf of his extended family.

4

Politics and Verbal Art: Heteroglossia in the Fono

In the last chapter, I discussed how the local hierarchies are reproduced and negotiated within the context of the fono, which is to be understood as a complex social event where communication takes place at different levels and through different channels. From an ethnography of spatial and temporal dimensions within the fono, we can learn how Samoans construct multiple versions of the same social order, giving the impression of a stable but at the same time flexible system, which has deep historical and mythical roots but is also permeable to contextual variation and innovation. In this chapter, I will go on to analyze in more detail both the content and the form of talk within the fono. I will show that from a comparison of the fono speeches with speeches in other social events we can gain an appreciation of the very goals of the fono as an important social drama in the community, where elaborate speechmaking is not simply a celebration of past glory and immutable structures but the acceptance of a real tension between past and present, order and breaches, stability and threats to the system. It is in this context that the lāuga style and content are adapted or, as it were, corrupted, to serve the ends of local politics and local justice. Rather than a world where aesthetic canons and social order coincide, the speeches in a fono intermittently describe and deal with contingent

This chapter is a revised and expanded version of my "Heteroglossia in Samoan Oratory," published in *Pacific Studies* 15. The central sections on interruptions are new. Special thanks to Paul Kroskrity and Pamela Rosi for comments on an earlier draft of this chapter.

events and real conflicts among community members. From studying the polysemic associations inherent in the genre lāuga as it changes from one event to another or from one moment to another in the same event, we can learn a great deal about the power of language to both adapt to and shape the contexts in which it is used (Duranti and Goodwin 1992).

Previous work on language and politics suggests that in certain domains of artistic performance, such as traditional oratory, there is a strong identification between a particular genre or style of verbal art and a particular version of the sociopolitical order. For Bloch (1975a), such an identification makes it difficult to introduce in the interaction modes of expression that threaten the order celebrated by the formal genre. In discussing the Merina of Madagascar, Bloch writes:

> The village Councils are nothing more then than particularly important examples of a much wider general kind of formalised oratorical occasions whose structure is the same and where social control is handled by the same procedures. On these occasions if you have allowed somebody to speak in an oratorical manner you have practically accepted his proposal. The reason is that the code adopted by the speaker contains within itself a set pattern of speech for the other party. (Bloch 1975a, 9)

Given these properties of traditional oratory, Bloch suggests that political leaders must adopt a different style in order to break out of the "non-historical, non-specific and highly ambiguous language which reduces events to being merely instances of a recurring eternal order" (Bloch 1975b, 25). Thus, for instance, in the case of the Tshidi oratory discussed by John Comaroff (1975), two codes, "formal" and "evaluative," are used for two different types of activities:

> The formal code will be used by a Tshidi orator when he speaks, among other things, about the chiefship and the values embodied in it, the rules which govern succession and incumbency, and commonly held indigenous views concerning the nature of government. The evaluative code, on the other hand, is utilised by a speaker, when, for example, he debates the past performance of an office-holder or the public actions of politicians. (Comaroff 1975, 150)

The two codes, which Comaroff defines as "ideal-types" (p. 149) but which are "grounded in empirical reality" (p. 150), can occur in the course of the same speech.

A similar dichotomy is described by Ann Salmond (1975) in discussing Maori oratory. Whereas greetings (*mihi*) and other opening parts of a public encounter in a *marae*—the central, ceremonial ground of a village—tend to be formal and celebratory of the past and of the common heritage, the topical speeches (*take*)[1] are more informal and do not follow the same aesthetic canons.

> The difference between formal and informal speeches is a very interesting one. The formal speeches establish relations between groups and allow both groups and individuals to vie for prestige within a tightly controlled framework of rules. These contests are at once easy to score because options are so limited, and difficult to play, requiring real finesse from the actors. The end results are judged in terms of *mana*. When stranger groups are meeting on the *marae*, they are in the territory of the traditional war god, and oratory is a tenuous bridge between them. Rules are broken only by accident or in anger, since at this point the encounter can still fail. It must be stressed, though, that not every encounter is a power struggle. Between friendly groups and kinfolk, *aroha* (love, solidarity, heart) is by far the most significant part of their meetings, and *mana* is irrelevant.
>
> In the informal speeches, on the other hand, the ground rules are almost non-existent, and prestige is less at stake, yet very real political influence is exercised. (Salmond 1975, 58)

In this chapter I will show that something similar is at work in Samoan oratory. In particular, I will suggest that Samoan speakers can act qua political actors by exploiting a traditional genre of verbal art, the lāuga, while adapting it to their political ends. The variation of the genre lāuga suggests that social actors can show respect for aesthetic canons while at the same time exploiting them for their own political ends. Drawing from the work of Bakhtin on the evolution from the epic to the novel, I will argue that in the context of a fono the ceremonial genre lāuga is mixed with other genres to serve different needs. At the same time, by framing the discourse in a fono as related but different from the discourse of ceremonial exchanges, the speechmakers can establish a context for real confrontation and, hence, for real political challenge. Rather than an epic genre that celebrates an immutable past projected toward a predictable future, the lāuga in a fono becomes the vehicle for political appraisal and political change. It is in this context that, as I discuss in chapter 5, brief narratives are told about human deeds and agency is constituted.

Variations across Contexts

A lāuga is a formal speech usually delivered by a professional speechmaker (*failāuga*) who controls and knows when and how to display traditional lore, including genealogies, proverbs, metaphors, as well as respectful words (*'upu fa'aaloalo*), that is, special words to be used when talking about and (usually) in the presence of high-status people during ceremonial exchanges and other formal occasions (Duranti 1992a; Milner 1961).

The word *lāuga* is used in Samoa for a wide range of speeches, some of which will not be discussed here. For instance, it not only covers traditional oratorical performances of all kinds but also has been extended to (Christian) church sermons, which lack the subdivisions characteristic of traditional lāuga (see table 4) and exhibit an overtly Western logic of expository prose that is different from local rhetorical strategies. Thus, sermons are dedicated to explaining a passage of written text (from the Bible), have a main theme (*matua*), and are based on a more extreme monologic model of communication. Despite the fact that during traditional speechmaking the orator has virtually exclusive control of the floor for an extensive time (several minutes), the audience routinely shows appreciation of the various points made by the speechmaker by responding with a timely *mālie!* 'well said!' or *mo'i* 'true'. During a sermon, however, no appreciation of the pastor's delivery is signified by the audience, although afterward, a few matai or deacons might individually congratulate him on his performance.[2]

When asked about it, Samoans are quick to point out that not all speeches casually referred to as "lāuga" are lāuga strictly speaking or in the true sense of the word. On any given occasion, there usually is one (more rarely two) true lāuga, with other (either preceding or following) speeches being seen as replies (*tali*) or simply discussions (*talanoaga*). Thus, for instance, in a ceremonial exchange, before a lāuga is delivered the orators present engage in a formal debate in which the best speechmakers compete to be given the right to deliver the speech on behalf of everyone else in their descent group, congregation, village, and so on. This debate is called *fa'atau* (literally 'buying' or 'selling') and is characterized by many lāuga features, such as long turns by the same speaker, conventional feedback by the audience, proverbs, metaphors, respectful words. Speeches during these negotiations, however, are not considered lāuga.

Even within a fono, the word *lāuga* can be used in referring to a chief's speech (e.g., the speech presenting the chief's opinion and binding decision), though only in a loose sense of the term. Strictly speaking, only the very first speech of the day is considered a lāuga. As I will discuss below, the rest of the speeches are part of the discussion (*tal-*

anoaga) of the agenda and do not closely follow the rules governing the performance of lāuga, although they incorporate many of their features. Although I once drew a sharp distinction between *lāuga* and *talanoaga* (Duranti 1984), which I saw then as two different genres, I now have come to the conclusion that the distinction is in fact one of degrees. Speeches delivered on formal occasions are always seen as some version of lāuga and in fact one can always use the term *lāuga* in referring to them—in other words, even the speeches that are part of the fono discussion or talanoaga could be called *lāuga*. What changes is the extent to which the speechmaker must conform to certain aesthetic canons, including the performance of the different parts of the speech. In the discussion part of a fono, the basic structure of the lāuga plan is much reduced. Furthermore, as I will discuss below, linguistic features characteristic of less formal occasions creep in to create an intertexuality that dramatically undermines the harmonic order implied by the more elaborate lāuga.

The Lāuga Plan

Despite idiosyncratic and contextual variation, even the most summary investigation of a few lāuga reveals a well-defined structure across contexts. The existence of a basic pattern composed of various parts is readily admitted and recognized by all orators, who can talk at ease about names for different parts, their order, and their content, give examples of the expressions used within each part, and discuss possible variation to fit the occasion. As I learned during my first attempts to discover the basic principles of lāuga performance through informal interviews, individuals may however differ as to their ability to provide a general (or ideal) plan that can explain specific contextual variants. For this reason, my categorization of lāuga organization is based not only on speechmakers' metastatements about the lāuga plan but also on recordings of actual performances and their discussion with knowledgeable performers.

Any lāuga is composed of several parts (*vāega*), typically from four to seven, with each part having a name and performing a different function. Some recent work by a Samoan scholar, T. F. M. Tu'i (1987; formerly Matā'afa 1985), has largely confirmed the prototypical *lāuga* plan I originally outlined on the basis of my 1978–1979 fieldwork. In

Table 4 *The Lāuga Plan*

Duranti (1981a)	Tu'i (1987)
1. *folasaga* (introduction)	1. *tūvaoga* (also called *folasaga* or *paepae-ulufanua*) (introduction)
2. *'ava* (kava)	2. *'ava* (kava)
3. *fa'afetai* (thanksgiving)	3. *fa'afetai i le alofa o le Atua* (thanks for the Lord's love)
4. *taeao* (mornings)	4. *taeao* (mornings)
5. *pa'ia* (sacred [titles])	5. *pa'ia* (sacred [titles])
6. *'auga o le aso* (foundation of the day)	6. *faiā or matā'upu* (agenda)
7. *fa'amatafi lagi* (clear the sky)	7. *fa'amatafiga o lagi* (clearing of skies)

table 4, the lāuga plan I outlined for ceremonies (Duranti 1981a, 1983) is compared with the one Tu'i (1987) proposed for the fono. The penultimate part in a ceremony, "foundation of the day," corresponds to the "agenda" in a fono, given that it is the time for announcing the reason for the gathering.

As I discuss in several works (Duranti 1981a, 1981b, 1983), the sequence and distinctions presented in table 4 should be seen as an ideal plan that is rarely fully realized. One of the qualities of a competent speechmaker is the ability to adapt this ideal plan to the contingencies of the day or even of the moment.

VARIATIONS IN LENGTH AND NUMBER OF PARTS

Length is an important element in the evaluation of a lāuga performance. Whereas a young or inexperienced orator might use speechmaking as an opportunity to show off his knowledge of traditional customs and hence go through each part of the plan, an experienced and skillful speechmaker knows when to be concise and when to be lengthy. Thus, for instance, the *folasaga* or introduction is used when the speech is given before the kava ceremony, but not when it follows it (as in a fono). This can be partly explained by the fact that both the folasaga and the kava ceremony perform similar functions. Thus, for instance, as shown in examples (5) and (6) below, they both declared the place and the time sacred and special:

(5) Folasaga from a *saofa'i*, a ceremony of installation of new matai titles. Performed by the orator Usu Utua'i in a loud voice.

17	Usu;	*uā:- . . . pa'ia 'ākoakoa le maoka legei*
		So:- this residence of chief is completely sacred
18		*ma le kupua legei. . . .*
		and this honorable village. . . .
19		*'ua pa'ia ma 'ua mamalu le aso.*
		The day is sacred and dignified.
20		*'ua pa'ia fafo*
		Outside is sacred
21		*'ua pa'ia fale*
		the house is sacred
22		*'ua leai se i se ā i le kaeao legei. . . .*
		there are no doubts this morning. . . .
23		*'o le kaeao ga liliu iai le kōfā i le Makua Iuli,*
		The morning decided upon by the Honorable senior orator Iuli,
24		*. . . ma le mamalu i le 'āiga.*
		. . . and the dignitaries of his family.

Example (6) presents the first few lines of the *solo* or poetic lines pronounced loudly and in a characteristically fast beat by the tufa'ava when he starts announcing the distribution of kava:

(6) Fono of April 7, 1979. The orator Manu'a (Ma) starts to call out the kava.

5	Ma;	*(aga)kogu le kaeao pa'ia ma le kaeao mamalu!*
		The kava of the sacred morning and the dignified morning!
6		*(1.0) le usuia o le aofia ma le fogo!*
		(when) the assembly and the fono has convened!
7		*(1.5) pa'ia Moamoa 'o le kua o Lalogāfuafua*
		Moamoa, the back of Lalogāfuafua, is sacred
8		*(o)ga afifio ai 'oukou 'āiga ma aloali'i!*
		since you chiefs and son chiefs have arrived!
9		*(1.5) alāla ai 'oulua makua ma le 'a'ai o Fogokī!*
		You two senior orators and the rest of the village of (the King) Fonotī have also appeared!

The similarities between the two segments become more transparent once we further interpret the content of each. In particular, line 17 in example (5) parallels line 7 in example (6), the only difference being that whereas the orator Usu only mentions the 'residence' (/maoka/) of the chiefs, Manu'a refers to /Moamoa/, the malae, or ceremonial ground, of the village and specifies that its location is at the "back of" Lalogāfuafua, the malae of the nearby village of Lufilufi. This difference reflects the different nature of the occasion: in the bestowal of a title the speechmaker concentrates on the family that gives out the title; in the fono, the relationship between the village and the nearby district is restated. Thus, the expression "back of" refers both to the physical location (Lufilufi could be seen as geographically "behind" Falefā) and to the social ties between the two polities (Falefā should stand "behind," so as to protect Lufilufi, which is the residence of the Tupua title).[3]

Line 19 in example (5) declares the day sacred (because of the occasion) while line 5 in example (6) declares the ceremonially more important part of the day, the morning, sacred. Lines 23 and 24 in (5) recognize the dignity of the titles of the families involved, especially the descent group of the senior orator Iuli, who controls the titles to be bestowed, while lines 8 and 9 in (6) are dedicated to recognizing the most important titles in the village as a whole, as contained in the village short fa'alupega (see chap. 2).

If the lāuga starts after the kava has been distributed, as in most of the fono I recorded, the orator is likely to leave out the folasaga and start from the kava part, which appropriately links the speech to the immediately preceding activity.

(7) Fono of April 7, 1979. First speech of the day, by the orator Taofiuailoa, abbreviated "Loa."

147	Loa;	*ia' makū fau*
		The strainer has dried out
148		*fa'asoa pa'ia i sē 'o ku'ua i le- (2.0) lā ikūvai,*
		(in) the sacred sharing by the one who comes from the- side of the water,[4]
149		*(1.0)*
150		*kagaka o le Kuiakua.*
		person of the King of Atua.
151		*kau'a'ao ipu o le kāeao,*
		The morning cups have been handed out,
152		*(1.0)*
153		*kaumafa fo'i (0.5) 'ava o le aofia ma le fogo*
		the assembly and the fono was also imbued with kava

If a speech is a reply (tali) or a follow-up to a previous lāuga—this happens in a fono when the beginning of the discussion is delayed— the orator who delivers the second speech may decide to leave out some of the parts already delivered in the first lāuga, like the mention of the agenda of the meeting, always a potentially controversial part of the speech (see chap. 4). In ceremonial exchanges, the orator may weigh the familiarity vis-à-vis the social distance between his group and the recipients of his speech as factors in deciding whether to be elaborate or restrained. In the following excerpt from a Sunday speech to the guest preacher after his sermon, for instance, the orator Loa uses the fact that the preacher was born in Falefā (also Loa's village) to move from the Thanksgiving (part three) directly to part seven, namely, the wishing of "clear skies" (see table 4):

(8) Lāuga delivered during a to'ona'i by the orator Loa, 1979.

    65   *ia' e lē fa'amakagauloaiga sa mākou 'upu* . . .
           I'm not going to make my speech (too) long . . .
    66   *e leaga 'o Falefā le gu'u*
           because the village (where we are) is Falefā
    67   *aga fa'apea 'o se isi gu'u*
           if it were some other village
    68   *e ke:* . . . *e ke susū mai iai.*
           that you [i.e., the preacher] come from
    69   *ia' = fagū e fa'akele aku ā gi a mākou 'upu.* . . .
           I would have for sure made my speech longer. . . .
    70   *ia' ae-* . . . *pau o le vi'iga o le Akua*
           So instead only the praising of the Lord

More generally, in a fono, the speeches delivered after the introductory lāuga never contain all of the parts listed in table 4. As I have discussed elsewhere (Duranti 1981a, 1981b), in the discussion part of the meeting, there is a "telescoping effect," whereby although the actual length of the speeches may vary and in some cases be even longer than the beginning lāuga, the number of parts shrinks down to three: (i) the thanksgiving, (ii) the discussion of the topic, and (iii) the closing blessing, with part (ii) taking the lion's share in speeches made during the more heated parts of the debate.

INTERRUPTIONS

    A speech may also be shortened because of the intervention of another speaker, who interrupts him, questioning the need or appropriateness of what is being said.

    A distinction must be made here between interruptions in a fono and in other contexts. The main difference between the two situations is the *key* in which the interruptions are carried out and interpreted.

Interruptions in the fono. In a fono, interruptions are often serious and are aimed at controlling the general demeanor of the event, in which participants are expected to show respect for the tradition (procedural rules included) and avoid emotional or uncontrolled rebuttals. In a fono, matai must be able to face one another and discuss difficult issues without getting too direct. The highly metaphorical language, full of respectful words, is an important tool in this process. If someone tries to quickly end the proceeding without paying proper attention to the protocol and hence to the importance of the occasion, or if someone becomes too direct and speaks his mind, the interaction is seen as degenerating into something other than a proper meeting. An immediate remedy for this kind of situation is to interrupt the speaker. Thus, in example (4) in chapter 3, when the high chief Alai'a-sā tries to preempt the discussion of his case by cutting off the second speaker, 'Alo, he is in turn cut off by Iuli, who manages to reestablish the canonical order of speakers, namely, orators first. Another example is provided in example (9), in which the old orator Matā'afa's heated response to Moe'ono's accusations is interrupted and eventually cut off with the help of three matai, the two senior orators Iuli and Moe'ono and the chief Tevaseu, who is from Matā'afa's part of the district, namely, the Falelua (next to Fagaloa Bay; see map 3 and fig. 18).

Matā'afa is here responding to an earlier proposal by Moe'ono to expel from the fono the matai from Sauano (Matā'afa's village) and Saletele on the basis of the allegation that they neglected their duty to attend the fono proceedings. In fact, everyone knows that what they neglected to do is to support Moe'ono in the local elections. Matā'afa here proudly counterattacks Moe'ono's allegation by reminding him of an old debt that Falefā contracted with the villages of Sauano and Saletele in a fight against the people of Amaile. The lengthy excerpt is necessary to give the full sense of tension and struggle involved in these kinds of confrontations and their interruptions:

(9) Fono of April 7, 1979.

1352	*Matā'afa;*	My village didn't beg for anything.
1353		I myself am eighty-two years old. . . .
1354		It is the sweat of my village.
1355		Your village didn't have any transport to Tuā (in Amaile)

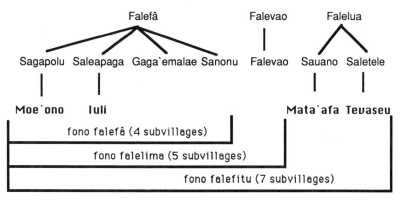

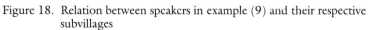

Figure 18. Relation between speakers in example (9) and their respective
          subvillages

1356		(you) came to our village to take our long boats
1357		to Amaile. . . . to take in them our people.
		. . .
1358		(When you) got there, the people from Lotofaga were there, (you) did everything, then came back.
1359		(To be part of your fono) was our reward from your parents
1360		from Ta'ele and Sale not long ago. . . .
1361		And now (you) tell me (you) want to expel us
1362		the Falelua did not ask for anything. . . .
1363		It was (a reward for) their sweat . . .
1364		it hurts my stomach to listen to these news
1365		because . . . stories are made and blow in the wind.
1366		You say something . . .
1367		there are a lot of matai here who don't know . . .
1368		the things that your fathers did (our-)
1369		Sale and . . . Ta'ele not long ago
1370		. . .
1371	*Moe'ono;*	Yes, Matā'afa!
		[
1372	*Matā'afa;*	Had we fought with Lotofaga
1373		the (villages of) Sauano and Saletele would have died.
1374	*Moe'ono;*	Matā'afa!
1375		. . .
1376	*Matā'afa;*	But the doing of these things,
1377	*Iuli;*	Matā'afa!
1378	*Matā'afa;*	What-?
1379	*Moe'ono;*	We got the point.

1380		I have told you what should fall on you
		[
1381	*Matā'afa;*	it's the same if we run our own villages
1382		we are happy to do it.
1383	*Iuli;*	Matā'afa!
1384	*Matā'afa;*	We will also elect our own M.P.!
1385		. . .
1386	*Moe'ono;*	Fine!
1387		. . .
1388	*Iuli;*	Matā'afa! . . . Please! . . .
1389		That's enough!
		[
1390	*Matā'afa;*	But saying that you will expel us . . .
1391		how can you say that if this village was going to get killed
1392		had we had a war with Lotofaga?
1393	*Tevaseu;*	Yes, oh chiefs!
1394	*Iuli;*	Matā'afa. . . . Ma- Matā'afa!
		[
1395	*Tevaseu;*	You two senior orators,
1396	*Iuli;*	That's enough.
		[
1397	*Tevaseu;*	and (the rest of) our village.
1398		. . .
1399	*Matā'afa;*	But when you say- you say to expel (us).
		[
1400	*Tevaseu;*	So now-
1401		Matā'afa has spoken.
		[
1402	*Matā'afa;*	as if we ca-
1403		came here and wanted to join (your fono).
1404	*Tevaseu;*	And this morning
1405		no, in front of the Lord . . .
1406		the praise and the thanksgiving
1407		as it has been delivered on this morning.
		[
1408	*Matā'afa;*	Look at the sweat (i.e., hard work) of the (i.e., my) village
1409	*Tevaseu;*	And this morning,
1410		this morning is like a fine mat being laid out on the malae. . . .
1411		No, here you have come chiefs and son-chiefs . . .
1412		you have arrived also, senior orators
1413		and all the other dignified titles.

After line 1408, Matā'afa finally yields to the chief from his own sub-district, Tevaseu, who succeeds in taking the floor and delivering a reconciliatory speech. Tevaseu would in fact manage to mention later the real reason for the present conflict, namely, the elections, but he would do so by embedding his complaints and his accusations within apologies and words of respect for the two senior orators and the rest of the matai from Falefā. Matā'afa overstepped the boundaries of proper public speaking and for this reason was not allowed to finish his speech. He turned around the threat of expulsion by reminding Moe'ono that it was the village of Falefā, many years before, that had asked the villages in Fagaloa to join the Falefā fono (as a reward for Sauano and Saletele's willingness to go to war with Falefā's matai against the village of Lotofaga). This was a way of shaming Moe'ono and quieting the younger matai by reminding them that they are too young to really know anything. But this kind of talk violates fono etiquette. To bring up old controversies or events that can be used against someone is very confrontational and thus particularly inappropriate in a public arena, unless it is done by those who have the right to act as public prosecutors, namely, Moe'ono and Iuli. The two senior orators' attempt to take control of the floor is thus a way of reasserting the authority of their titles. Matā'afa, however, could not be stopped easily. He was older than anyone else in the assembly and used his age and knowledge to challenge Moe'ono's authority (see line 1353: "I myself am eighty-two years old"). It was only the intervention of the chief Tevaseu, from the same part of the district, that finally convinced Matā'afa to give up the floor. From the beginning of his speech, Tevaseu's tone was very different from Matā'afa's and from that of the two matua, Iuli and Moe'ono. He speaks slowly and softly. His voice is soothing and manages to calm down the audience. His way of speaking is very different from the prototypical style of oratorical speechmaking. It is more appropriate to chiefs, who, in contrast to orators, are expected to show restraint in all circumstances. In this sense, whether they planned it or not, Matā'afa and Tevaseu are working in perfect synchrony by complementing each other's style and producing the desired effect: they neutralize Moe'ono's attempt to punish their villages and they keep the right to stay in the fono with Falefā. Despite the fact that Moe'ono has more authority than Matā'afa, he cannot carry on his alleged plan without the support of the other members of the fono. By creating a tense and apparently volatile situation, Matā'afa successfully stops Moe'ono from persisting with his accusation. Moe'ono loses support as the interest of the council rapidly switches to trying to contain the shame produced by Matā'afa's emotional recounting of past events and commitments.

Interruptions in events other than fono. Lāuga in social events other than the fono are more frequently interrupted and, as a consequence, shortened. This typically takes place before or just at the beginning of part five, the *pa'ia*, or sacred names (see table 4). An orator from the opposing side 'catches the lāuga' (*seu le lāuga*), that is, cuts it short, by reminding the speaker that there is no need to go through all the sacred names of the parties or families involved in the transaction. This is a way of avoiding the public exposure of genealogies and at the same time shortening the speech and getting on with the rest of the ceremony. The two parties overlap and try to overdo each other with a powerful voice and eloquent phrases, until one of the two, typically the one who was delivering the speech, gives up and shortens his speech. This interruption has dramatic tones which are reminiscent of the confrontational style illustrated in example (10) below, but the "key" (Bauman 1977; Hymes 1972b) of the performance is different. Although the exchange sounds like an argument, their confrontation is ritualized and highly predictable and thus is not expected to cause bad feelings. The orator who is interrupted during a ceremonial lāuga—unlike an orator who is interrupted during a speech in a fono—explicitly accepts the invitation to cut down his speech and resumes the right to the floor in order to conclude his performance. The orator who interrupted, in turn, thanks him for agreeing with his request. An example of this kind of exchange is provided in example (10) below, where the orator Usu is interrupted by the orator 'Auga, who asks him to leave out the *gafa* 'genealogy', from his speech.

(10) Saofa'i, 1979.

143	Usu;	'o le 'ā goga ia 'o le pa'ia o kaeao (2.5)
		May the sacred days stay as they were
144		'a 'o kūlaga (2.5)
		as for the positions
145		auā se fa'afofoga aga i lau kōfā le Makua
		may Your Honorable senior orator hear
146		ma le mamalu i loukou 'āiga, (2.0)
		and the dignity of all of you chiefs
147		auā gafa lege- le gafa legei
		because this- this genealogy
148		e fāgaua 'upu o loukou 'āiga
		gives birth to the words of your families
		[
149	'Auga;	ia' Usu,
		Well, Usu,

150	Usu;	auā la gofo gei. because this (new) title. [
151	'Auga;	uā (?) well, (?)
152		'ou fia fa'alakalaka aku I would like to approach you
153		'o lo'o 'e fekalai (2.0) while you are giving your speech
154		leai e le 'o se:- kuli 'ua vale (2.0) no it's not that you said something- wrong
155		'ae fa'apea lo'u kāofi (1.0) but this is my opinion
156		gi ā fa:- (1.0) if (you)-
157	Usu;	ia' 'Auga, Well, 'Auga,
158	'Auga;	leai e le 'o gi gofo ga si'i mai i fafo. no these are not titles that come from outside.
159		(0.5)
160	Usu;	leai ge'i e faikau mai lau koofā le Makua Iuli. No, don't read it that way, Your Highness Iuli. [
161	'Auga;	(leai) (? ?) No (? ?)
162	Usu;	ma le mamalu i loukou 'āiga, And the rest of your chiefs, [
163	'Auga;	e iai lo'u kāofi fa'apea. This is the way I see it.
164	Usu;	fa'apea e alo fa'akamala le Ga'ukaala Don't think that the Ga'utaala ((a particular descent group))
165		legei auā lo kākou gogofo ai. doesn't value our relationship. [
166	'Auga;	ia' 'ua 'ou maua aku Okay, I got it
167		'ua 'ou iloa I know
168	Usu;	ioe. Yes.
169	'Auga;	'a e alo igā fa'apa'ia gofo, (0.3) and do go ahead and give the titles now,
170		'a 'o le gafa, but the genealogy,

171	Usu;	ia'
		Okay
172	'Auga;	ia'.
		Okay.
173	Usu;	ia' e fa'apegei.
		okay, this is it.
174	'Auga;	(ua lava) ka'akia.
		(It's enough) drop it.
175	Usu;	'o le 'ā uma sa'u kāofi.
		I shall conclude.
176	'Auga;	ia' fa'afekai.
		Okay, thanks.

Usu then resumes his speech and, leaving out the mention of the family's genealogy, moves on to explain the importance of a matai title and to list the qualities that the people being made matai need to acquire for their new status (see Duranti 1983).

In conclusion, interruptions are often performed to avoid the public mention of past events, genealogies included, which can bring up potentially controversial issues and thus either escalate the tension already present in a fono or break the frame of reached agreement typical of speech performances during ceremonial encounters.

The Lāuga as an Epic Genre

Like the traditional oratorical genres discussed by Bloch (1975a), Salmond (1975), and others, the prototypical Samoan lāuga (in ceremonies and the first one in a fono) celebrate mythico-historical characters and places, eternal values, and immutable hierarchies. They represent, in other words, the ideal model of social life, where things are beautiful (*matagofie mea 'uma*) and the world is in harmony. This is a world in which things are immutable—one of the recurrent lines of some lāuga is in fact *e le'i liua* '(it) has not changed' followed by matai titles and ceremonial address forms. The sacredness of the titles, their dignity, for instance, is thus portrayed in these lāuga as something that comes from the past (*vavau*) and reaches eternity (*fa'avavau*): *'o pa'ia mai le vavau e o'o i le fa'avavau*. The speechmaker professes his belief in these titles and their immutability (*'ou te talitonu* 'I believe' is a recurrent phrase in certain lāuga).

Much of the speech is dedicated to praising and recognizing powerful figures and events that are depicted as above human control. Thus, the "thanksgiving" (part three) recognizes the Lord's power to bring an end to life on earth and thanks Him for allowing this particular occasion to take place. The "mornings" celebrates important events in the history of Samoa, such as the arrival of the gospel. The "sacred (names)" reminds everyone of the power of mythico-historical figures and their descendants, who are depicted as the "gods on earth."

Overall, like the idealist philosophers, Hegel in particular, criticized by Marx, in these speeches the Samoan speechmakers present to their audience a model of the universe where the traditional social order, with its hierarchies and values, is given historical and philosophical justification. In many ways, the world and style of these lāuga is reminiscent of what Bakhtin (1981) described as characteristic of the "epic" as opposed to the "novel" in Western literature:

The world of epic is the national heroic past: it is a world of "beginnings" and "peak times" in the national history, a world of fathers and of founders of families, a world of "firsts" and "bests." . . . The epic . . . has been from the beginning a poem about the past, and the authorial position immanent in the epic and constitutive for it . . . is the environment of a man speaking about a past that is to him inaccessible, the reverent point of view of a descendent. (1981, 13)

The style and discourse of the epic, like the style and discourse of the lāuga, is removed from everyday discourse, where one may find open-endedness, indecision, indeterminacy (Bakhtin 1981, 16). Instead we find certitude, and, with it, a world of established hierarchies. Instead of knowledge of contingent facts, we find memory. Creativity is manifested in the way in which the past is re-evoked and not in the manner in which the present (through the past) is reevaluated:

The absolute past is specifically evaluating (hierarchical) category. . . . In the past, everything is good: all the really good things . . . occur *only* in this past. The epic absolute past is the single source and beginning of everything good for all later times as well.

In ancient literature it is memory, and not knowledge, that serves as the source and power for the creative impulse. That is how it was, it is impossible to change it: the tradition of the past is sacred. There is as yet no consciousness of the possible relativity of any past. (Bakhtin 1981, 15)

Bakhtin's view of the epic world is thus very similar to the social world described by Bloch as characteristic of formalized speech, that is, traditional oratory. It is a world that cannot be changed because it is beyond the realm of human activity. In this type of speech, the social system is presented in such a way that one cannot explicitly argue against its premises, at least not without stepping out of genre.

Formalized Language and Power

As I discussed earlier, Bloch (1975a) argued that the strict formal canons of much traditional oratory condition and hence coerce speakers to accept what has been said or presupposed by other speakers:

It is because the formalisation of language is a way whereby one speaker can coerce the response of another, that it can be seen as a form of social control. It is really a type of communication where rebellion is impossible and only revolution could be feasible. It is a situation where power is all or nothing. (p. 20)

For Bloch, the formalized language used in traditional oratory typically works outside of the canons of empirical evidence and logical reasoning whereby contradiction is possible. In traditional oratory, contradiction would not be possible because there is only one truth. Thus, following each statement there is only a limited set of other possible statements, each of which substantiates the prior one and cannot be denied by empirical evidence or by logical argumentation.

Bloch's position has been widely criticized for his "deterministic" view of the relationship between language and social order (see Brenneis and Myers 1984; Burling 1977; Myers and Brenneis 1984; Paine 1981) and for his assumptions about what constitutes "formalization" or "formal event" (see Irvine 1979). In fact, his is an attempt to invert the "vulgar" materialists' view of the unidirectional impact of the base (economic structure) on superstructure (e.g., law, religion, art) by stating the fundamental role played by language in human praxis. In comparing his proposal with my data on Samoan oratory, I have become convinced that, with some minor modifications, we can maintain Bloch's generalization while complying with some of his critics' points. What we need to do is to move beyond idealization of language, speech genres, and formalization and look at concrete examples of how language is used in political arenas.

The Samoan data on oratory across events suggest that Bloch's argument about the constraining force of formal oratory should be contextualized. It might be accurate for some situations but not for others.

At the same time, we would not want to say that in one case language is "formalized" but in the other it is not. Lāuga are performed in all kinds of public situations and they are always radically different from everyday conversational speech. What we need to understand is not only the form and content of what is being said but the key in which the speech is delivered. We also need to understand the surrounding events, what the speech follows and what it is a prelude to.

Thus, for instance, in ceremonial contexts (outside of the fono), the lāuga celebrates the day as sacred because of the perfect match of what the matai planned and what has resulted out of successful negotiations. The performance of the speeches in these cases typically celebrates a found agreement: between the family of the groom and the family of the bride in an exchange of dowry, among the members of the extended family first and then between the family and the village in the installation of a new title, between workers and those who commissioned them a job, and so on. Whereas in these contexts the lāuga is the final act of an often long series of negotiations, in juridico-political arenas such as the fono, the lāuga opens the meeting and hence is delivered before the discussion of the agenda, that is, before participants engage in argumentation, searching for the truth (*mea tonu*) and for the right solution (*mea sa'o*). In a ceremony, the world found by the speechmaker before he delivers the main speech of the day is a world of reassessed order, a world, that is, where an equilibrium has been found between the demands of different parties (viz., employers and employees, family and village, village and village, family of the groom and family of the bride, etc.). The world the speechmaker finds at the beginning of a fono is instead one of disorder, contrast, and disagreement, a world often tinted by strong feelings such as resentment, anger, envy, misunderstood or misplaced pride. Accordingly, the first lāuga in a fono opens the meeting by reassessing the way things were (the "absolute past" of Bakhtin's epic) and the way things should be (the normative order). To solve the crisis, which the convocation of the meeting recognizes, participants must reconcile the world of past and eternal values with the contingent world, full of uncertain truths, conflicting narratives, and divergent perspectives.

It is here that the contrast between formalization and verbal art on the one hand and political, pragmatic goals on the other is acted out. The same ethos that keeps the tradition alive through symbolic-communicative acts such as the ceremonial lāuga also enforces the need to expose differences, disagreement, ugly facts, violations, faults, and individual and group responsibility. As in other Pacific cultures (see Watson-Gegeo and White 1990), it is also a Samoan local belief and practice

Table 5 *Comparison of Features of a Lāuga in a Ceremony and in a Fono*

Ceremony	Fono
1. Before the lāuga, there is a debate (*fa'atau*) about who should deliver the speech.	1. There is no debate.
2. The speechmaker is recognized as skillful (*poto*) (he is the one who won the debate [see 1]).	2. The speechmaker is the one who holds a particular title and/or role in the meeting.
3. The number of lāuga is known beforehand (usually two parties—e.g., guests and hosts, family of the bride and family of the groom—deliver one speech each). The reply (*tali*) to the first lāuga may in some cases partly overlap with it. This may or may not be seen as competitive (see 8).	3. The number of lāuga may not be known in advance.
4. The lāuga is part of an exchange, that is, of a complex ritual of reciprocity.	4. There is no exchange of goods.
5. People typically evaluate the beauty of the performance.	5. Usually no comments are made about the performance.
6. The speech often represents an agreement of some sort.	6. The speech does not represent an agreement but the beginning of a negotiation process.
7. The speech is usually addressed to a particular group or lineage within the village.	7. The speech is addressed to the entire village or assembly, which may include several villages.
8. The speechmaker is often formally interrupted (*seu*) by the other party, who might be testing his skills.	8. Interruptions are rare and confrontative.
9. Once the speech is over, no parts are added, that is, no corrections are made.	9. Another, senior matai may correct or repair a faulty performance (e.g., if the speechmaker left something out).
10. The address forms and titles mentioned are those relevant to the occasions.	10. Part of the speech is dedicated to greeting or recognizing all the most important titles in the village.
11. The speech is usually delivered in a high volume and with a distinct voice quality (e.g., guttural).	11. The voice of the speechmaker conveys a sense of "routine job" in a normal to low volume.

continued

Table 5—*Continued*

Ceremony	Fono
12. The speechmaker usually takes off his shirt and shows his tattoo (if he has one).[a]	12. The speechmaker usually wears a shirt.
13. There is often compensation for the speechmaker.	13. There is no compensation for the speechmaker(s).

[a]The tatoo I refer to here is called a *pe'a*, lit. 'flying fox.' It covers a man's body from his abdomen to his knees, is performed by a specialist (*tufuga*), and involves a protracted, painful process that young men usually undergo in groups.

that the return to social harmony and mutual love (*fealofani*) requires the exposure of the ugly (*matagā*) facts. During such discussions, those who have violated the law must be confronted with their responsibility, shamed if recalcitrant, and punished. If a political decision must be taken, the different positions must be presented, evaluated, and a consensus must be reached.

This process, full of dangers and uncertainties, cannot however take place in the prototypical lāuga format. Like the end of the epic and the birth of the novel discussed by Bakhtin (1981), the new set of contents and implicit worldviews needs new forms of expression. This is accomplished not only by introducing a number of changes in the content and style of the lāuga but also by reframing the performance through the audience's response and other features of the event. See table 5 for a comparison of some features of the lāuga in a ceremony and the first lāuga in a fono.[5]

All of these features point to the fact that in the ceremonial lāuga both the speaker and the audience are more committed to the "performance aspects" of speechmaking as discussed by a number of scholars, including R. Bauman (1977) and Hymes (1975). More attention is paid to the way in which the speech is delivered. There is "an assumption of accountability to an audience for the way in which communication is carried out, above and beyond its referential content" (Bauman 1977, 11).

In a fono both the speaker and the audience are less concerned with performance per se and some of the canons of verbal art are lifted. In a fono, there is not much enjoyment of the lāuga performance; participants are too worried about what's coming up next. They are silently rehearsing their own speeches or trying to anticipate the other parties' moves in the forthcoming debate. In this way the problem of the contrast between faithfulness to artistic form and content, on the one hand, and faithfulness to contingent, pragmatic needs, on the other, is partly resolved by downplaying, in political arenas, the artistic dimensions of ceremonial speechmaking.

Variations within the Fono

After the opening speeches, the fono discourse is further removed from the epic form. In going from the beginning of the event, when the first lāuga is performed as an opening speech, to later on in the discussion part, when the issues of the day are presented and analyzed, the matai's language turns into a truly hybrid genre, which still utilizes the lexicon and other aspects of lāuga but at the same time allows for features of talk and register markers which are not typical of the epic genre and even less of the formalized language as described by Bloch.

In particular, when compared to ceremonial speeches, political speeches are characterized by the use of various codes, registers, and perspectives that violate the "code consistency" and the "increased code structuring" that Judith Irvine (1979) associated with formalized language and events. In other words, in the fono, after the initial lāuga, the consistency of the code and the restrictions imposed on what can be said are partly modified toward the creation of a "blurred genre" in which multiple voices and multiple perspectives can be heard. This is a domain of speaking which more clearly reflects what Bakhtin called *heteroglossia*, that is, the combination of centrifugal forces in language which move away from centralization and unification toward a language that "represents the co-existence of socio-ideological contradictions between the present and the past, between differing epochs of the past, between different socio-ideological groups in the present, between tendencies, schools, circles and so forth" (Bakhtin 1981, 291).

FEATURES OF HETEROGLOSSIA

The features of the language of the fono discussion that constitute its heteroglot nature, especially when compared with the more controlled and unified character of the lāuga, include:

(a) mixing speech registers or codes
(b) more pronounced display of affect
(c) invocation of personal identities
(d) use of quoted direct speech
(e) more dialogical exchanges
(f) logical argumentation (especially "if-then" propositions)
(g) mention of negative deeds (especially in complaints and accusations)

(a) Mixing speech registers. Whereas the first lāuga is consistently full of respectful terms (*'upu fa'aaloalo*) for matai's actions, feelings, relations, and possessions (Duranti 1992a; Milner 1961), later on in the discussion part (talanoaga), next to the respectful words we also find ordinary and even profane words, as shown in examples (11) and (12):

(11) Fono of January 25, 1979.

> 249   *Moe'ono;*   *oi kālofa!*
> oh too bad!

(12) Fono of March 17, 1979. Samoan text in Duranti (1990a, 474).

> *Moe'ono;*   I also spoke on that day
> when you had come to the house.
> "A., stop, there is an important affair (going on)."
> Oh! But you came back outside
> (you instead) repeated those words
> "Fuck off! Asshole! Prick!"

These are words that would never appear in a ceremonial lāuga, but they can be said, embedded in reported speech, in the recounting of the events that are being evaluated.

Other kinds of mixed codes include the use of English loanwords, as shown in examples (13), where the English borrowing *sikolasipi* (from *scholarship*) is used, and (14), where we find the informal *suipi* (from *sweep*), a metaphor from card playing—not a very "dignified" activity—in place of the Samoan *mālō* (see line 420 in example 21 below).

(13) Fono of January 25, 1979.

> 329   *Moe'ono;*   *ai ua iai le agaga fa'apea 'o ia*
> maybe this is the way he sees it
> 330   *'ua sikolasipi.*
> PST scholarship
> (he) had a scholarship.

(14) Fono of January 25, 1979.

> *761   Usu;   kau ke <u>suipi</u>.*
> (we) sweep up (i.e., win).

(b) More pronounced display of affect. As shown in examples (11) and (12) above, the display of affect is also more common in talanoaga. The explicit appeal to feelings is also expressed by means of such linguistic particles as the vocative and endearing postnominal suffix *e*, as shown in (15) and (16):

(15) Fono of April 7, 1979. Moe'ono is trying to convince Savea to withdraw his suit against the M.P.

> *416   Moe'ono;   ia' Savea<u>e</u>.*
> So, <u>oh</u> Savea.

(16) From Saofa'i, 1979. Tevaseu tries to cool people off after the orator Matā'afa has scolded the matai from Falefā—see example (10) above.

> *1393   Tevaseu;   Aiga<u>e</u>!*
> <u>Oh</u> Chiefs!

(c) Invocation of personal identities. In the talanoaga, personal names may be used next to titles. Although this is something that happens only when there is possible ambiguity between two or more parties sharing the same title—as in the case of the Savea title, which was split between Savelio and Sione—it demonstrates a concern for individuals that violates the epic vision of ancestral powers remaining unchanged and unaffected by individuals' actions or (mis)deeds:

(17) Fono of April 7, 1979.

> *159   Moe'ono;   ia' 'o lea fo'i ua:-*
> So now also-
> *160   'ua koso fo'i le va'a o le Sa'o 'Ese'ese.*
> the boat of the Sa'o 'Ese'ese has been pulled in (i.e., he is running for office).
> *161   le afioga iā Savea Sioge.*
> His Highness Savea Sione.

(d) Use of quoted direct speech. Heteroglossia is also constituted by the display of multiple perspectives as produced by the use of reported speech, which is a common device to insinuate the possibility of alternative views and discording voices (Vološinov 1973). Although speakers in ceremonial lāuga may refer to the speech of other orators in their speech, they do so only in indirect forms. In the fono

discussion part we find instead *quoted direct speech* (see also Macaulay 1987):

(18) Fono of April 7, 1979. The female orator Tafili is speaking on behalf of her brother, the chief Savea Sione.

2886	Tafili;	'o lea lava 'ou ke kaukala aku ai, . . .
		Now is the time that I am speaking, . . .
2887		e leaga 'o 'upu gei 'ou ke kaukala iai,
		because these are the words I am talking about,
2888		" 'ua fa'akau Savea e Igu i kupe" . . .
		"Savea has been bought by Inu with money" . . .
2889		ia 'ua kakau ai lā ga kulāfogo 'upu gā,
		well those words must be (challenged in) court,

Not only are verbs of saying referring to someone else's previous speech and to specific wordings used by others much more common in the discussion part but speakers also quote and question one another's statements.

(e) More dialogical exchanges. In a few cases, especially when there is strong disagreement (as shown in example 10 above) or need to clarify some obscure point, the macro-turn format (see chap. 3) of the fono speeches breaks down and quasi-conversational exchanges take place. Instead of the conventional and predictable back-channel cues by the audience (e.g., *mālie!* 'well said!'), in the discussion part of a fono, we may find two or more speakers engaged in question-answer pairs or assertion-evaluation sequences that introduce a flavor of everyday conversation in the otherwise highly controlled and ritualized style of public speaking:

(19) From Saofa'i, 1979.

1384	Matā'afa;	We will also elect our own M.P.!
1385		(1.0)
1386	Moe'ono;	Fine!

(20) Fono of April 7, 1979. Chief Savea has just finished delivering a speech that defines his position. Senior orator Moe'ono speaks again.

3186	Moe'ono;	I am not very clear
3187		(about) these words I am taking note of
3188		whether they are words (said by) Inu
3189		or by one of our people (about)
3190		the forty (dollars) that Inu paid
3191		so that you would run in the elections.
3192		That is what I would like to get clarified.
3193	Savea;	Well Moe'ono I am approaching you again

3194		. . .
3195		(since) our assembly wants to get an answer from me
3196		. . .
3197		those very words were by a matai in this village.
3198	*Moe'ono;*	Words by a matai in this village?
3199	*Savea;*	This village.

In this last example, which is one of the rare cases I observed of requests for clarification during a fono, despite the respectful words and the ceremonial phrases (e.g., "words I am taking note of" or "I am approaching you"), the exchange comes closer and closer to a conversation between Savea and Moe'ono instead of a series of speeches in which each of them globally assesses the other's words without making himself vulnerable to the other's immediate response.

(f) Logical argumentation. Alternative views and comparisons between past and future events are also achieved by the recurrent exploitation of logical argumentations in the form of (not always explicit but equally well understood) "if-then" statements.

(21) Fono of January 25, 1979.

419	*Moe'ono;*	*'a kākou ō ko'akolu (1.0)*
		if all the three of us go (i.e., run for office)
420		*'ua mālō Lufilufi. (2.5)*
		Lufilufi will have won.
421	*?;*	*mālie!*
		Well said!
		[. . .]
486	*Moe'ono;*	*auā e vaivai Iuli*
		because (if) Iuli is weak
487		*'ou ke vaivai fo'i.*
		I am also weak.
488	*?;*	*mālie!*
		Well said!

These rhetorical figures are common in the fono discussion and violate the characterization of formalized language presented by Bloch, for whom:

Formalized language is . . . non-logical and any attempt to represent it as such, whether by a paraphrase into ordinary language which implies "explanation" or by the use of tabular representation containing a logical form, is misleading. (Bloch 1975, 21)

(g) Mention of negative contributions and bad deeds. As I will discuss in more depth in the next chapter, it is in the context of

the fono discussion that a different kind of short narrative appears in the fono speeches, when words for celebrating the eternal values of the ideal social system are replaced or mixed with everyday deeds, that is, with accounts and stories of what people are up to now as opposed to what supernatural powers did in the eternal past or what the matai do now as the heirs of the sacred ancestors. In a ceremonial lāuga, when people's deeds are mentioned, they are typically positive contributions or important prerogatives that define someone's social role in the ceremonial context and the community as a whole. In the discussion part of the fono, we encounter instead deeds that are presented as harmful or dangerous. As we shall see in chapter 5, in the fono discussion agency thus takes on a different flavor.

It is in the context of these kinds of data that ethnography becomes particularly valuable if not indispensable. In order for us to assess whether a given statement should be seen as a complaint or an accusation, we need to know a great deal about the events under discussion as well as about community values.

METALINGUISTIC AWARENESS

These features of the fono talk indicate that we must think of "formality" or "formalized language" as variable not only in a cross-contextual and cross-cultural sense, as suggested by Irvine (1979), but also intra-contextually. In contexts such as the Samoan fono, rules are more or less, sometimes progressively, altered in the course of what is defined and perceived as the same event. The style of the opening lāuga is different from both the style of lāuga in other events (see table 5) and the style of the speeches in the following discussion part. This is not a feature of fono speech that goes unnoticed by its producers. The matai in a fono are quite aware of the plasticity of the genre lāuga, as shown by Moe'ono's explicit invitation, after the first introductory lāuga, to talk things out, to *talanoa* 'chat, discuss':

(22) Fono of April 7, 1979.

398	Moe'ono;	ma:- 'o lo kākou aso,
		and- our day,
399		'o lea fa'auso loa le kākou aofia . . .
		now our assembly is open for discussion . . .
400	?;	mālie!
		Well said!
		[

401	Moe'ono;	'o lea ua fa'akigo mai makā'upu e-
		now that the topics have been clarified by-
402	?;	mālie!
		Well said!
403	Moe'ono;	'oe le Laukogia.
		you the Lautogia (title referring to first speaker).
404		makā'upu e uiga i le Falelua . . .
		the topics about the two subvillages . . .
405		kākou kalagoa muamua i ai.
		let us first <u>talk</u> about them.
406		. . .
407	Loa;	(mā)lie!
		Well said!

One of the functions of the conventional phrase 'o le 'ā fa'auso le aofia (or, other times, 'o le 'ā fa'auso le fono), which literally translates as 'the meeting will be (from now on) in a brotherly style (fa'a-uso)', is to release participants from complying with the strict canons of lāuga performance (for instance the parts listed in table 4) and allow them to introduce features of less formalized and more colloquial talk to fit the needs of the discussion and bring about a different discourse context.

Metacommunicative statements of this nature also abound in the rest of the discussion as several of the participants explicitly frame their own speech as "discussion" or "talk":

(23) Fono of January 25, 1979.

| 685 | Usu; | 'ou ke kaukala aku ma la'u amio kogu. |
| | | I am talking (to you) with honesty (lit. 'with my true spirit'). |

The use of such expressions paradigmatically contrasts with phrases like /'ou ke kalikogu/ 'I believe, trust', which, as I mentioned earlier, characterize the ceremonial lāuga.

Conclusions

The Samoan data suggest that rather than maintaining an absolute distinction between "formalized language" and "conversation," as one might infer from a strict interpretation of Bloch's (1975a) argument, we take into consideration cases in which traditional ceremonial speechmaking bends, without breaking, to the needs of political speechmaking and a mixed, spurious genre is created (such as, for in-

stance, in the talanoaga part of a fono). Like Bakhtin's novel vis-à-vis
the earlier epic, speechmaking in a political event such as the fono is in
a parasitic relation to the more prototypical lāuga: it uses its parts,
tropes, lexicon, grammar, and at times even its name,[6] but it also infil-
trates it with a type of discourse and frames it with a number of acts
that belong to other texts and contexts (see table 4). For this reason,
each individual speech within the discussion part of the fono can also
be called "lāuga," but only in a loose, evocative, and at the same time
"corrupt" way. When pressed, Samoans will always recognize that in a
fono only the opening speech(es) are "real" lāuga. Even those, however, are not as aesthetically pleasing as ceremonial lāuga. Thus, it is not
by accident that most of the times I asked to meet a good speechmaker,
I was taken to someone who was well known for his skills in ceremonial
settings and not in political arenas. In this respect, Tūla'i's invitation to
go to the fono (see chap. 2) was unusual. Perhaps it was an answer to
what he must have perceived as my curiosity about the political scene
in the village rather than an invitation to hear "real lāuga." Had he
taken me to a different kind of event, I would have developed a different
notion of Samoan speechmaking. In particular, I might not have been
able to connect it with the expression of agency, which is the subject
of the next two chapters. The issue of grammatical framing which I will
discuss next is directly connected with the expression of narrative accounts in which certain actions are described as initiated and at least in
part controlled by an individual or group. Such narrative accounts are
only possible in a lāuga style that combines the expression of shared
values with truths that are instead debatable (Lindstrom 1992). Argu-
able actions and blameful agents can only surface in the type of heter-
oglossic discourse context described above.

5

The Grammar of Agency in Political Discourse

Over the years that followed my first experience in Western Samoa I felt as if I had a professional split identity. Part of me was intrigued by the artful speechmaking I recorded in the fono and in other social events. Another part of me was continuing to do work on Samoan grammar, trying to make sense of grammatical patterns across social contexts. This double allegiance was well reflected in my 1981 doctoral dissertation, which, despite the repeated efforts by the members of my dissertation committee to make me write it more like a conventional linguistics thesis, contained more material on oratory than on syntax or morphology. Over the next few years, as I was moving closer to anthropology, I often felt my "grammatical" side slipping away. Despite numerous attempts at synthesizing my more strictly linguistic work, for several years I was unable to publish or finish a single piece based on my grammatical analysis. Everything I published about Samoa was instead devoted to oratory, conflict management, and the role of intentionality in local interpretive practices. There were times when I was particularly frustrated by the difficulties of integrating my grammatical work with my interest in Samoan oratory and politics. I felt that the time and energy spent collecting and analyzing various types of gram-

This chapter is a revised and expanded version of my "Politics and Grammar: Agency in Samoan Political Discourse," published in *American Ethnologist* 17. I would like to thank the four anonymous *AE* reviewers for their helpful comments and Kristin Fossum, the editorial associate at *AE*, for helping me improve the organization and style of the original paper.

matical patterns was being wasted in unsuccessful attempts at planning a "sociolinguistic grammar" of Samoan language, a project that seemed overwhelming even to some of my more sympathetic colleagues. Nevertheless, I never completely abandoned the idea of a possible and useful link between Samoan syntax and Samoan politics. In fact, I occasionally discussed issues of syntax and morphology with a few people and especially with my wife, Elinor Ochs, who in the meantime was producing several studies of child language acquisition and found several of my observations and findings relevant and in some cases similar to hers (see Ochs 1982, 1986, 1988). One particular set of observations was especially intriguing to both of us: it had to do with the expression of agency in Samoan discourse. In the adult and in the child language data alike, we had noticed three interrelated phenomena: (i) a tendency for utterances in spontaneous discourse to have only one nominal complement, which usually was not the subject of a transitive clause; (ii) a tendency not to express human agents as full subject of transitive clauses; and (iii) a widespread use of genitive constructions or "possessives" for expressing a number of semantic roles, including agents (see chap. 6 for further discussion of these three phenomena). In the summer of 1983, we presented our preliminary findings at the Linguistic Institute at the University of California, Los Angeles, in a class on discourse and grammar taught by Sandra Thompson and Paul Hopper. It was not until the fall of 1986, however, that we managed to sit down together and write a grant proposal to the National Science Foundation to systematically examine our Samoan data with respect to the three phenomena mentioned above. As part of this project, we also planned to transfer a portion of our handwritten transcripts to computer disk. The National Science Foundation's positive response allowed us to embark in this new study, which lasted from the summer of 1987 until the fall of 1990. This chapter discusses one result of that study, namely, my own analysis of the expression of agency in political discourse. In the next chapter, I will extend the same analysis to everyday discourse.

As I will show in what follows, the Samoan matai engaged in a fono have access to a variety of linguistic resources for expressing, implying, or denying agency, and they employ them to sustain or undermine different versions of politically important "facts." Through a close examination of the specific linguistic resources (including morphological, syntactic, and discursive structures) found in the fono speeches, we can come to a better understanding of the ways in which certain social actors in the community maintain, acquire, or juggle the authority needed to control their political destiny and fashion a future in which the traditional system can survive, while at the same time adapting to changing socioeconomic and cultural conditions.

The Content of Political Speechmaking

In chapter 4, I contrasted the performance of the speeches in the fono with that of similar speeches in other social events. In that discussion I was mostly concerned with speechmaking as verbal art and with the adaptations and mutations of the same genre, the lāuga, across contexts and social goals. In that context, I did not say much about the actual content of the fono discussion. In this chapter, before examining the specific linguistic features used to express agency, I will describe the ways in which the participants in the event handle the difficult topics of the agenda of the meeting. I will discuss how matai bring up the problems, conflicts, and disagreements that caused the meeting to be convened and how they face the difficult task of accusing, blaming, and scolding one another, maintaining respect for the social hierarchies and without completely undermining the ultimately reconciliatory nature of the event.

With these themes in mind, let us turn to the introduction and subsequent discussion of the topics of the day in the fono proceedings.

THE UNFOLDING OF THE STORY

As I mentioned in chapters 3 and 4, in a fono, a section of the first speech is dedicated to the announcement of the agenda (see table 4). This section comes rather late in the speech, right after the lengthy ceremonial greetings of all the major lineages in the village and before the speech's final section, which is the wishing of good health to the chiefs and orators who are present. Its embedding between those two highly complimentary parts, where the sacredness of the audience is acknowledged and celebrated, already hints at the difficult character of the agenda. The announcement of the agenda is at once a report about some past events and a recognition of the troublesome nature of those events. In announcing the topics of the day, the first orator is also hinting at a public accusation about a party whom he should honor or

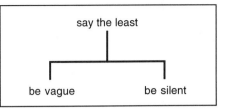

Figure 19. Strategies for dealing with the agenda topics in the first speech in a fono

protect. This conflict is typically dealt with through one basic strategy: "Say the least." In the meetings I recorded, this strategy took one of two forms: (i) "Be vague" or (ii) "Be silent," that is, "Don't say anything at all about the topics of discussion" (see fig. 19). The former strategy was usually preferred over the latter.

Strategy one: "Be vague." When the agenda is mentioned in the first speech, we typically find very general descriptions of the events that have precipitated the meeting. Here is one example:

(24) Fono of March 17, 1979. First speaker of the day.

> *Loa;*   *ia 'o- pei 'o makā'upu o le aofia ma le fogo,*
> so as for the topics of the assembly and the fono,
> →   *... 'o lo'o iai- (...) ka'akia i- i pā'aga*
> ... there are ... (they) concern the two buddies
> →   *ia o- o V[NAME] lava ma: le afioga iā A[NAME]*
> V. [orator] himself and His Highness A. [chief]
> →   *(...) oga 'o le aso le kākou pāloka.*
> ... because of the day of our elections.
> *ia ... ka'ilo gā po 'o iai ma gi si makā'upu,*
> so ... poor me I don't know if there are other topics,
> *... ia' 'a 'o le 'ā- lumāmea lava i le aofia*
> ... well (they) will be further in front of the assembly
> *ma le fogo gi si fo'i makā'upu*
> and the fono any other topics
> *'o lo'o (...) iai kokogu o le kākou aofia. (...)*
> that there ... are inside of our assembly. ....

The level of vagueness itself is in fact negotiable, as in a meeting in which the senior orator Moe'ono repeatedly asked the first speaker to reformulate the agenda until he began to produce more specific statements (see Duranti 1988, 22–24).

Strategy two: "Be silent." The second strategy is simply "don't say anything." In this case, the first speaker of the day skips the part dedicated to announcing the agenda of the meeting. This strategy was implemented in the following cases:

(a) In two meetings, the first speaker skipped the announcement of the agenda in his speech. It's important to realize that the agenda is the only part ever skipped by this one orator in the meetings I recorded. This omission was repaired in the following ways: In one case (January 25), as shown in example (25) below, Moe'ono, the senior orator acting as the chairman of the meeting, made the announcement himself when his turn came to open the discussion. In the other case (April 7), when the speech was over, Moe'ono prompted the first orator to mention the agenda (Duranti 1990a).

(b) In one meeting, in which there were four introductory lāuga before Moe'ono opened up the discussion (talanoaga) part of the meeting, the second, third, and fourth orators did not repeat or elaborate the agenda. They said either that the agenda had already been mentioned by the first orator or that they didn't have much to say about it. This avoidance indicates that even a retelling might be problematic until other, more powerful or more directly involved parties have spoken.

To the extent to which these two strategies appear to be violations of one of Paul Grice's (1975) maxims of cooperative behavior, namely, "be informative," they are but an example of polite behavior in situations that threaten loss of face, as predicted by Penelope Brown and Stephen Levinson (1987). The speakers seem to be trying to save the public "face" of those being tried by withdrawing information that is relevant to the ongoing interaction. There is however something problematic or at least only partially accurate in this interpretation, given that later in the meeting there will be plenty of face-threatening acts against key defendants (see Duranti 1988, 1990a). It seems instead that the vagueness about the agenda is structurally bound to the beginning of the meeting. It is only then that even the most powerful and outspoken speaker is vague. An example is provided in example (25), where the chairman, Moe'ono, takes it upon himself to introduce the topic that was skipped by the first speaker, the orator Loa: the question of the forthcoming elections and the relationship with the nearby village of Lufilufi. A few weeks earlier, the matai from Falefā had committed themselves to skip the secret ballot and unanimously support the incumbent M.P., the matai Fa'amatuā'inu (often abbreviated "Inu") Mailei from Lufilufi. In exchange, Lufilufi matai assured the fono of Falefā that no other matai from their village would run against Inu. Now, the situation has completely changed, with another matai from Lufilufi and three matai from Falefā, including Moe'ono, all running against one another.

(25) Fono of January 25, 1979.

Moe'ono;	*'ae 'o lo kākou aofia ma le fogo,*
	but our assembly and the fono,
	(0.8) 'o le 'ā fa'auso loa. (1.5)
	. . . the discussion is open. . . .
	uā e le'o se fogo o le kī ma le kolo.
	because it is not a very serious matter.
?;	*mālie!*
	Well said!
Moe'ono;	*leai. 'o le fogo- (2.0) o lo kākou kofi faipule*
	No. It's a meeting . . . of our M.P. representative
	o lo kākou ikū ma Lufilufi. (3.0)
	of our side with (the village of) Lufilufi.
	ia. 'o le 'ā aga'i loa iai o kākou māfaufauga.
	Right. We will bring forward our thoughts.
	i le asō.
	Today.

The only reference to the background events is the mentioning of the M.P. representative in the district (/lo kākou kofi faipule/). No word is spent at this point on the internal rivalry among the three matai in the village (the senior orators Moe'ono Kolio and Iuli Sefo, and the young chief Savea Sione) who are running for the same M.P. post. Nor is anything said about their respective stance vis-à-vis the earlier agreement to support the incumbent M.P from the nearby village of Lufilufi. Only later on in the speech will Moe'ono launch into a long and detailed appraisal of the situation, in which each of these elements will be spelled out from his point of view and evaluated.

These facts suggest that the vagueness of the first announcement of the agenda is conventional but for reasons different from the definition of the offenses or crisis as threatening loss of face to some specific party. To understand what the beginning vagueness is about we must think of the fono discourse not only from the point of view of the oratory that is being performed but also from the point of view of the complex *narrative* that is being woven in and around it. One of the features of narratives—to be understood as sequences of events temporally linked to one another—as described by William Labov (1972b, 363–364), is that they contain "abstracts," that is, sections with general statements about the basic point of the story. The agenda of the meeting is, in a sense, such an abstract. The problem, however, is that it is an abstract of a story about events that still need to be put together. That is, the agenda of the fono is an abstract of a multi-authored narrative about truths yet to be negotiated. This can explain why the speaker should not, or perhaps could not, "give out" the details of the story at the beginning of the meeting. The story implied in the abstract-agenda does not yet exist on the floor or in anyone's mind, at least in the shape it will take during the meeting: the form and content of the narrative are negotiable and must be collaboratively constructed by the participants, bit by bit, speaker after speaker, turn by turn. As strongly asserted by Moe'ono in a meeting where he was scolding the titleholders from a particular subvillage for not attending the meetings, "It is the government by many that makes a village safe!" (/'o le ko'akele o faipule e saogalemū ai se gu'u/). This view implies a variety of voices, that is, a succession of "tellers," each of whom brings a little piece of the story, a small contribution to the greater mosaic the matai are jointly assembling, each of whom contributes to the heteroglossia characteristic of fono discourse (see chap. 4).

In this perspective, contrary to Grice's maxim, to be informative at the beginning of the meeting would be the opposite of being "collaborative." It would preempt what is in fact both the style and the goal of the fono as part of a *social drama* (Turner 1974), namely, the "slow disclosure" of the inciting events and their assessment vis-à-vis the normative order they challenge or test. A detailed narrative at the time of the announcement would imply that the issues are already settled. It would assume an agreement that should not be taken for granted. It is precisely the uncertainty of a final solution that gives meaning and value to this as well as to most if not all social transactions (Bourdieu 1977).

Thus, in a fono, it is rare to hear one person tell a detailed story about the events that brought about the present crisis. Usually, instead, bits and pieces of the events will be revealed through a variety of grammatical and discursive frames. The choices that a speaker makes in referring to an event not only support a particular view of the event but also constitute (i.e., both entail and instantiate) a particular stance vis-à-vis the issue at hand. Indirectly, such a choice may reinforce a certain image of the speaker's role and stature in the political arena. This means that the *linguistic frames* (see Fillmore 1975, 1977) for a particular event in the fono must be explained both as communicative strategies to insure an adequate "flow" of information (Chafe 1980; Du Bois 1987) and as social acts that index political positions and particular claims to power. Such claims are made, justified, and sustained through acts of moral approval (praise) and moral condemnation (blame, accusation). For this reason, as I will discuss again in chapter 7, in addition to thinking about discourse as being regulated by an *information flow*, we should also think in terms of a *moral flow*, that is, a progressive and cooperative framing of characters and events in terms of their positive or negative value vis-à-vis community standards as defined in the ongoing interaction. Grammatical framings such as the ones I will discuss in the rest of this chapter have pragmatic and metapragmatic functions (see Silverstein 1985a, 1985b), in that they not only tell us about the events, they also say something about what the events mean to the speaker and what they should mean to the audience. The differences in the ways in which different social actors choose to tell or describe the facts are relevant for our understanding of the relation between discourse and social structure on the one hand and discourse and political process on the other. In the next section I will introduce some of the grammatical resources available to speakers to frame events and participants' roles during the discussion of the agenda.

Grammatical Structures as Framing Devices

Languages offer a variety of resources for describing events, states, properties, and relations in and with the world. Thus, for instance, in English the following three sentences may be seen as describing roughly "the same" event:

(a) The decision has been made.
(b) The chief has made the decision.
(c) We have heard the chief's decision.

Each of these three sentences presents a slightly different framing of what could be otherwise conceived of as the "same" event. Furthermore, each of the sentences commits the speaker to slightly different claims about what happened and about the participant structure of the reported event. The framing of the role of the chief, for example, varies from nonexistent in (a) (it may or may not be known from the context), to directly involved and initiating the event in (b), to presumably less directly involved in the action in (c) (where the chief is depicted as the originator of the message but not necessarily the one who delivered it). In order to understand such choices, we must first understand the system of which they are part, that is, the range of alternative forms available to the speakers and the linguistic contexts in which they appear (Ervin-Tripp 1972).

The Expression of Agency in Samoan Grammar

In Samoan grammar, a distinction is made between the subject of transitive clauses, which is marked by the preposition *e*—see (d) below—and the subject of intransitive clauses, which is not usually marked by any preposition—see (e):

(d) '*ua fa'atau*   *e*   *le tama*   *le suka*.
    TA   buy   ERG   ART   boy   ART   sugar
    The boy has bought the sugar.

(e) '*ua alu*   *le tama*   '*i*   *le maketi*.
    TA   go   ART   boy   to   ART   market
    The boy has gone to the market.

Samoan, in other words, distinguishes subjects that are Agents from other kinds of subjects. This system of case marking makes Samoan quite different from languages like English, where the category "subject" can be fulfilled by a variety of semantic roles (see E. L. Keenan 1984), including Agent (f), actor (g), experiencer (h), instrument (i), or patient or undergoer (j).

(f) [The boy] chased the dog.   [Agent]
(g) [The boy] went to America.   [Actor]
(h) [The boy] saw the dog.   [Experiencer]
(i) [The stone] killed it.   [Instrument]
(j) [The dog] died.   [Patient/Undergoer]

In Samoan only the noun phrase corresponding to [The boy] in (f) could be marked by the preposition *e,* as shown in (k).[1] In all the other cases, the subject of the English sentence would be expressed either as a prepositionless noun phrase—compare (l), (m), and (o)—or as an instrumental noun phrase, with the preposition *'i* 'with, by'—as in (n):

(k) *Na tuli [e le tama] le maile.*
     PST chase ERG ART boy ART dog
     [The boy] chased the dog.

(l) *Na alu [le tama] 'i Amerika.*
    PST go ART boy to America
    [The boy] went to America.

(m) *Na va'ai [le tama] i le maile.*
     PST see ART boy PREP ART dog
     [The boy] saw the dog.

(n) *'Ua pē ['i le ma'a].*
    PST die INSTR ART stone
    (It) was killed [with a/the stone].

(o) *'Ua pē [le maile].*
    PST die ART dog
    [The dog] died.

This system of case marking is found in many other languages of the world and has been called "ergative" or "ergative-absolutive" by linguists (see Chung 1978; Comrie 1978; Cook 1988; Dixon 1979; Fillmore 1968; Silverstein 1976). In these languages certain types of subjects, namely, Agents, are distinguished from other kinds of subjects, namely actors, experiencers, and instruments. Therefore, the subject of a sentence like (f) would be marked differently from the subject of sentences like (g)–(h). Thus, a crucial morphological (and sometimes syntactic) distinction is made, not between subject and object but between the subject of transitive clauses (marked by the ergative case)—see (k)—and the subject of intransitive clauses—(l) and (o)—which is marked in the same way as the object of the transitive clause—*le maile* in (k)—namely, by the absolutive case (zero preposition in the Samoan case). In Samoan, the preposition *e* before the noun phrase *le tama* in (k) is the ergative marker. I will hereafter refer to the subject of transitive clauses as the "ergative Agent" (in Samoan the absolutive marker for the subject of intransitive clauses and the object of transitive clauses is zero, that is, has no overt marking[2]). In figure 20, I show the canonical pattern of transitive clauses with full noun phrases ("verb" is here an

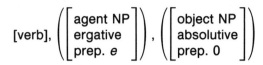

Figure 20.   Canonical word order pattern

abbreviation for "verb complex," that is, a predicate phrase that includes, in addition to the verb, tense and aspect markers, negation, clitic pronouns, and deictic particles).

The commas, a convention I am borrowing from G. Gazdar et al. (1985), indicate that the order of elements in figure 20, verb-Agent-object, is variable. The parentheses around the agent NP (agent noun phrase) and the object NP indicate that they are optional, namely, that either one of them can be left out of a transitive clause through a grammatical process called "zero anaphora," whereby the Agent or object of a transitive clause can be referred to or implied without having to have an overt pronominal trace (see chap. 6). Thus, not only verb-Agent-object sequences but also verb-Agent, verb-object, and verb alone are grammatical in Samoan. Although there is a tendency in my data for the verb to appear before the other syntactic elements (see also Cook 1988 for arguments in favor of verb-Agent-object as the unmarked word order in statements), other orders are also found, for example, verb-object-Agent, object-verb-Agent, Agent-verb-object (in the last case, which represents only 6.7 percent of the Agents found in the transcripts of two entire fono [7 cases out of 105],[3] the preverbal Agent cannot be preceded by the preposition e and is instead marked by the predicative particle/topic marker 'o, zero, or the adversative conjunction 'a. For the purpose of this study, the subject of transitive clauses will be called "ergative Agent," regardless of whether it is marked by the ergative marker e[4] and regardless of whether it co-occurs with an overt, that is, lexical object[5]—the capital A of *Agent* is intended to define it as a linguistic rather than social category, although, as I will argue below, the two will often merge. This means that what I consider salient in the following analysis is not so much the presence of a noun phrase with the ergative marker e—which however does mark the great majority of Agents—but the presence of an independent subject of a transitive clause, which happens to be marked by the ergative e in postverbal position. It is these lexically expressed Agents that were difficult to find in our earlier stages of fieldwork, and it is these noun phrases that I will discuss in the rest of this chapter. As I will discuss in chapters 6 and 7, their rarity is not restricted to Samoan discourse but is part of a more general phenomenology that needs explanation.

Ergative Agents in Fono Discourse: Claims of Accountability

The system I just described offers its speakers the possibility of explicitly and unequivocally assigning to a particular referent/concept the semantic role of *Agent,* to be understood here as *willful initiator of an event that is depicted as having consequences for either an object or animate patient.* It also offers observers and analysts of Samoan language use the possibility of monitoring the expression of agency in a particular speech event. Given what was said above about the participants' reluctance to define the background events and agency in the beginning part of the meeting, the appearance of utterances with ergative Agents constitutes an important and noticeable departure from that trend and hence becomes extremely informative for assessing the political climate and specific political alliances within any given situation.

Human Agents in the Fono Discussion

An analysis of the transcribed corpus of fono speeches shows that transitive clauses with ergative Agents are not very frequent—a generalization that confirms independent findings by Du Bois (1987) based on other languages and discourse genres (see chap. 7). However, when we analyze a large corpus of data, we find a sufficient number of cases to allow us some first generalizations about their use. Thus, in a transcript of an entire fono (April 7, 1979) of about 3700 lines, with each line roughly corresponding to a clause, I found sixty-six examples of utterances with ergative Agents expressed by full noun phrases, that is, lexically. In the transcript of another fono (January 25, 1979), out of a total of 750 lines comprising two particularly animated speeches (one of which was by the senior orator Moe'ono), I found thirteen cases of ergative Agents.[6]

When ergative Agents do occur, we find some recurrent patterns: they often appear in speech acts where a party, be it an individual, a group, or a deity, is held or made accountable for some act or way of doing something. That is, the use of transitive clauses with explicit Agents coincides with statements in which the power of certain individuals or groups to affect others through their actions or to initiate or cause events is at least acknowledged, if not more explicitly given credit or blamed. Transitive clauses with ergative Agents are also commonly found in statements about what a certain person, group, or legislative body is expected (or not expected) to do. In other words, the pattern outlined in figure 20 often appears with utterances that recognize someone's accomplishment or power to do something. The parties whose power and deeds are recognized or praised[7] above those of everyone else are the Christian God (/le Akua/), the polity as a whole (/le gu'u/ 'the village'), or its components, for example /'āiga/ 'the chiefs' (see chap. 2) or specific subvillages. Also common is the use of ergative Agents with utterances that express negative assessments such as complaints and accusations. Thus, we find that the speaker with the highest number of ergative Agents in his speech is the senior orator Moe'ono, who is considered the chairman of the meeting and typically acts as a prosecutor or instigator (sometimes in conjunction with the other senior orator in the village, Iuli). Moe'ono is the one who opens the discussion after the first introductory lāuga and explains the charges against the defendants or the problem for the community.

The recurrent pattern of agency expressed by ergative Agents can then be seen as an opposition between the unquestionable power of the deity and the polity (and its branches) who exist outside of the here and now, on the one hand, and the social actors who behave and act within historical time, on the other. While the former are usually shown to work at maintaining the social order or typically portrayed as doing what is expected of them, the latter are represented as challenging it through their (hence often improper) deeds. Example (26), from a speech by the high chief Salanoa, shows how the role of the Almighty is brought into the events of the day: He is the creator and the one to whom we owe happiness on this earth.

(26) Fono of April 7, 1979.

> 1911   Salanoa;   *e*   *fa'alava*   *e*   *le Akua mea 'uma.*
> TA CAUS+enough ERG ART Lord thing all
> The Lord makes all things sufficient.

1912	*le aso lā legei ma le mākou fa'alogo, (...)*
	this day and (given) what we heard, ...
1913	*ia' e leai so mākou leo.*
	well, there are no words (lit. 'voice') of ours.
1914	*pau lea kākou si'i le vi'iga i le Akua.*
	The only (thing) let us raise the praise to the Lord.
1915	*'ua faia <u>e le Akua</u> mea kekele,*
	<u>The Lord</u> has done many things,
1916	*kākou ke fiafia ma kākou olioli ai!*
	for which we are all happy and we rejoice!

The Lord can also be made responsible for inspiring a "Christian solution" to the crisis—that is, one of reconciliation and forgiveness:

(27) Same meeting, earlier on.

720	Salanoa;	*'o le aso fo'i 'ou ke lagoga,*
		Today I also feel (that)
721		*e iai ā le auala e amai <u>e le Akua</u>*
		TA pro EMP ART road TA bring ERG ART Lord
		here really is a way brought (to us) <u>by the Lord</u>,
722		*e fa'afilemū a'i se makā'upu,*
		with which to soften some item on the agenda,

Human actors as well can be responsible for good deeds, as shown in example (28), where the work done by the first speaker is recognized[8]:

(28) Fono of April 7, 1979.

424	M;	*si'i <u>e le kōfā</u> i le Laukogia le vi'iga*
		raise ERG ART Highness from ART (title) the praise
		His Highness the Lautogia[9] (has) given the praise
425		*ma le fa'afekai i lo Kākou Makai.*
		and ART thank to ART + IN we-INC Lord
		and the thanksgiving to Our Lord (lit. 'Our Matai').

But human actors are more likely to disrupt what God has done or not comply with what the polity expects of them than to deserve praises, especially those human actors who are talked about in a fono, which is a structure designed to repair "trouble."

After the first ceremonial speech of the day, the reason for the current crisis starts emerging from more explicit statements, like the one in example (29), where the senior orator Moe'ono (*M*) accuses the people from the nearby village of Lufilufi of having betrayed the agreement made during the campaign for the national elections.

(29) Fono of January 25, 1979.

>84   M;   *ia' (0.5) ma e kaukala aku ai lava- (2.0)*
>   so, and to really talk about-
>85   *ma 'o le 'ā fo'i ('ou koe f-)*
>   and I will also- (I again ex-)
>86   *koe fola mālamalama aku fo'i le mafua'aga*
>   again to really explain the reason
>87   *'ua mafua ai oga kākou fa'apegei.*
>   for which we have come to be like this.
>   [. . .]
>94   *oga   'ua soli   e   Lufilufi   le   kākou*
>   because TA betray ERG Lufilufi ART our-INC
>   *māvaega*
>   agreement
>   because Lufilufi has betrayed our (common) agreement

In example (30), from a meeting held two months later, the same speaker directly attacks the junior orator V. for something he claims V. did on the day of the elections. Again, we find the ergative Agent (in this case represented by the emphatic pronoun *'oe* [singular 'you']) in an utterance that makes explicit the nature of the accusation—an accusation, by the way, that will be repeatedly denied by the defendant:

(30) Fono of March 17, 1979.

>*Moe'ono;   (. . .) le   ā   le   mea*
>   ART What ART thing
>   For what reason
>   *'ua 'ē faga mea leaga ai   e   'oe   le   gu'u*[10]
>   TA you feed thing bad PRO ERG you the village
>   have you spread bad things (in) the village
>   *ma   isi   iku'āiga 'upu makagā?*
>   and other kind word ugly
>   with other kinds (of) ugly words?

Finally, in example (31), from yet another meeting, the other senior orator, Iuli, sums up his series of complaints about the orator Loa's behavior with a concluding statement in which Loa is represented as an ergative Agent:

(31) Fono of April 7, 1979.

>3400 Iuli;   *mea   lea   'ua fai   e   Loa.*
>   thing this PST do ERG Loa
>   This is what Loa has done.

Examples of this sort are common among transitive clauses with ergative Agents. The pattern is the same: the attribution of agency to a party typically coincides with an implicit or explicit assignment of responsibility. Depending on the nature of the referent—for example, whether divine or mortal, the meaning of the verb, and the discourse context—the attribution of agency can constitute an act of praise and positive recognition of authority or an act of condemnation for events that should not have occurred (cf. Besnier 1990a).

In more culture-specific terms, the use of transitive clauses with explicit agents often seems to contribute to the actualization of Polynesian *mana*, meant as an unstable and mobile potency that needs to be activated in concrete acts, speech acts included (see Shore 1989, 142; Valeri 1985, 99–101). In particular, the data presented in this study suggest that the transfer of mana from the gods to mortals, which has been analyzed as typically realized through ritual speech (Valeri 1985, 153–154), may also be seen as characteristic of political speech. In a sense, there is nothing surprising about this, given the close connection in ancient Polynesia between political and religious power. The potency represented by mana was what gave chiefs both political authority and special spiritual powers that made them dangerous and hence 'taboo' (*tapu*) to commoners' touch or close proximity. At the same time, as shown in chapter 4, at least in contemporary Polynesia, political and (non-Christian) religious-ceremonial discourse must be distinguished. This means that we need more in-depth grammatical analyses of ancient ceremonial speeches before making any generalizations or comparisons.

Mitigated Agency

If the use of transitive clauses with ergative Agents is strongly associated in Samoan political discourse with the assessment or assignment of responsibility, and if, as argued earlier in this chapter, part of the struggle in a fono is a linguistic one, namely, a confrontation over the definition of the causes or reasons for the crisis, we should expect two opposite trends in the fono discourse with respect to the expression of agency: while certain participants will try to assign agentive roles to certain other parties and in so doing will imply their accountability in either saving the polity or damaging it, other participants will try to resist those linguistic definitions and attributions. In the following three sections I will discuss linguistic strategies that resist or "mitigate" negative attributions. I will concentrate on three such strategies: (i) mention of Agent via alternative case marking; (ii) self- or other-abasement formulas within transitive clauses; and (iii) reported speech.

MENTION OF POTENTIAL AGENT VIA ALTERNATIVE CASE MARKING

In Samoan discourse, agents can be mentioned through alternative case markings. These other grammatical forms provide alternative resources for mitigating responsibility. I briefly discuss here two such case marking strategies: the encoding of agents as so-called "oblique objects" and as genitive modifiers. In the first strategy, a human participant in a described event is marked with a preposition *i* or *iā* 'from' instead of the ergative marker *e*.

With this *i* or *iā* case marker, the human agent who is the initiator of the event or action is framed as a source of a transitive act rather than as an ergative Agent. In such cases, the speaker lets the listener infer the potentially causative relationship between the referent of the source and the action described by the predicate.

In example (32), the orator Tafili describes her brother Savea's suit against the M.P., which is the cause of much worry and regret for some members of the village council, as originating 'from Savea' (/iā Savea/) rather than as being brought 'by Savea' (*e Savea*):

(32) Fono of April 7, 1979.

> 2826   *Tafili;*   *'o   le   makā'upu,   'o   lea- 'ua-*
> PRED ART   topic   PRED now   TA
> (as for) the topic, (that) now- has-
>
> 2827   *'ua lafo   kāofi   iai   le   kalosaga   iā   Savea*
> TA   state opinion   PRO ART   petition   from   Savea
> the petition <u>by</u> (lit. 'from') <u>Savea</u> has already been filed

In example (33), near the beginning of the same meeting, when the orator Fanua gives his first speech of the day and refuses to take a stand on the issue, he justifies his position by hinting that he has not received instructions from the high chief of his subvillage, Salanoa (see /Salagoa/ in line 449):

(33) Fono of April 7, 1979.

> 448   *Fanua;*   *e ui fo'i ga 'o legā e afio mai Lealaisalagoa,*
> although Lealaisalanoa has now arrived,

449   e   le'i   aumaia   se   kōfā   iā
             TA   NEG+TA give+CIA ART   opinions from
             Salagoa ma-
             Salanoa and
             no opinion has been given from Salanoa
450   ... ua le lava mai fo'i Iuli i legei faleakua.
             ... and also Iuli is not present from our subvillage.

In the second case-marking strategy, the agent is marked as a genitive modifier, with the same marking as possessors (either *o* or *a*) (see Duranti 1981a; Ochs 1988; Duranti and Ochs 1990). An example of this kind of case marking from informal conversation is given in example (34), where the deacon A. tells the pastor about his son Eki's food preparation for our research group:

(34) Pastor and Deacon.

24   A;   fai   le   umu kalo a   Eki ma   lu'au
             do   ART oven taro of Eti and palusami
             Eti made baked taro and palusami
             (lit. 'Eti's baked taro and palusami (was) made')
25   e fa'akali mai ai.
             to wait   DX   PRO
             to welcome (them) with it.

This case marking has the effect of focusing on the object (or patient) rather than on the human initiator or cause of the event. As with oblique object marking, the speaker leaves the listener to infer agency. It could be argued that line 24 is about the making of the taro rather than about Eti making the taro. This case marking can be used in situations, like example (34), where the speaker wants to mention and at the same time de-emphasize someone's contribution to a given task or achievement—in this particular instance, since Eti is an untitled person, and A.'s own son, it would seem inappropriate for A. to boast about Eti's doings or praise him. The genitive form /a Eki/ 'of Eti' cannot be interpreted as a possessive, given that it would be culturally inappropriate to think of a young, untitled member of the family as owning the food offered to high-status guests.

Similar examples are found in the fono speeches. In example (36), for instance, the chief Savea reframes an event mentioned earlier by his sister, using genitive marking instead of the ergative marker used by his sister. Example (35) presents the sister's initial utterance and (36) Savea's reframing. In (36) the verb is still /kokogi/ 'pay', but the character

Inu (/Igu/) has a less-active relationship with the money and Savea is not in the syntactico-semantic role of patient:

(35) Fono of April 7, 1979. Tafili, Savea's sister, reveals the source of trouble, the rumor that has forced Savea to file a suit against the M.P. Inu.

2887	T;	e (le)aga 'o 'upu gei ou ke kaukala iai,
		because these words I am going to talk about,
2888		"*ua fa'akau Savea e Igu i kupe.*" ...
		PST buy Savea ERG Inu with monies
		"Savea has been bought by Inu with money." ...
2889		*ia 'ua kakau ai lā ga kulāfogo 'upu gā,*
		so it has been necessary to try in court those words,

(36) Later in the same meeting.

3089	Savea;	e leai ā se kupe a Igu o maimau
		TA NEG EMP ART money of Inu PRED wasted
		there is no money of Inu's wasted
3090		e kokogi ai sa'u fāsefulu kālā ...
		TA pay PRO my forty dollars
		to pay my forty dollars ...
		(or 'to pay forty dollars for me')

The use of the nonspecific article *s-* (in *sa'u* 'my') further reinforces the hedging quality of the statement, which should be translated as 'to pay some forty dollars of mine' (see Mosel and Hovdhaugen 1992, 261–262).

Genitives are often found in defense statements such as the following, where the orator V. defends himself and the chief A. from the accusation of having used offensive language toward the fono members on the day of the elections (see example 30 for the accusation):

(37) Fono of March 17.

V;	'ou ke mālamalama fo'i i a'u 'upu ga fai.
	I TA clear also to my words PST say
	I also understand my words (that were) said.
	(lit. 'I also understand my words [that] say')
	'a 'o le Akua lā e silasila mai.
	but PRED ART Lord there TA see DX
	But the Lord sees (that)
	e augapiu ma sa'u 'upu ga fai.
	TA devoided with my words PST say
	there were no words of mine (that were) said.

And later on, defending his chief, A.:

V; e   leai   se   'upu   a A̲. [NAME] *ga   faia.*
   TA NEG ART word of   A.   PST say + CIA[11]
There are no words of A̲. [NAME] (that were) said.

Compare the last defense line with the following one by another orator who is pointing out in an accusatory manner the damage that the events have brought to the chief A. In this case we find the chief A. mentioned in the role of ergative Agent, precisely to highlight rather than downplay his accountability and the accountability of those who acted to damage his reputation:

(38) Fono of March 17, 1979.

> *Fanua;   e   leai   se   mea   lelei   e   maua   e̲   A̲.* [NAME]
>   TA NEG ART thing good TA get ERG   A.
>   there is nothing good (that) A̲. [NAME] got (out of this)

The use of the negative with ergative Agents is not unusual and, as in this last case, often implies the appropriateness of its positive counterpart: "he didn't, but he should have."[12]

The power struggle between different parties in the fono is in these examples reconstituted through the choice of specific case marking that reorients or frames the degree of agency by certain human participants. Powerful actors are more likely to define others as ergative Agents when they want to accuse them of something. Less powerful actors can try to resist such accusations by suggesting alternative linguistic definitions of events and people's roles in it. The struggle between prosecution and defense is thus often played as a linguistic exercise whereby those in power try to get clear and punctual definitions whereas those who want to resist them try to diffuse the tension and the accusations by undermining the framing of events as directly involving human agents.

SELF- OR OTHER-ABASEMENT FORMULAS IN TRANSITIVE CLAUSES

As discussed earlier, the use of ergative Agents in political discourse implies a concern with the actions of the referent of the agent noun phrase. This is typically the case either with important social actors and social bodies or with defendants whose actions are portrayed as the source or cause of a current crisis. As shown in the previous section, speakers may however downplay the importance of certain parties (themselves included) by using certain mitigating strategies. Yet another strategy is one in which the speaker uses a transitive clause with an ergative Agent and at the same time mitigates the impact of his or her assertion by lowering the status of the agent referent. This is a complex act reminiscent of what Gregory Bateson (1972) called the "double bind" situation, where a speaker simultaneously sends out two contradictory messages. In the Samoan case, the speaker uses a type of clause and case marking that, according to our analysis, highlights the role of the referent of the agent noun phrase but at the same time defines the agent participant as a worthless being whose actions should not be taken too seriously or could not possibly seriously affect anyone. In this strategy, ability to initiate the action is implied but at the same time responsibility is mitigated. This kind of self- and other-abasement formula often occurs in replies to accusations or acts that threaten loss of face. An illustration is provided in example (39). The scene is the end of a long fono (on April 7, 1979) from which I have taken several of the examples quoted above. The discussion is finally over, the senior orator Moe'ono would like to have a closing kava ceremony but has just been told that there is no more kava left. He then turns to the researcher (myself) and using a fake and humorous title, "Alexander the Great"— a common pun on my name—asks:

(39) Fono of April 7, 1979.

> 3751 Moe'ono; ia' Alesaga (le) Sili,
> Well, Alexander (the) Great,
> 3752 uā ua 'uma ga kusikusi?
> so TA finish COMP write-write
> so, is all the (busy) writing over?
> 3753 'o ā ea gā mea e kusikusi
> PRED wh- QU those thing TA write-write
> (e) 'oe?
> ERG you
> What is that you keep writing all the time?
> 3754 Others; (laughter)

In the second question (line 3753), which is a reformulation of the first one, Moe'ono escalates the assignment of responsibility by changing from an agent-less question ('is all the [busy] writing over?') to a full transitive clause with an ergative Agent (e 'oe '[by] you')—the reduplicated form (/kusikusi/) of the verb /kusi/ 'write' conveys the sense of a frequent and repetitive action (as if I had been writing a lot, hence too much). Utterance 3753 is thus an example of one of the typical uses of transitive clauses with an explicit agent noun phrase, namely, a criticism, if not an accusation. At this point, the chief Fuimaono comes to my rescue, and he does so in a remarkably skillful manner that leaves Moe'ono momentarily unable to match Fuimaono's reply with the same wit and hinted scorn of his own original question. All he is left with is a meager overlapping *oh!* right after the first part of Fuimaono's response.

(40) Fono of April 7, 1979.

3755	*Fuimaono;*	*'o a kou vagaga ā ma saugoaga lea*
		PRED of you speech EMP and speech that
		It's your honorable speech (of senior orators) and
		the honorable speech (of the chiefs) that
3756		*ua- (.3) kusikusi uma lava e le kama.*
		TA write-write all EMP ERG ART boy
		<u>the boy</u> has been all really writing.
		[
3757	*Moe'ono;*	*oh!*
		Oh!
3758		(Voices of people leaving)
3759		(Someone laughing)

The two respectful words *vagaga* 'honorable speech (of a senior orator)' and *saugoaga* 'honorable speech (of a chief)' do the first part of the job (see Duranti 1992a). The researcher, Fuimaono suggests, is just writing down the honorable, hence beautiful and important, speeches that Moe'ono and the chiefs have been giving.[13] What could be more appropriate? Moe'ono is reminded of his power and his status. He should behave accordingly, that is, with dignity and restraint: he can be pleased or indifferent but certainly not too concerned, especially given the fact that the one who is writing is just a "boy" (see line 3756). In his reply, Fuimaono maintains the transitive clause format with the frequentative verb form /kusikusi/ and with the ergative Agent, but changes the description of the latter from a pronoun (*'oe* 'you') to a definite description (*le kama* 'the boy') that clearly lowers my status. In so doing, he manages to accomplish several goals at the same time: he avoids contradicting Moe'ono's implicit assertion that I have been willfully and busily writing down something, he downplays my responsibility by describing me as a "boy," and implies praise for the "boy" who has been writing down the important words of important people. Similar examples are found in other parts of the proceedings—in, for instance, cases where the speaker presents what he thinks or feels (which can be expressed with a transitive verb, e.g., /lagoga/), and uses the genitive /lo'u/ in the expression /lo'u kāofi vaivai/ 'my weak opinion' instead of the first-person pronoun to identify the agent, as in example (41):

(41) Fono of March 17, 1979. The orator Nu'u closes with a long speech that is partly an apology for his chief's misbehavior.

> Nu'u;   'ua lagoga   e   lo'u   kāofi   vaivai
>   TA   feel   ERG   my   opinion   weak
>   My weak opinion feels (that)
>   'ua   kali   le   Akua   mo   le   aso   legei.
>   TA   answer   ART   Lord   for   ART   day   this
>   the Lord has replied today.
>   (i.e., a Christian solution has been found)

In this case, several strategies are used at once to create what could be called a "polyphony of stances." The speaker objectifies his own thinking through a third person referent (the opinion), and, while giving it prominence through the ergative marking, also suggests a less direct agency through genitive marking (the possessive *lo'u* 'my'), and mitigates the importance of the act through the lexical choice of the adjective *vaivai* 'weak' to modify the term 'opinion' (/kāofi/).

What is important here in terms of the constitution of agency is that such uses of transitive clauses with "abased agency" co-occur with certain kinds of speech acts (e.g., apologies or diffusion of loss-of-face-threatening acts) and are produced by speakers in certain kinds of contexts. In fact, we might say that such forms help define the speech act and the context as of a certain kind. Thus, for instance, when the high chief who speaks on behalf of all the village chiefs gives his opinion, he uses the same verb found in example (41) (/lagoga/), but instead of the self-abasement form /kāofi vaivai/ 'weak opinion', he uses the first-person (emphatic) pronoun: /a'u ke lagoga/ 'me (I) feel' (fono of April 7, 1979). The social hierarchy is linguistically sustained and activated by the ability of certain social actors to define themselves as willful and responsible agents whose actions or feelings matter for the rest of the community.

These last few examples have shown that the same linguistic strategies used to define a third party's involvement and responsibility with respect to a given event can also be used to define the speaker's responsibility. In fact, in any act of speaking, by assigning responsibility to others, speakers are also themselves implicitly assuming responsibility. By engaging in definitions of others' doings, speakers take stances that might have consequences for others' as well as for their own well-being. It was the problematic nature of any kind of "definition" that guided us in the earlier discussion of the announcement of the agenda at the beginning of the fono. In the next section, I will briefly discuss a strategy to deal with definitions that have already been given and need to be assessed. As we shall see, reported speech can offer a solution to the perils of accepting someone else's definition of a given state of affairs.

EMBEDDING OF A TRANSITIVE CLAUSE
IN REPORTED SPEECH

Reported speech has been shown to be a very powerful tool allowing authors (or speakers) to take distance from a particular statement or to infiltrate it so as to include their own views in a third party's quoted speech (see Besnier 1990a; Brenneis 1984; Haviland 1977; Macaulay 1987; Vološinov 1973). These strategies are also used in the fono, where we find accusatory transitive clauses with fully expressed agents sometimes framed as reported speech. An example of the use of reported speech in a fono is provided in example (35), where, after much discussion about a "problem" between one of the village chiefs (Savea) and the district M.P. (/Igu/), the chief's sister (herself an orator) reveals the source of the problem to be the accusation her brother is trying to fight in the capital's courts.[14] The example is here reproduced as (42):

(42) Fono of April 7, 1979. Second topic in the agenda.

> 2887   *e (le)aŋa 'o 'upu ŋei ou ke kaukala iai,*
> because these words I am going to talk about,
> 2888   *"'ua fa'akau Savea e <u>Iŋu</u> i kupe."* ...
> TA   buy   Savea ERG Inu with monies
> "Savea has been bought by Inu with money." ...
> 2889   *ia 'ua kakau ai lā ŋa kulāfoɡo 'upu ɡā,*
> So those words must be tried in court,

The statement in line 2888 is a difficult one for the speaker to make. In reporting an accusation against her brother, she is also reporting one against the M.P. Putting the accusation in reported speech mitigates the force of her speech act and allows her to reveal an important piece of information—and hence to "tell the story"—without assuming full responsibility for it.

A similar case is provided during the discussion of another issue, in the same meeting. In this case, the orator Fa'aonu'u questions Iuli's accusation against Loa (see example 29 above). In his reply to Iuli's invective, instead of making the accusation his own or blatantly rejecting it, Fa'aonu'u repeats it maintaining Iuli's authorship, via reported speech, but undermining the accusation by framing it as an indirect question and hence giving it a dubious shade:

(43) Fono of April 7, 1979.

> 3455   *pei oga e:- . . . vagaga iai . . .*
> as you say [R] . . .
> 3456   *po'o Loa ua f- . . . ua:- fai se pepelo i lo kākou gu'u*
> whether Loa . . . s- . . . said some lie to our village
> 3457   *po 'o Loa ua fa'afefea.*
> whether Loa had done this or what.
>
> (Free translation: 'As you have said, Loa would . . . have said some lie to our village, Loa would have done this or that.')

At times the reported speech strategy and the change of case marking can be combined, as in the following example, where the orator Fa'aonu'u once more reframes Iuli's words in asking for clarification:

(44) Fono of April 7, 1979.

> 3462   *po 'o Loa po 'o le ā ga (??)*
> Loa- what is that (??)
> 3463   *le   mea   a   Loa   ua   fai? . . .*
> ART thing of Loa PST do
> Loa did? . . .
> (lit. 'Loa's thing that (??) (was) done?')
> 3464   *'o le koe fa'afesili aku lea i- i lau kōfā le Makua.*
> This is what I am asking to Your Highness, the senior orator.

In line 3463, Fa'aonu'u changes Iuli's words from a transitive clause with an ergative Agent, namely *e Loa* (see example 29) to a clause in which Loa is the genitive modifier (*a Loa*) of the noun *mea* 'thing'.

Agency and Power

The more we learn about the ways in which linguistic codes and variables are used and integrated into ongoing social processes, the more we realize that language does not simply reflect the world, it also shapes it, fashions it. Power exists, externally, with its weapons, armies, jails, and other such material agents and institutions, but the authority for specific acts—like any other form of social action—must be achieved. Thus, it is appropriate to say that the choice of specific linguistic framings for people's actions, beliefs, and feelings does not simply reflect existing power relations, it also constitutes them. The linguistic code seen as a process rather than as a structure is one of the "technologies" through which power and social structure can be sustained and renegotiated. In our discussion, this becomes particularly apparent when we realize that the linguistic forms used not only index a speaker's stance with respect to a given issue or accusation but also help constitute the "facts" under discussion and hence the grounds for the final resolution by the village council. Finally, the very act of using assertions with explicitly mentioned agents—especially when coinciding with accusations or blamings—constitutes an assertion of a participant's power to speak his or her mind. Thus, with the exception of the "safe" recognition of God's power or the importance of the chiefs, the village, or other political entities, the process of constructing agency can be a dangerous process that can place the speaker in a vulnerable position. Those who are being defined as "agents" (through utterances with ergative Agents) and their allies may fire back and seek revenge. If this is the case, the number and types of ergative Agents in a matai's speeches can be used as an index of the type of public persona he wants (or is able) to project.

In the speeches I collected in 1979, the speaker who uses the highest number of ergative Agents is the senior orator Moe'ono (see chap. 2 on his status in the village), who uses more ergative Agents than any of the other matai, including the other senior orator, Iuli, and the high chief Salanoa (see tables 6 and 7).[15]

Moe'ono was perceived by many as the most powerful leader in the community; his actions and words were feared by most people, and it was also partly due to his political wisdom and energy that the village maintained its integrity throughout its most difficult crises (see Duranti 1981a, 1990a for more information on the events during and after the 1978–1979 political campaign). While sitting in the fono and then later listening to the speeches I had recorded, I often felt that if there had been no crises, Moe'ono would have created some. His strength was in building unity out of potential divisions. He used any kind of conflict to redraw the meaning and boundaries of the system, to test other matai's commitment to tradition. His role in the community was quite

Table 6 *Ergative Agents by Speakers during the Fono of January 25, 1979*

Speaker	Status	Number of Ergative Agents
Moe'ono	Senior Orator	16
'Auga	Orator	5
Usu	Orator	4
Iuli	Senior Orator	3
Tui	Orator	3
'Alo E.	Orator	3
Loa	Orator	3
Tafili F.	Orator	1
Fulumu'a	Orator	1
Matā'afa	Orator	0
Salanoa M.	Chief	0
Tevaseu	Chief	0
Savea Savelio	Chief	0
Total		39

Table 7 *Ergative Agents by Speakers during the Fono of April 7, 1979*

Speaker	Status	Number of Ergative Agents
Moe'ono	Senior Orator	18
Iuli	Senior Orator	10
Salanoa A.	High Chief	9
Matā'afa	Orator	6
Savea Sione	Chief	6
Fanua	Orator	4
Tafili	Orator	4
Loa	Orator	3
Fa'aonu'u	Orator	2
Alo F.	Orator	2
Tevaseu	Chief	1
Fuimanono	Chief	1
'Upu	Orator	0
Total		66

Table 8 *Number of Ergative Agents Referring to God by Speakers during the Fono of April 7, 1979*

Speaker	Total Number of Agents	Agents Referring to God
Moe'ono	18	0
Iuli	10	1
Salanoa A.	9	9

different from that of the other high-ranking titleholders. The high chief Salanoa Aukusitino, for example, was more a symbol of power than an actual mover. He was considered politically astute, someone who would always look for the best possible compromise and avoid harsh words and direct confrontations. This public perception is well represented in the types of ergative Agents he uses. Despite the relatively large number of ergative Agents he produced on April 7, when we look at what they refer to, we find that they all refer to God. All of Salanoa's nine full transitive utterances with an ergative Agent expressed[16] have "the Lord" (*le Atua*) or "the (Holy) Spirit" (*le Agana*) as the agent noun phrase (see table 8). These figures are in contrast with Moe'ono's ergative Agents during the same meeting, none of which refer to God,[17] and Iuli's, with only one ergative Agent referring to 'the Lord' /e le Akua/. Thus Salanoa would seem to have been concerned not with directly blaming those who had violated the rules—a job that he left to Moe'ono and Iuli—but rather with reestablishing harmony and social order by invoking the legitimacy of the highest power of all.

Moe'ono and Iuli, however, use ergative Agents in more varied ways. First, as I mentioned earlier in this chapter (see examples 29, 30, and 31), their ergative Agents are often part of complaints and accusations against specific parties. Thus, for instance, in the fono on January 25, eight of the ergative Agents produced by Moe'ono (50 percent of his total; see table 6) referred to the village of Lufilufi, which Moe'ono was very much trying to cast as the villain in the current political situation. But Iuli and Moe'ono also use ergative Agents in speech acts in which they work at reinforcing the unity of the polity as a whole. Thus, four of Moe'ono's and three of Iuli's ergative Agents on April 7 refer to the village as a whole (/le gu'u/). Moe'ono also uses the ergative Agents in statements about what various people are expected to do. In these cases, agency is used to define attributes of specific groups of people or types of persons.

Conclusions

One of the lessons of this exercise is that grammar is closely tied to politics and, more generally, to ethics—namely, which actions are acceptable or even laudable and which ones are unacceptable and blameful. In other words, given a particular grammatical system (for instance, one in which Agents are marked as special), speakers exploit it to do their job as social actors, that is, in this case, community leaders and members of an ever-evolving sociopolitical unit. When we look closely at the grammatical form of the utterances produced by matai in a fono, we find that the frequency of certain types of grammatical patterns is correlated with the nature of the event and the political roles of its participants. Some of these aspects seem predictable. Thus, for instance, we are not surprised to learn that the two senior orators who act as prosecutors do in fact often use transitive clauses with ergative Agents more often than most of the other matai. It is their role to assign responsibility, including blame, to members of the assembly. They also have the rank to do so without risking immediate retaliation or physical aggression by the people they accuse. At the same time, such a subtle way of constituting agency allows for finer distinctions. How often one uses ergative Agents, for which purposes, and about whom are all elements that contribute to define a person's stance vis-à-vis a specific issue while at the same time contributing to the more general construction of that person's persona in the political arena. During the tenure of Moe'ono Kolio and Iuli Sefo, for instance, there was no question that Moe'ono was more outspoken and politically more aggressive. How did people come to such a perception? In part, I am arguing, through the impression left by the linguistic choices he made during his public speeches in the fono, including his rhetorical style of using a higher percentage of utterances in which specific parties would be linguistically framed as initiators of events that were presented or understood as detrimental to the well-being of the community.

In a highly hierarchical but at the same time dynamic social system like the Samoan one, in which a title is a necessary but not sufficient means to rise to power, individuals must use a variety of resources for defining their own social persona. A fono is the political arena in which this work mostly gets done, the context in which the secret strategies prepared in more private meetings are tested. Words alone do not create the world, but they certainly contribute to make inner selves known and opinions available and hence vulnerable to the scrutiny of others. A hesitation in the voice, a confused description, an ambiguous claim, a direct accusation, the reframing of someone else's words: these and other linguistic elements help build an image of the situation which may or may not support a particular proposal. They also help build social identities. The grammar of fono speeches is fascinating precisely because it displays the same complexity and the same subtleties as the other semiotic resources discussed in earlier chapters: the use of the social space in the fono house, the exploitation of any temporal sequence into a ranking occasion (viz., in the kava ceremony, in the order of speakers). It is only by juxtaposing all of these elements that we can hope to reach a more adequate understanding of Samoan social structure, its hierarchies, and the rise and fall of particular actors.

In my own experience, the realization of the close connection between the grammatical patterns I had gone to study in their own terms and the political contexts I found them embedded in represents the end of a long detour, an eventful and richly meaningful ethnographic journey in which language and politics came together to close off an interpretive circle. But, of course, this would be only a conventional closure. In the real cycle of everyday life, there are no circles but only spirals. From one conclusion we move on to new hypotheses and to the search for new interpretive horizons. It is with these thoughts in mind that I will venture into the next chapter to offer some evidence of how the very same linguistic strategies I found in the fono speeches are also used in other, more mundane settings.

6

From Political Arenas to Everyday Settings: The Grammar of Agency across Contexts

In the previous chapter, I have shown that the use of transitive clauses with Agents fully expressed tends to correlate with speech acts in which the speaker recognizes someone's accomplishments. Such a recognition, in turn, can be seen as an assignment of responsibility to the referent of the Agent, which can be characterized as doing something positive (viz., that the speaker and the community like to see done) or something negative (viz., that the speaker and the community do not like to see done). Such speech acts exhibit interesting correlations. Positive actions are routinely ascribed to God, whereas negative ones are typically ascribed to humans, namely, in our case to members of the fono or other parties in the district who have caused a crisis by their (hereby defined as) inappropriate actions—some of the morally "negative" actions can even be expressed in negative clauses, that is, by stating what a certain party has *not* done. In the fono, then, we find transitive clauses with fully expressed Agents ("ergative Agents") often embedded in or constitutive of two types of speech acts: (i) praising or giving credit (especially to the Lord for his power and mercy) and (ii) blaming or accusing (either individuals or groups). In chapter 5, I stressed the political force of these constructions, suggesting that, in the fono arena, they are potentially powerful tools through which matai can shape the political agenda of their own community in at least two ways: (i) by directly portraying certain parties as willful and powerful agents—namely, as parties who can affect through their actions the actions of others—and (ii) by indirectly supporting their own standing in the community as important participants, whose words are indeed deeds—namely, they can, through praises and accusations, make a difference. I also showed that speakers can try to oppose or resist such moves by mitigating agency through a variety of linguistic strategies, such as non-agentive (viz., genitive) case marking, reported speech, and affect-loaded expressions. In this chapter I want to extend the analysis of the social work that grammatical constructions can do by comparing the use of ergative Agents in fono speeches with their use in more mundane interactions. I will show that, contrary to what is often assumed in linguistic and anthropological studies of verbal interaction, there are strong similarities between the ways in which certain grammatical constructions are used in an institutional setting such as the fono and more "private" interactions among family members, friends, or acquaintances. The similarities in the ways in which transitive clauses with ergative Agents are used in spoken Samoan suggest that there is a powerful "grammar of praising and blaming" at work, to be thought of as a set of grammatical resources that shape one's perception of a party's worth and standing in the community. Such a grammar, which directly links linguistic constructions with notions of person, social status, and moral values, indicates that we might have to revise or at least enrich the categorization of the acts of praising and blaming proposed in speech act theory, where these acts have been respectively classified as "expressives," that is, as acts in which speakers express their attitude about a given state of affairs, and as "assertives" (Searle and Vanderveken 1985), that is, as acts in which speakers represent views of how the world is. It would seem that, at least in the contexts I have analyzed, praising and blaming do more than that. They are important social acts through which speakers can in fact affect the way the world is.

The Expression of Agency across Social Situations

The extent to which what I have said about language and social context in ceremonial and political events has any relationship to what Samoan speakers say and do in other contexts, especially in more mundane or secular activities, is an important issue for a number of reasons. Methodologically, establishing a positive relationship between what is found in formal or institutional contexts and informal or everyday contexts is a way of responding to criticism of the particular tradition on which I originally grounded my research, namely, the ethnography of communication (Bauman and Sherzer 1974; Gumperz and Hymes 1972; Hymes 1974a). This school of linguistic anthropology has been accused in the past of being too concerned with ritual encounters and formal speech genres and of having little to say about more mundane types of interactions (Bloch 1976; Moerman 1988, 11). Theoretically, similarities as well as differences between grammatical usage across contexts can shed light on a number of issues, including the nature of the process by which a given utterance is assigned illocutionary force—the type of speech act it represents—and the political nature of what we might think of as private or less consequential activities. As we shall see, although the utterances in which ergative Agents occur may not be explicitly marked as praising, blaming, or accusing, the discourse context in which they occur and, in particular, the participants' reactions to the use of such utterances suggest that rather than representing the world or the speaker's stance, they are perceived as affecting the social world in rather dramatic ways.

THE FONO VERSUS EVERYDAY
CONVERSATIONAL INTERACTION

Since the very goal of a fono is usually to repair some damage to the well-being of the community, whose ideal harmonious existence or, in Samoan terms, mutual love (*fealofani*), has been upset, it could be argued that it should not come as a surprise that the mentioning of actions and their initiators through transitive clauses with overt Agents is strongly correlated with acts of criticism or even accusations against those who are being held responsible for the present state of affairs. For similar reasons, given the emphasis on restoring harmony in the community, one should also not be surprised to find God's deeds and power recognized and praised. After all, as the central political institution in traditional Samoan communities, the fono is designed to reinforce a view of political authority as directly linked to supernatural power. What used to be the Polynesian ancestral mana is now redistributed between a number of entities and recognized as: the Christian God's power (e.g., His power to eliminate any member of the village council at any time, as many metaphors used in the opening speeches remind everyone present, and hence His good will to make the ongoing meeting possible), the matai's power (e.g., their power to control the land and hence the natural resources as well as the labor force in the community), and, finally, the power of old and new "spirits" (*aitu*) who inhabit familiar places and are still feared by some Samoans. It is about the first two kinds of power that fono participants are especially concerned.

In other words, Samoan fono, like American trials and congressional debates, are about the constitution of the social order in an explicit and to some extent predictable way. Participants are expected to argue with one another and try to make their version of reality win over someone else's. To the extent that reports about what a party has done are embedded in such arguments, they will be used to make that party look either good or bad. We know that in a juridical or political arena, there is no reporting just for the sake of storytelling. As I discussed in chapter 5, in the fono as well there is no *neutral* recounting. In these contexts, transitive clauses with explicit reference to responsible agents (represented as "ergative Agents") are part of larger narratives in which political and ethical landscapes are built for others to assess.

A question I want to entertain in this chapter is whether the strategies and expectations found in such a competitive and status-conscious context as the fono transfer to other more ordinary settings, when participants' political and economic standings do not seem to be at stake as they obviously are in a fono (see Howard and Kirkpatrick 1989, 90–91). More specifically, I will investigate whether the uses of transitive clauses found in the fono transfer to contexts in which the participants (or some of them at least) do not even seem to have any real political power or high status to defend in the eyes of the community at large. In the following pages I will show that in fact the association between the use of ergative Agents and acts of praising or blaming are quite common in much less institutional settings, such as interactions among acquaintances, friends, or family members sitting in front of a plate of food. These are parties who are apparently just there "to make conversation" (*talatalanoa*) or to "gossip" (*faitala*).[1] As we shall see, the difference between institutional settings (such as the fono) and everyday settings lies not so much in the use of the linguistic strategies discussed in chapter 5 but in the range of participants who have access to such strategies as well as in the more immediate response that they evoke, partly although not exclusively due to the type of turn-taking system that characterizes conversational interaction as opposed to speechmaking arenas.

In Search of Fully Expressed Agents

As I wrote in chapter 2, when we started to collect linguistic data, we were struck by how few examples of ergative Agents we encountered in our transcripts.

When we began collecting speech data, we were still influenced by common expectations in linguistic research that transitive clauses with Agents fully expressed—for example, by a full noun phrase (the man, the girl, the chief)—should be fairly frequent in everyday discourse. That is, we expected such utterances as *the boy broke the plate, the kids ate the cake, Sina cut the breadfruit.* In fact, in analyzing our transcripts, we soon discovered that this was not the case. The relative paucity of ergative Agents in naturally occurring discourse seemed to be due to a number of factors. A consideration of these factors can be helpful for an assessment of the relative frequency of this particular grammatical form across speech activities.

First, much of household interaction (which constituted the bulk of our data, with a final corpus of 18,000 pages of handwritten transcripts) is made of directives, often shouted out to younger members of the extended family. Grammatically, such directives are expressed by imperative forms which in Samoan, as in English, usually do not include the subject/addressee. Our tapes are full of imperative forms such as /gofo lelei/ 'sit properly', /kū i luga/ 'stand up!', /'aua/ 'don't!', /sau e kakau lau kāgamea/ 'come to hang your laundry', /alu ave mea lea le keige lale/ 'go (and) take that thing (to) that girl (over there)', and so on, in which the subject (semantically either an actor or an Agent) is not expressed. As shown by Ochs (1988, 109), even when women in the house use transitive clauses (either in declaratives or in yes-or-no questions), they tend to express the Agent much less often than men do in formal settings such as the fono.

Second, as I mentioned in chapter 5, in Samoan conversation, not only imperative forms but declarative sentences as well are often elliptical and the Agent is one of the arguments of the verb that is more likely to be omitted. This is possible in Samoan because of a grammatical feature, also common in other languages, called zero-anaphora, that is, a form of reference that operates without overt pronominal forms for certain kinds of arguments, including, in this case, subjects of transitive clauses. Thus, for instance, in the following utterance taken from an

interaction between a mother and her young child, the referent of the
subject of the predicate /pu'e le aka o 'oe/ 'take(s) a picture of you' is
left out and is understood from the context:

(45) Pesio, book 16.

> *Mother; kū   i   luga   e   siva   se'i   pu'e   le   aka   o   'oe.*
> stand PREP top to dance so-that take ART picture IN you
> Stand up to dance so that (she) will take your picture.

In other cases, the referent of the Agent of the transitive verb has
been introduced in the immediately prior discourse and is not repeated
(cf. Du Bois 1987). Example (46) shows a case in which the transitive
verb /sasa/ 'cut' (lit. 'hit') is part of a complement clause connected
to a main verb /mafai/ 'be possible, can', which also does not have the
subject expressed. For both verbs the subject is understood as being the
man Tui (/Kui/) who was just mentioned in the immediately prior
clause, as the subject of the predicate *ma'i* 'sick':

(46) Inspection. A group of matai is inspecting people's lawns to see whether
they have complied with the order to clean up and cut the grass. Orator T.
arrives in front of the land of one family which has not finished cutting the grass
on the side of the road.

> *T;   Fisaga! 'ā ma'i Kui ua   lē   mafai   ŋa   sasa   le   auala.*
> Fisaga if sick Tui PST NEG can COMP hit ART road
> Fisaga! If Tui is sick (he) can't cut the grass.
> *sau   'oe   e   sasa   ī   i   le   auala lea.*
> come you COMP hit here on ART road this
> You come to cut (the grass) here on this (part of) the road.

In example (47), a sequence taken from a conversation among three
young men in which one tells the story of a Dracula movie he saw in a
theater in the capital, speaker T. mentions the character in line 137
(/le koea'iga/ 'the old man') and then proceeds to tell a series of predicates about him, including two transitive verbs, /kolosisi/ '(to hit with
a) cold chisel' in line 143, and /ku'i/ 'give a blow' in line 145, without
mentioning the character again (not even by means of a pronoun):

(47) Dracula.

> *137   T;   ŋa   alaku   ā   le   koea'iga   ma-*
> PST go + DX EMP ART old-man with-
> the old man went (there) with-

138		*le piẟisipa'u ma le mea -hh*
		ART crowbar and ART thing
		the crowbar and the thing- -hh
139		*(1.5)*
140		*ma (le-)*
		and (the-)
141		*(1.2)*
142	S;	*kolosisi?*
		Cold chisel?
→ 143	T;	*ma le kolosisi kolosisi ai ((LG)) le keiẟe hehe!* [2]
		and ART chisel chisel PRO ART girl
		and the cold chisel (to) strike the girl with it ((LG)) hehe!
		(lit. 'and the chisel (to) chisel with-it the girl')
144	Si;	*kolosisi fa'afea?*
		chisel like-what
		(He) struck (her) like what?
→ 145	T;	*ku'i le maẟava.*
		strike ART stomach
		(He) struck the stomach.
		[
→ 146	S;	*ku'i fakafaka 'ā,*
		strike chest TAG
		Struck (the) chest, right?
→ 147	T;	*mm. ku'i. 'ē'ē:!*
		Mm. (He) struck. (She) scream(ed)!

In line 147, even the subject of the following predicate referring to a different character (the girl in the story) is left implicit and must be recovered from the context.

Thus, in Samoan, as in other languages (see Du Bois 1987), transitive clauses typically contain a verb and an object rather than a verb and the Agent, given that usually the referent of the Agent already has been introduced in the immediately preceding discourse (Ochs 1988, 108–117). In other cases, as shown in example (45), the identity of the Agent can be recovered from the nonverbal context.

Furthermore, in many cases, when the referent of the understood Agent in the depicted event is expressed (either as a full pronoun or as a noun phrase), it is often in the form of a genitive or possessive modifier. Thus, a common syntactic frame for transitive verbs in Samoan is also verb-object, but in the Samoan case the object noun phrase is at times a complex one, which includes a genitive noun phrase (NP) (see fig. 21).

As indicated by the angle brackets, "Gen" (Genitive) can appear transitive verb + [$_{np}$ det + { gen pro } + nom + { gen NP }]

Figure 21. Structure of transitive verb plus complex np (with genitive)

transitive verb, [$_{np}$ ergative Agent], [$_{np}$ object (= absolutive)]

Figure 22. Structure of transitive clause with fully expressed ergative Agent
and object (in the absolutive case)

either before or after "Nom" (a category corresponding to the part of
a noun phrase represented in X-bar syntax in generative grammar [see
Radford 1988] by N' or N̄). Semantically, Gen can play a number of
roles, including the Agent (seeDuranti and Ochs 1990). This pattern
is shown in the following passage in which the verb *fai* 'do, make' is
first followed by a possessive modifier that refers to the beneficiary of
the action—/a lākou mea'ai/ 'their food' means 'food for them' in line
19, example (48)—and then to the Agent in line 20—/mākou kofe/
'our (exclusive) coffee' means 'the coffee we made':

(48) Pastor and Deacon.

> 19   A;   *fa'akali mai   agapō.   fai   a   lākou mea'ai*
>   wait   DX past-night do of   they food
>   We were waiting last night, (we) made food <u>for them</u>
> 20   *fa'aSāmoa=fai   le   mākou   kofe.*
>   Samoan-way make ART we EXC coffee
>   Samoan style = <u>We</u> made coffee.

The pattern in figure 21 is thus more common than the canonical
transitive pattern shown in figure 22 (cf. fig. 20 in chap. 5).

More generally, in Samoan we often find genitive constructions with
either transitive or intransitive predicates used to describe situations that
in other languages (e.g., English) might be described by subjects of
transitive clauses.[3] This means that when the Agent is actually mentioned in Samoan discourse, its force is potentially greater than in languages in which subjects of transitive clauses cover a wider range of
semantic cases.

In the next section, I will start examining the use of transitive clauses
with ergative Agents expressed in everyday conversations.

The Politics of Everyday Interaction I: Blaming

Fully expressed ergative Agents are also found in casual conversations. In these settings, in which we cannot rely on institutional roles and specific event-bound expectations, it is harder to assess the illocutionary force of the utterance in which the agent is mentioned. In addition to the ethnographic information we might have about the participants and their previous interactions, we also need to be particularly sensitive to *local* contextual features, including the discourse context in which the transitive clause appears. If they appear at all, transitive clauses with fully expressed Agents are likely to appear in narrative segments and when a speaker either gives out the punch line of the story or provides some background information about a character. Thus, for instance, in the narrative reproduced in example (49), Chief Tui (a pseudonym) recounts what happened to his watch. The punch line in this first round of the story (which will later develop into a multi-authored narrative with a more complex plot) is line 49, where he says that "someone" (/le kagaka/, lit. 'a person') has taken his watch. In this context, this utterance can be interpreted as an accusation, given that it clearly assigns responsibility to a third party and hence blames the thief for the loss of his watch.

(49) The watch. Chief Folafola [F] has just arrived at the house of Chief Palu [P] and has been ceremonially greeted. After a brief pause, chief Tui [T] starts telling him a story. All names are pseudonyms.

```
42        (2.0)
43   T;   ke iloa   le   mea  mālie Folafola
          TA know  ART  thing funny Folafola
          Do you know the funny thing, Folafola,
44        lea   e   kupu  iā  a'u?
          that  TA  happen to  me
          that happened to me?
45   F;   'o     le   ā?
          PRED  ART  what
          What is it?
46   T;   i   le   pō   fo'i  ga  kāko(u) kalagoa kalagoa
          in  ART  night also  PST we-INC  talk    talk
          In the night (when) we talked and talked
47        (kou-)  'o    a'u  moe
          PL     FRED  I    sleep
          (your-) I sleep
```

48		ŋa'o a'u
		only I
		only me

→ 49   'ae   'ave   *(e)*   le   kaŋaka la'u uaki.
       CONJ take (ERG) ART person my watch
       and (advers.) someone takes my watch.

50   (1.0)

51   F;   'ave lau uaki?
       take your watch
       Takes your watch?

52   P;   'ave le uaki.
       take ART watch
       Takes the watch.

53   (1.0)

That line 49 is an assertion with potentially serious consequences is shown not only by the nature of the proposition expressed, namely, that someone has taken something that belonged to the speaker, but also by chief Folafola's surprised response, which is confirmed by chief Palu in line 52. Ethnographic information is here crucial for assessing the seriousness of the speech act in line 49, which has all the prerequisites of an accusation: chief Tui is from another village and a guest in Folafola's and Palu's village, where the conversation is taking place. For him to say that *someone* took his watch during his last visit not only claims that someone, a thief, is responsible for the disappearance of his watch, it also implies a certain amount of co-responsibility by the people in the village and, hence, by the chiefs Folafola and Palu, who should do a better job of running the place. Although this exchange is about an incident that is not sufficiently serious to receive the attention of the village fono, it represents a type of verbal exchange which is not too different from the kind of reports that might lead to the convocation of a fono.

The potential seriousness of the accusation expressed in a transitive clause in which an Agent is expressed is not restricted to contexts in which chiefs are talking with one another. By looking at everyday encounters among common people and youths, we realize that there are conflicting forces and opposing parties even in the apparently most ordinary settings. Even when people seem to be "off stage" and engaged in very mundane, almost private exchanges, their utterances can turn into accusations that need to be rebuked. Thus, even among family members and friends, the use of a transitive clause with an Agent can provoke the reaction of the person who has been assigned the responsibility of the action, just as a similar type of sentence may provoke the reaction of a matai in a fono. Given the rules for turn taking in conversation as opposed to a fono, however, in a conversational interaction we can immediately see the effects of an utterance on other parties and hence make an evaluation of how participants themselves interpret it.[4] In particular, we can try to reconstruct the kind of illocutionary force they assign to it. In the following exchange, taken from a family dinner videotaped in the summer of 1988 in Falefā, we find a series of transitive clauses that escalate from apparent innocuous "reports" to potential accusations. The sequence discussed here begins with the little girl O. making a request to her mother, Savali, whom she calls "Vali,"[5] for a banana. When she is handed over a small slice of a large banana, O. reacts with a conventional complaining expression (/ui! va'aia!/ 'ehi, look at that!'), which gets reprimanded by the mother with an /ei!/ in line 512.

(50) Dinner Number 3. The dinner is almost over. The mother (Savali, often abbreviated /Vali/), father, and several of their children are still at the table, eating. The youngest girl, O., who has been up from the table for a few minutes, makes her request for a [piece of] banana and walks toward her mother, Vali.

506		(7.0)
507	O;	Va//li, sa'u fa'i?
		Vali ART + AL + my banana
		Vali, may I have a banana?
508	Vali;	(? ?) ((very softly, to father?))
509	Father;	mh? ((to Vali))
		Mh?
510		((Vali reaches for a piece of banana and hands it over to O.))
511	O;	ui va'aia![6]
		oh see + CIA
		Oh, look! ((implying that it is too small))
512	Vali;	'ei!
		Hey! ((reacting to the complaint))

At this point, Mika, a teenage boy who is in the kitchen area and has been serving the rest of the family during the dinner, informs everyone that O. has already eaten a (piece of) banana:

513	Mika;	//ga 'ai fo'i laga fa'i. ((from the kitchen))
		PST eat also her banana
		(She) already ate her (piece of) banana.

This utterance is a transitive clause that adds to the irritation people in the house are starting to feel toward the little O. In line 513 the Agent of /'ai/ 'eat' is not expressed as an ergative Agent, but as the possessive /laga/ 'her', following the more common pattern defined in figure 21. At this point, another, more specific request by O., which is accommodated by the mother, provokes an explicit complaint by R., O.'s older sister, in line 516.

> 514 O; *(ē) 'aumai   le   mea   fo'i gale!*[7]
>   VOC bring ART thing EMP there
>   Give me that one (piece) over there!
>
> 515   ((Vali complies with O.'s request by switching the piece of
>   banana from the plate next to her))
>
> 516 R; *'ē!   'o   lo'u   igoigo   ia   i   amio   a*
>   hey FRED my hate EMP PREP behavior of
>   *le   la'ikiki // lea.*
>   ART little   that
>   Hey, I am really disgusted with the behavior of this little one.

When O. insists again and the mother accommodates her one more time by giving her a different and larger piece from the plate, sister R. interprets O.'s unreasonable demands for everyone: R. just wants the biggest piece.

> 517 O; *leai, lea, e lē:, e lē (le) kipi::.*
>   No, (no-/this) is not, that's not cut.
>
> 518   ((Once more, Vali switches the piece of banana with a
>   bigger one from the plate and gives it to O.))
>
> 519 R; *maga'o   ā   e   fa'akelē   aga   ia.*
>   want EMP TA make-big her PRO
>   (She) wants hers to be the biggest.
>
> 520 O; ((Coughs))

It is here that one of the two boys at the table, V., O.'s cousin, intervenes. The information he releases (something that in fact others might have already known but were not saying) gets O. off the hook by redirecting everyone's attention to someone else's actions. V. says that O.'s request cannot be accommodated because someone else, Kilisimasi, O.'s older brother, has already eaten the biggest piece. V. conveys this information by means of a complex sentence that has in it a transitive clause with a fully expressed ergative Agent (*e Kilisimasi*):

> 521   V;   'Ae ua uma oga ave *e* *Kilisimasi*
>   but PST finish COMP take ERG Kilisimasi
>   le mea k(h)e(h)l(h)ē.
>   ART thing   big
>   But <u>Kilisimasi</u> has already taken the big one ((laughing)).

This utterance is a lot more than a simple explanation of why O.'s request cannot be satisfied. Done jokingly, this is a kind of verbal "friendly fire" by Kilisimasi's cousin, who manages to switch (or at least to distribute) the accusation of selfishness from the little girl to her older brother. That this utterance is understood this way by the participants and in particular by Kilisimasi himself is shown by his immediate response in line 522: another transitive clause with a fully expressed ergative Agent, another assertion of responsibility for a recent action. This time it is the boy's attempt to turn things around by reassigning responsibility to someone else, namely, his mother, Savali.

> 522   K;   'o la'u mea lea ga aumai e *Savali*.
>   PRED my thing that PST give-me ERG Savali
>   That's the one that <u>Savali</u> gave me.

Rather than taking care of things, this statement gets Kilisimasi in trouble, given that it hints at the co-responsibility of an adult for the present state of affairs. This is certainly not acceptable by Samoan standards. Without directly commenting on Kilisimasi's response, his mother finds a way of reminding him that he has overstepped the limit. She does so not by directly addressing the issue of the piece of banana but by picking on the fact that he is standing at the table while everyone else is sitting. If he is done eating, he has no reason to be at the table and should leave.

> 523   Vali;   'ua uma na 'ē 'ai? ((to K.))
>   PST finish COMP you eat
>   Have you finished eating?
> 524   K;   ((nods))
> 525   Vali;   alu ese lā'ia ma igā.
>   go away then from there
>   Then get away from there.
> 526   K;   'o lea e sau e avaku le mea lea.[8]
>   PRED this TA come COMP take-DX ART thing this
>   I've come here to take this thing.

Kilisimasi's attempt this time to involve his father—by invoking an earlier instruction by his father to pick up a plate ("this thing") and take it somewhere—will not save him. He will have to leave his position without having had a chance to justify his actions. His cousin V.'s partly humorous stroke in line 521 has made Kilisimasi morally pay for his young sister's spoiled behavior.

Examples of this kind are not too rare in our transcripts. In ordinary conversation, as well as in the fono, transitive clauses describing some-one's deeds are frequently embedded in acts of blaming or accusing someone.

We can now return to example (1) in chapter 2, here reproduced as (51):

(51) Pastor and Deacon.

> A; 'ae ga fai mai ā   e   lākou
> but PST do DX EMP ERG they
> But they did (it) (for us)

As I discussed in chapter 2, this was the only example with a fully expressed ergative Agent (/e lākou/) in an entire transcript of fifteen minutes of intense conversation mostly between two participants: a pas-tor and one of the deacons in his congregation. When we reexamine this utterance with the functions and contexts of this type of grammat-ical construction in mind, it is not difficult to see that it is part of an act of blaming. The speaker, A., the deacon, is complaining to F., the pastor of his village, that during a recent meeting, a family from another village had given them a carton of biscuits. But the family doled out the biscuits instead of letting A. and the other members of the congregation from Falefā decide how they wanted to divide it. The utterance in (51) is part of a longer narrative in which A. describes how he and the other deacons from Falefā had collected some money to give the family who was hosting them and then saw that they were going to be given a box of biscuits:

(52) Pastor and Deacon.

> 94 A; 'ave 'uma ā   i le āiga. ioe=
> give all EMP to ART family yes
> (we) did give everything to the family. yes=
> 95 F; =o:.
> Oh.

```
96        (1.0)
97   A;   'aumai lea    e-    e    le'i    'aumaia  lā   fo'i lele-
          bring   that  COMP-  TA  NEG + PST  bring  ADV also that
          They bring it (to us) to- they also didn't bring that-
98        uā      'ua  mākou  va'aku   ā    ua
          because PST  we-EXC see + DX  EMP  PST
          'avage   le   p- pusa   masi.
          take-DX  ART  box    biscuits
          because we saw (that) (they) had brought the box of
          biscuits.
99        'ae     le'i     'aumaia    lā   iā   mākou=
          but  NEG + PST  bring + CIA  ADV  to   we-EXC
          But (they) didn't bring (it) then to us=
100  F;   = mm.
          Mm.
101  A;   'ae  ga  fai mai  ā    e   lākou
          but  PST  do  DX  EMP  ERG  they
          but they did (it) (for us)
```

The complaint about the breach of etiquette is here not only expressed by the use of the transitive verb with the ergative Agent (/e
lākou/); it is also conveyed by the use of other linguistic markers such
as the adversative conjunction 'ae 'and/but' at the beginning of the
turn in line 101 and the emphatic particle ā after the verb complex / ga
fai mai/.

In everyday settings, unlike political arenas, the range of participants
who use full transitive clauses to assign responsibilities to third parties
is wider and not as controlled by status and rank considerations. Judging
from people's reactions to such utterances, however, they seem to be
taken just as seriously by the participants. The assignment of responsibility can be equally important in institutional settings and in informal
interactions.

The Politics of Everyday Interaction II:
Giving Credit

Transitive clauses are not only found within sequences in
which someone is singled out for some deed that turns out to be seen
in a negative light; they are also used for positive assessments. In political arenas, as I illustrated earlier on, positive actions tend to be the
prerogative of the supernatural (viz., God) or are acknowledged as part

of specific social roles. In ordinary conversation, however, the range of referents who are made responsible for positive deeds is wider and may need to be constructed over several utterances or turns. I will illustrate this use of transitive clauses with ergative Agents with examples from a conversation among four women who are having a midday meal after having worked for a couple of hours cleaning up a house that belongs to their religious congregation. As they jokingly assured me when I asked permission to video record their interaction, their talk contains a considerable amount of 'gossip' (faitala) (see note 1), that is, stories about and evaluations of other people in the village, talk about episodes of their lives which should not be discussed publicly. These are usually stories about people's bad deeds, about stealing, getting drunk, damaging property, having affairs. In the midst of these bad behaviors (*amio leaga*), there are, however, a few good things to report. Occasionally, the four women single out someone for praise. As is typical in stories— in good stories, that is—good characters are needed to make the bad ones look bad, just as bad characters are needed for the good ones to exist. Although transitive clauses with full agents usually do not contain in themselves evaluations, that is, explicit indications of how to assess someone's deeds, conversationalists' reactions are good indicators of such assessments. In fact, they are important moves in the process of co-constructing moral interpretations of the events that are being re-counted. As prior studies of narratives in conversation have shown (Labov 1972b; Ochs et al. 1992), all narratives oscillate between two poles: a moral one in which people and events are assessed for their ethical values (which ultimately must coincide with those of the narrator's), and a practical-theoretical one in which solutions must be jointly found to the "problems" presented by the narrators. The first exchange in example (53) begins at the point in which one of the women, Vg., introduces a new topic for another woman, Malue (M.) to expand on: the man Masi's trip to New Zealand to visit a woman named Moana.

(53) Women eating. Malue, who is the most junior in age and status with respect to the other three women, has been moving back and forth in the house delivering food and tea. She has just fetched a towel from T., who has finished eating, and has handed it over to Vt., when Vg. addresses her. While returning to her place and without turning to face Vg., she starts reporting on the events she has been asked about.

> 1147　　*Vg;*　　*ali'i⁹ Malue,*
> 　　　　　　　　Lady Malue,

1148   M;   *'oe.*[10]
            Yeah.
1149   Vg;   *'o Masi e alu iā Moaga, 'ā?*
            Masi has gone to Moana, hasn't he?
1150   M;   *'ī.*
            Yeah.
1151   *(3.5)*
1152   *e alu i le fa'aipoipoiga a loga akali'i.*
            (He) is going to the wedding of his son.
1153   Vg;   *mm.*
            Mm.
1154   M;   *le (a Masi ?)*
            The (? Masi ?)

At this point, T.'s and Vg.'s curiosity has grown and they prompt Malue to give more information.

1155   T;   *'o ai?*
            Who?
            [
1156   Vg;   *e ā?*
            What?
1157   *(1.0)*
1158   M;   *le akali'i o: Masi,* ((softly while she starts to sit down))
            Masi's son,
1159   *fai mai 'o le akali'i o Masi i le si fafige.*
            they say that (he) is Masi's son from another woman.
1160   *(0.5)*
1161   *('o ia) sā fai ā lā e Moaga,*
            (He is the one) <u>Moana</u> adopted back then,
            [
1162   ?;   *(?   ?)*
1163   M;   *'o laikiki le kamaikiki.*
            the boy (was) little.
1164   ?T;   *mm.*
            Mm.
1165   ?Vg;   *mm.*
            Mm.
1166   *ia' lā 'ua 'ave aku ā (e si) keige ia o Moaga,*[11]
            So, he was then taken by the (dear poor) girl Moana,
1167   *ia' lea lā ua fai laga fa'aipoipoiga*
            now he is having a wedding
1168   *lea ua kokogi mai ai le pasese 'o Masi lā e alu ai.*
            for which Masi's fare has been paid to go to it.
            [

1169   *Vg;*   *māgaia le loko alofa o Moaga.*
What a loving soul Moana has.
[
1170   *M;*   *ioe.*
Yes.

As it turns out, this is a story about a man in the village, Masi, who has left to go to New Zealand to his son's wedding. The relevant exchanges here are lines 1162 and 1166. In 1162, Malue recounts that the woman Moana had adopted Masi's son, a child Masi had from a woman other than his wife. This is expressed with a transitive clause and an ergative agent (/e Moaga/). This piece of information is given a positive reading by Vg., who shows appreciation for Moana's deed (line 1163). When told about Moana's further generosity of having sent money for Masi to travel to New Zealand to attend his son's wedding, Vg. expresses herself even more openly with a strong positive evaluation in line 1169: she was right, Moana does indeed have a great heart! Although the affective maker /si/ in line 1166 was originally transcribed by a young woman in the village who was very familiar with the participants' voices, it could not be heard later by myself and other native Samoan speakers using more sophisticated technologies. The very possibility of its occurrence as perceived by the first transcriber, however, highlights another feature of these assessments, namely, the existence or need, in some cases, of more explicit hints as to how to interpret their moral value. The particle *si* is a type of affective article that invites empathy for the referent it introduces (Ochs 1988, 172–183). It is expected to make the listener feel sorry for the referent. When used to introduce the Agent in a transitive clause, it indicates the type of attitude that the speaker has toward the referent/concept of the agent. A clear example is shown in example (54), from the same conversation among the four women. In this case, in recounting the story of a young man, Falalili'i, who had destroyed a house, allegedly while under the influence of drugs, Vg. adds background information to make her audience appreciate even more the terrible damage done by him. She does so by reminding everyone that the house that had been destroyed is the same one that another man also named Falalili'i had come back from New Zealand to repair (line 1311).

(54) Women eating.

1302   *Vg;*   *ka'ei*[12] *uma   ā   le   fale.*
break   all   EMP   ART   house
(He) broke the whole house.

1303   *fai mai Ti'a e fai le lākou   ko'aga'i*
say DX Ti'a TA do ART their Sunday meal
Ti'a ((Vg.'s husband)) said that they were having the
Sunday meal

1304   *'ae sau le fe'au.*
and come ART business
and* the problem came up.
*"and" is a kind of adversative conjunction, almost,
but not quite, a "but."

1305   *kagi mai Ola e   alaku iā Leukele   e-*
cry DX Ola TA go + DX to Leutele COMP
Ola (is) crying (she) goes to Leutele[13] to- (tell him)

1306   *(0.5)*

1307   *e   ka'ei uma le fale o-*
TA break all ART house of
(that) the whole house of- is broken

1308   *(3.0)*

1309   ?;   *(?)*

1310   Vg;   *fa'ako ā uma ā   ga   koe fai fa'amalama*
just EMP finish EMP COMP again do window
e   si kama   o   Falalili'i ga   sau,
ERG AFF boy PRED   F.   PST come
The boy Falalili'i, who had come (from New Zealand),
had just finished repairing the windows,

As I mentioned in chapter 2, in all of these narratives it is crucial to have an ethnographic understanding of the events that are being discussed. A Samoan from another village or someone fluent in the language but removed from the everyday life in a Western Samoan village might miss some important assumptions and implications hidden in the words spoken here. In this case, for instance, not only do the two main characters have the same name (Falalili'i), but the only reference to the second Falalili'i coming from New Zealand is elliptically expressed in the phrase /ga sau/ 'PST come' in line 1310. Much is assumed by the participants here about the spatial and economic points of reference in the community. In this case, to 'come' (/sau/) to fix a house means to come back with cash earned abroad. Such an endeavor is thus much appreciated precisely because of its cost: hard physical work in a foreign land and emotional separation from one's kin. It is in the context of this experiential world that the good deed of the second (and older) Falalili'i and the bad deed of the first one must be understood. Finally, the second (and good) Falalili'i is a 'boy' (/kama/) only affectively speaking and in relation to the other Falalili'i who is earlier described as a /kamaikiki/ 'little kid'. The second Falalili'i is a *'dear poor* boy'

(/si kama/) because of what he did and not because of his age. De-scriptors like /kama/ 'boy', /kamāloa/ 'man', and /koea'iga/ 'old man' are often used in conjunction with the affective particles (si in this case) and without much consideration of the actual age of the person about which they are predicated.[14]

The continuation of the exchange reveals more details about the events, including the summary by Vt. of the things done by the (bad) 'kid' (/kamaikiki/) in line 1316 (again with an ergative Agent), and the good thing done by the village, namely, the fine given to Ola's husband, who was responsible (in lines 1321 and 1324).

1312	T;	mm.
		Mm.
		[
1313	Vg;	'ae alu Faleologa
		But (after) Faleologa leaves (to go back to New Zealand)
1314		ae ka'ei le fale.
		but break ART house
		(he) breaks the house (in many pieces).
1315		'ua- 'ua igu i mea fo'i i:- 'o maluaga.
		PST PST drink[15] PREP thing also from PRED marijuana
		(They) had- had smoked also some marijuana.
→ 1316	Vt;	'ua fai e kamaikiki.[16]
		PST do ERG child
		The young one did (it).
1317	Vg;	mm.
		Mm.
1318		'ae fai ifo.
		but do down
		But (they) find out.
1319		fai mai,
		say DX
		(They) say,
1320		(1.0)
→ 1321		fa'asala ai le ko'alua o Ola.
		CAUS+fine PRO ART spouse of Ola
		Ola's husband (has been) fined for it.
1322		(0.5)
1323	Vt;	mm.
		Mm.
→ 1324	Vg;	e le gu'u.
		ERG ART village
		by the village.

The final statement (produced across several turns, from 1321 to

1324) about the action taken by the /gu'u/ 'village' gives credit to the local authorities for reestablishing order.[17]

Illocutionary Force of Transitive Clauses with Agents

Most, if not all, of the examples of transitive clauses with ergative Agents discussed in this chapter are examples of what John Searle called "assertives" or "representatives" (Searle 1976), that is, speech acts in which the "direction of fit" is from the words to the world. According to Searle, this means that in this type of speech acts the speaker tries to match, with words, an already constituted world. As shown in this chapter and in chapter 5, however, many of the transitive clauses are very typically understood as part of larger exchanges through which claims are made, among other things, about the moral qualities of a party (be it a person, group, or entity) or his or her responsibility for a given event. Rather than simply describing an already constituted world, these utterances are at least part of important social acts through which speakers try to affect the world and often succeed at it. Although they do not contain explicit reference to verbs of judging or praising, they are to be understood as part of such acts when seen in the larger context of the narratives or conversational exchanges they are found in and when they are matched with the necessary ethnographic information about the events and characters they portray.

For Charles Fillmore (1971), verbs of judging imply a set of role concepts or participants such as the "affected," the "defendant," and the "judge." They can also be distinguished from one another in terms of different presuppositions. The difference between accusing and criticizing, for instance, is that in the first case the speaker-judge is *presupposing* that the situation caused by someone's actions is bad, whereas in the second case the judge is *stating* that the situation is bad. In giving credit, a judge establishes that someone is responsible for something which is assumed (presupposed) to be good. In praising, the speaker says that something good has happened and someone is presupposed as responsible for the situation.

These are useful analytical distinctions that help us make sense of certain types of semantic differences in a particular category of English verbs. Similar distinctions are made by Searle and Daniel Vanderveken (1985, 190) in discussing different types of assertives. These discussions, however, are largely, if not exclusively, based on abstract examples, that is, individual sentences thought out by the researcher without a clear understanding of the potential and actual contexts in which they might be used. When we examine how "judging" is done in real life, or at least, in our case, in Samoan discourse, we find that people usually do not make explicit the performative verbs that would qualify their assertions as different types of claims about the world. In other words, speakers do not qualify their judgments as blamings, accusations, or praises. On the contrary, they leave the force of their utterances to be figured out and, more often, to be co-constructed by others. It is the context that carries the illocutionary force of an utterance, and it is the other participants in the interaction, with their responses, assessments, counteraccusations, and affective stances, who provide the stuff out of which an interpretation of speech is made possible, for them first, and for us, later.

Conclusions

The findings discussed in this chapter suggest that there are indeed striking similarities between the ways the grammar of blaming and praising operates in political arenas and the way it functions in everyday settings. In other words, the data presented here suggest that it is not only in events like the fono that participants are constantly assessing one another's doings with respect to some presupposed qualities or standards, but that in fact *moral judgment* is a constant feature of any kind of human interaction, whether the participants are people of high status and influence, young children making claims about the food on the table, or women telling stories about bad deeds and good deeds in the life of the village. The data presented in this chapter also suggest that rhetorical strategies employed by skillful speechmakers in a fono are first learned in the discourse of everyday interactions, where children participate in confrontations about rights and duties and listen to stories about people whose deeds are in some cases to blame and in other cases to praise (see also Schieffelin 1990).

To account for these phenomena, in the next chapter I will propose a *moral flow hypothesis,* namely, a perspective on grammatical framing that sees utterances in discourse as organized by the need or want to construct a moral world in which characters and events are continuously evaluated over against an emergent, jointly achieved, although not necessarily agreed upon, ethical perspective.

7

Conclusions

___

In this book, I have tried to rescue words, phrases, utterances, narratives, and speeches out of their unobtrusiveness, their misleadingly "natural" status in the midst of ordinary or not-so-ordinary activities, and I have tried to expose them for what they are, namely, constructed and construing social acts, which ultimately make sense only within larger sociopolitical contexts. I have used audiotapes, ethnographic fieldnotes, and video recordings of spontaneously occurring events in a traditional Western Samoan village to build an argument in favor of an approach I would like to call *ethnopragmatic*. By this term I mean a double-sided, inherently eclectic and interdisciplinary analytical enterprise that relies on detailed grammatical descriptions on the one hand and ethnographic accounts on the other. The "ethno-" component is documented by various extensions of traditional ethnographic methods and the close attention to the sociocultural context of language use, which includes an understanding of specific linguistic activities as embedded in and constitutive of locally organized and locally interpretable events. Chapters 2–5 have, each in its own specific way, given information on how I first came to merely witness the Samoan fono and later started to appreciate it as a complex speech event that displays multiple, albeit "coherent," versions of the social order in a traditional Samoan society. None of the events implied by or referred to in the fono speeches could be understood without lengthy conversations with knowledgeable participants. Such conversations were always departing from or centering on detailed transcripts of the actual talk produced at the fono (see chap. 2 on transcription).

The "pragmatic" part of "ethnopragmatic" is meant to evoke a long tradition of study of the connection between language and context as defined in a number of disciplines, including philosophy, linguistics, semiotics, psychology, and anthropology (see Leech 1983; Levinson 1983; Verschueren 1991).

The connectedness of linguistic forms to the context of their use is something that has long been the subject of formal as well as informal accounts of the meaning of linguistic expressions. The need to rely on extra-linguistic context for the interpretation and use of certain linguistic forms, in particular so-called deictic terms—in English such terms as *I, you, here, there, this, that*—laid the foundations for a science of language which recognizes the link between human speech and its surroundings (Lyons 1977). Such surroundings include very physical things, such as houses, rooms, and courtyards (Lawrence and Low 1990), as well as cultural practices, that is, social activities in which human actors exchange and/or produce labor, values, and other kinds of goods (Hanks 1990). What I have elsewhere called a "linguistics of human praxis" (Duranti 1988) becomes possible only when we go beyond ethnographic accounts on the one hand and grammatical descriptions on the other, and we put the two together. The result of this union should, I hope, be more than the sum of its parts. This was indeed the original goal of the ethnography of speaking approach (see Bauman and Sherzer 1975). Such an agenda is being revitalized as we improve our research methods and our understanding of the interactional basis of grammar.

To say that pragmatics, the study of language in and as context, is inherently "ethno-" means to recognize the importance of the *local* level of language usage for an understanding of what linguistic forms contribute to social life, political life included. We can venture into adequate realms of speculation which include our assessment of what the actors are up to only if we abandon whatever stereotype we have of the "ordinary" speaker going around and producing utterances and replace it with real people speaking real words in real social interactions. This is not a call for an extreme empiricist position: only what we hear and record should be studied. Abstractions, intuitions, and deductions can be fruitful. After all, speakers themselves engage in such activities. This is, however, a call for a study of linguistic practices that are grounded in what words mean to the people who use them in the course of their lives. We need to know what Samoan chiefs are up to when they get together if we want to start to make some sense of the narratives they produce in the midst of archaic metaphors and long-winded speeches. We also need to know something about people's accountability and sensitivity when we interpret a story about a theft or one about an adoption (chap. 6). In fact, in each of these cases, the very way in which we choose to characterize the episode under discussion must take the lead from the way the participants themselves chose to do it. As we have learned from studies of syntax and semantics, language is a very powerful instrument in framing events and constructing particular versions of realities. What I have tried to show in this book is that those frames are not just cognitive maps or individual memories. They are also moral and political statements that classify deeds and their agents according to and against the background of local worldviews, including local versions of good and evil, generous and selfish, savy and inept, respectful of tradition and forgetful of the past. An ethnopragmatic approach to grammatical analysis provides us with the analytical tool kit to start making sense of grammar as an interactional resource—that is, in our case, as an instrument for sustaining claims of accountability in which members of the community can give credit to those who deserve it and blame those who have stepped out of the acceptable social path. Grammar is "good to communicate with" just as (according to Lévi-Strauss) animals are "good to think with." Grammar offers a vast range of categorical distinctions that can be reshuffled and blended with other semiotic resources to create a potentially infinite number of shaded rather than sharply drawn cultural distinctions.

In the following sections I will briefly outline what I see as the major contributions of this book.

Ethnographic Linguistics

Methodologically, I have tried to show that there are different ways of studying grammar and making sense of its patterns of use. The analytical path that we choose in investigating syntactic patterns is defined by a series of presuppositions about the relationship between language and social life. In my case, such a relationship was illuminated by specific fieldwork conditions (discussed in chap. 2). My induced interest in traditional speechmaking toward the very beginning of my fieldwork led me to a type of research that was different from the research I had originally planned. Instead of concentrating on individual utterances extracted from conversational *discourse,* I became exposed to long and complex speech *events* in which often more than twenty or thirty people participated. The words people exchanged in the fono I attended were unequivocally ingrained with notions of hierarchy, tradition, and justice. The eloquence of the speechmakers in establishing what they perceived as the correct frame for the ensuing discussion and for the definition of the ideal type of polity linked their speaking to other speech events in the community, namely, rites of passage and ceremonial exchanges of various sorts (see chap. 4), as well as more mundane everyday exchanges (see chap. 6). In each case, I was confronted with archaic and not-so-archaic speech forms and speech genres that underwent considerable permutations according to the context in which they were produced and the goals for which they were working. In all of these events, I was struck by the obvious relevance of a variety of semiotic resources such as the seating arrangement, the distribution of kava, the order of speakers, and the nature and length of various speech genres (see chaps. 3 and 4).

Faced with this data, so different from the data I expected to investigate, I had to resort to ethnography to make sense of what people were saying. I could not just take utterances out of their natural environment, that is, out of the struggle of which they were an integral part, and create examples for linguistic analysis. Those utterances were inextricably connected with the contexts in which they had been used. They were part of the social events they helped constitute. I needed to know about what went on before and sometimes after a fono in order to make sense of what was being said during a meeting, who was being talked about, and which grammatical forms were being used. The organization of the interaction in different parts of the fono proceedings gave out important hints about who was being perceived as important and for what reasons or purposes. The place where people sat and whether or not they were offered kava to drink during the opening kava ceremony were among the acts that helped construct the social hierarchy relevant for the occasion and established the interpretive frame for what was to follow. The order of speakers was also important, and it had to be understood vis-à-vis the nature of the event.

During my fieldwork, I tried to keep track of these interactional dimensions and I discussed them with members of the fono. They constituted the basis for my own understanding of the fono as a speech event (cf. Duranti 1985; Hymes 1972b). A speech event approach means, above all, that we use the knowledge of the activity people are engaged in to make sense of the kind of speech they use. At the same time, recent developments within linguistic anthropology, sociolinguistics, and the study of talk-in-interaction have made us more and more aware of how speech itself can be constitutive of the activity participants engage in (Duranti and Goodwin 1992). It is this mutually constitutive relationship between language and context that I tried to capture in the preceding chapters.

Conflict and Grammar

The Samoan fono are dynamic, dramatic, and in some respects unpredictable events. What is particularly interesting in these events from the point of view of linguistic analysis is that the struggle for power in them takes the form of a linguistic confrontation, with participants juggling different versions of past events and different images of certain people's actions and responsibilities. As I discussed in the previous chapters, the grammatical form of utterances becomes an integral part of the political process whereby the local hierarchy is reconfirmed or challenged. Those who object to a particular framing of the past have at their disposal a set of grammatical constructions that they can use to resist the responsibility or blame implied in a prior stretch of discourse. They can, for instance, suggest a different or less definite agency (chap. 5). This is accomplished through a series of grammatical strategies available to Samoan speakers for mitigating agency (e.g., case marking, humbling descriptions of the speaker/agent, reported speech). Overall, the availability of these alternative grammatical forms points to the power of words (even very small ones) in shaping the political life of a community and negotiating actors' responsibility for ongoing political and legal processes. The "alternation" and "co-occurrence" rules discussed by Susan Ervin-Tripp (1972)—a reformulation of Ferdinand de Saussure's paradigmatic and syntagmatic oppositions—have a political power both at the institutional and everyday level that sociolinguistic and ethnographically oriented studies have only started to uncover. In the study presented in this book I have tried to make the readers as aware as possible of the need for a tight collaboration between ethnographic and grammatical studies. In such an interdisciplinary enterprise, which linguistic anthropologists must be the leaders of, we need to evaluate the different contributions that each subdiscipline and perspective can bring to the basic problem of any study of linguistic performance: Why this form now?

The Grammar of Human Agency: From Information Flow to Moral Flow

It is with these issues and questions in mind that we must reappropriate discourse analysis as a legitimate and leading area of study for anthropological inquiries. It is in the context of such an enterprise that grammatical choices must be reframed as socially significant. Is this a new form of "linguistic relativity"? It certainly is a way of rethinking the issue of the relationship between language and culture—but in a new context, in which both language-specific and universal tendencies must be considered. The Samoan linguistic phenomena presented in the previous two chapters acquire then a new importance when we compare them with research conducted on similar issues in other, unrelated languages. In particular, the relative occurrence of different types of grammatical roles has attracted the attention of several researchers in the last few years. Thus, for instance, discourse analysts have noticed the low proportion of utterances with fully expressed agents in spoken discourse. J. Du Bois (1987), working on Sacapultec (a Mayan language), tried to understand this phenomenon from the point of view of the information that is allegedly being processed by the speakers and hearers. In this perspective, the use of a particular grammatical form is explained in terms of what Chafe (1987) called *information flow*. According to this approach, the way in which an argument of the verb is grammatically expressed (e.g., by a pronoun vs. a full noun) or left implicit (by a "zero" form) depends on whether or not it represents a "concept" (a category including what I have been loosely calling "referents") that is currently "active" or in a person's focus of consciousness. Thus, Du Bois writes:

An already active concept tends to be realized linguistically in an attenuated form (in some languages, by an unstressed pronoun; in others, affixally); it may even be omitted from verbalization (what is often interpreted as nominal "zero anaphora" or "deletion") (Chafe 1976, 31; 1987). A previously inactive concept is often realized as a full NP, sometimes with a strong stress. According to

Chafe, concepts which have been active become semi-active after a period of not being mentioned. (1987, 816)

In this approach to the organization of information in discourse, a concept that has been active is called "given" and one that has been inactive is called "new."[1] Du Bois extended Chafe's framework to explain the *grammatical framing* (see section "Grammatical Structures as Framing Devices" in chap. 5) given to events in discourse. He argues that arguments comprising "new information" typically appear in either the subject or object role (what in ergative languages would be expressed by the "absolutive"—see chaps. 5 and 6) but not in the Agent role. In this perspective on linguistic performance, the choice of a particular verb (e.g., intransitive vs. transitive) or a particular description (e.g., full noun vs. pronominal form) is seen as due to the sequential organization of information in discourse:

Speakers often select an intransitive verb not for its conceptual content or semantic one-placeness, but for its compatibility with constraints on information flow. (Du Bois 1987, 831)

As mentioned in chapter 6 (and more fully discussed in Duranti 1981a, Ochs 1988, and Duranti and Ochs 1990), the most common type of utterance in Samoan discourse is

Verb + Absolutive

(i.e., intransitive verb plus subject, or transitive verb plus object), and the referents of Agents are also typically understood from either the previous discourse context or from the physical context. The referents are not usually represented by lexical material, for example, by nouns. They are, in other words, usually "given" information and are expressed according to Chafe's predictions, namely, by anaphora. But what about those cases in which Agents *are* expressed as lexical arguments? What about all the cases discussed in chapters 6 and 7? I have been suggesting that those cases are a small but socially significant part of sentence types in Samoan narrative accounts. The traditional information-flow framework correctly predicts that those cases usually involve "new" information, that is, concepts or referents that have not been mentioned recently and should not be in the hearers' active (i.e., short-term) memory.[2] But the extension of the information-flow framework proposed by Du Bois (1987) cannot tell us why these utterances—however small a percentage they constitute—have been produced at all.[3] The ethnographically informed analysis presented in this book suggests a possible explanation, namely, the highly charged and hence politically or ethically "marked" nature of explicit reference to Agents. It is on the basis of the cases discussed earlier in this book that I tentatively propose here to look at the low occurrence of Agents in discourse from another perspective, namely, the *moral-flow hypothesis*. This hypothesis says that in addition to cognitive constraints and requirements (i.e., regulated by the information flow), discourse proceeds by building moral worlds, in which characters are introduced and assessed as examples of moral types, whose actions and attributes are either to be praised or to be condemned. Although with a different goal and different constraints, this is true in institutional settings as well as in more mundane contexts. When we analyze the shape of grammar in use, we must thus take into consideration the goals the participants themselves are, either consciously or unconsciously, striving toward. The constitution of a moral world in which people and other entities are characterized as willful instigators of certain events—that is, Agents—is an essential part of political discourse as well as of everyday speech. In the fono context, it is the village hierarchy and the meaning of rank that are discussed and reassessed. What does it mean to be a chief? What does it mean to show respect? Who should be in charge of making important decisions for the community? What are the values implied by the concrete actions of the members of the village council? In answering these questions, sometimes indirectly and sometimes directly, fono members continuously redraw not only a political but also a moral map of their community. In everyday conversation, people are engaged in a similar enterprise, while dealing with a set of values and expectations contiguous to but not necessarily identical with the values and expectations discussed in the fono. When we look at the stories that are told in a face-to-face conversation among friends or family members in a Samoan village, we find assessments about the value of adoption and the importance of sharing food among siblings; we encounter expressions of respect and compassion for those who left the village and went to work abroad. Out of the flow of discourse, that is, out of the ways in which speakers construct the sequence of utterances that form a locally coherent conversation, we can extract real judgments about real people who become icons of an ideal moral world. It is in these activities, that is, moral activities, that utterances really "mean" something to their producers and consumers. It is in this perspective that we can make sense of the importance of talk for the well-being of individuals as well as of their community. Talk is therapeutic (Watson-Gegeo and White 1990) because it is not just about exchanging new information. It is about assessing moral values. Without a moral flow, verbal interaction would be meaningless. Machines exchange information. People exchange moral assessments. Politics is the practice of making those assessments part of institutions by elevating them to pragmatic principles and policies that have collective import. Politics is about selecting the people who can fit the descriptions of the icons created by the moral flow. As I have tried to show in the preceding chapters, the use of ergative Agents in narratives is an important part of this enterprise.

Narrative Accounts

The technique by which knowledge about the background facts is revealed in a fono is reminiscent of what filmmaker and critic Stefan Sharff (1982) has called "slow disclosure": crucial facts are revealed one bit at a time (see also Ochs, Smith, and Taylor 1989). In a fono, however, the time lapse in the reconstruction of certain events is introduced not so much to build suspense but as part of a dialogical process whereby different voices must be heard. Powerful social actors assess each other's stance and decide when the right moment has come for revealing or using a certain piece of information. The mention of certain actions can become emblematic of the mood of a group or of a particularly powerful party. In a political arena, and probably always in more mundane contexts, there is never neutral recounting. This is the aspect of language use and language structure studied as "affect" (see Besnier 1990b for a review of the literature). Telling the facts, saying who did what to whom, is always potentially face-threatening and carries political consequences. The use of a verb that takes an ergative Agent and an object noun phrase (in the absolutive case) defines an act as *transitive,* that is, it depicts an event as involving a willful (typically human) actor whose actions have sometimes permanent, sometimes temporary consequences for a patient or for a state of affairs. As I have suggested in chapter 5, in the fono context, such a grammatical form contributes to two kinds of action: (i) it helps constitute important social agents (those whose actions make a difference), and (ii) it works as a pointed, accusatory finger toward someone for his or her (hence blameful) doings. By using a transitive clause with an explicit Agent, certain events and social actors are brought to the foreground, their initiators are singled out, and the act is defined as having consequences for a third party (or object) (see Hopper and Thompson 1980). This means that the activation of certain information, for instance mentioning someone's name and what he or she did, should not be dealt with simply as the transmission of information from a speaker to an audience. It is also (and perhaps always) part of more complex social acts whereby political and ethical personae are constructed (see Appadurai 1990).

Samoan Politics

Samoan chiefs and orators within a fono display a compelling ability to deal with the problems and crises affecting their community. The subtleties of their strategies to suggest, convince, remind, scold, frighten, forgive, and ultimately make of any crisis an occasion for reassessing the very foundations of the social order are impressive. Such reassessments take to a large extent the form of linguistic performance. It is then to language that we must also pay attention if we want to understand the past and make predictions about the political future of Samoan culture. The linguistic strategies discussed in the previous chapters are powerful mechanisms that will be in one way or another part of the struggles that lie ahead. In a culture that so strongly identifies political acumen with verbal skills, the path toward the future must be also a path of words, the conflict over definitions must be also a conflict of linguistic framings, the solutions to be found must also be ways of speaking.

Appendix

Abbreviations in Interlinear Glosses

Although in many cases I have given only a free translation of the Samoan utterances and speeches analyzed in this book, when I discussed certain aspects of Samoan grammar I found it necessary to provide word-by-word and in some cases morpheme-by-morpheme interlinear glosses. Here is a list of the abbreviations for grammatical categories used in the text:

AFF   affective article (sing. *si*, plural *nai*)

AL   alienable possession (*a*)

ART   article (both specific, *le*, and nonspecific, *se, ni*)

CAUS   causative prefix (*fa'a-*)

CIA   verbal suffix of various shapes, including C(onsonant)+i+a (e.g., *gia, mia, sia, -ia,* and *-a*) (see Cook 1988)

COMP   complementizer (*e, ona*)

DX   deictic particle (*mai, atu, ane, ifo*)

EMP   emphatic marker (*ā*)

ERG   ergative marker (*e*)

EXC   exclusive, a category used for plural personal pronouns—see INC, below

IN   inalienable possession (*o*, as in *lo'u isu* 'my nose' as opposed to *la'u ta'avale* 'my car')

INC   inclusive, as in *tātou* 'we (all)' as opposed to *mātou* 'we (not including the addressee(s)'

NEG   negation (*lē* or *le, le'i* in the past tense)

NOM   nominalization suffix (*-ga*)

PRED   predicate particle (*'o*); also used for cleft sentences and topicalization

PRO   pronoun

PST   past tense—used for different types of past tense markers, for example, *'ua*, which marks an event that has happened in the past but is framed as being relevant to the current temporal frame (as defined by the linguistic or extralinguistic context), and *na* (usually /ga/ in the transcript), which marks a remote, perfective past

QU   question particle (*ea*)

TA   tense/aspect marker—usually used for *e*, the unmarked tense marker which also acts as a complementizer (COMP)

Notes

1. Introduction

1. For a more in-depth analysis of Samoan kinesic behavior associated with ceremonial greetings and the process of entering a house already occupied by others, see Duranti 1992b.

2. When a person becomes a matai, the matai title (*suafa*) replaces the person's birth name and from that moment on, under most circumstances, everyone, including members of the person's family, uses the matai title. Sometimes, especially when there is potential ambiguity between two people who hold the same matai title, people use the matai title followed by the birth name.

3. Several authors studying other Polynesian societies distinguish among various "styles," such as *formal* and *informal* (Salmond 1975, 62–63), or *homiletic, persuasive, expressive, manipulative,* and *informative* (Firth 1975, 42).

2. Methods as Forms of Life

1. These are two ideal types rather than actual models closely followed by practitioners. In the real world of field experience, researchers in one paradigm may occasionally borrow from the other when they find it useful or necessary.

2. In fact, as pointed out by Willaim Samarin (1967, 1n), earlier definitions of anthropological linguistics are even narrower than field linguistics, at least as practiced by Samarin and other well-known field linguists. Harry Hojer (1961, 110), for instance, gave the rather limited definition of anthropological linguis-

tics as an "area of linguistic research which is devoted in the main to studies, synchronic and diachronic, of the languages of the people who have no writing."

3. A similar point was made about the culture of certain groups in the United States, namely, American Indians, by Susan Philips (1983).

4. On this point, see also Dreyfus's (1991, 62–63) insightful discussion under the rubric "The Transparency of Equipment." Although "transparency" clearly captures in English the sense of this property of tools, I prefer to use here the term "unobtrusiveness" used in the English translation of Heidegger's work because "transparency" is used as the translation of the German *Durchsichkeit*, a term which, in my reading, has a different meaning from the property discussed by Dreyfus and alluded to in the present discussion:

> The sight which is related primarily and on the whole to existence we call *"transparency"* [Durchsichkeit]. We chose this term to designate 'knowledge of the Self' in a sense which is well understood, so as to indicate that here it is not a matter of perceptually tracking down and inspecting a point called the "Self," but rather one of seizing upon the full disclosedness of Being-in-the-world *throughout all* the constitutive items which are essential to it, and doing so with understanding. In existing, entities sight 'themselves' [sichtet "sich"] only in so far as they have become transparent to themselves with equal primordiality in those items which are constitutive for their existence: their Being-alongside the world and their Being-with Others. (Heidegger 1962, 186–187)

5. What I am saying here should not be interpreted as implying that women cannot or do not hold matai titles in Western Samoa. They can, although they rarely do. In chapter 3, I will briefly discuss a rare case in which a female matai participated in a meeting of the village council.

6. "Promptly" should be qualified. Bilingual native speakers with whom I was working first had to learn to ignore the English word order, otherwise they tended to match the English verb-medial sentences (subject-verb-object) with Samoan ones instead of the more common verb-initial order (verb-subject-object) of Samoan syntax. The verb-medial word order has an effect on the morphology of the noun phrase, given that when the subject-agent noun phrase precedes the verb, it loses the ergative marking. This is shown in (b) below, where the noun phrase *le tama* 'the boy' takes the topic/predicative marker *'o* instead of the ergative marker *e* (other changes take place here, e.g., the verb takes the suffix -*a* when the agent is fronted; see Cook 1988).

(a) *'ua pu'e   e   le   tama   le   i'a   i   le   'upega.*
    PST catch ERG ART boy ART fish in ART   net
    The boy caught the fish in/with the net.

(b) *'o le tama 'ua pu'ea le i'a i le 'upega.*
    (It was) the boy (who) caught the fish in/with the net.

In chapter 5, where I discuss the ergative pattern in some detail, I will stop using the notion of "subject" for transitive verbs and follow R. W. Dixon (1979) in calling noun phrases like *le tama* in (a) and (b) above "ergative Agents," regardless of the word order they occur in (viz., post- or preverbal) or the presence of the ergative marker *e*.

7. I return to this example in chapter 6.

8. See Charles Briggs (1986) for a detailed discussion of the methodological

problems (and some of their solutions) in eliciting linguistic knowledge embedded in performance.

9. For different versions of Falefā's fa'alupega, see Krämer 1902/3 and *O le Tusi Fa'alupega o Samoa* (1958).

10. I am following Samoan orthographic practice of capitalizing the word *'Āiga* to emphasize the difference between this use of the term and its more common counterpart ('extended family'). A reason to capitalize this use of the word is that it is perceived and used as a proper noun rather than as a common noun.

11. When Iuli and Moe'ono are present, instead of the third-person dual form *lā'ua* (the two of them), the second person form *'oulua* (you two) is used.

12. Despite the fact that Moe'ono was sometimes addressed as the "father" of the village, the plural term *matua* (here translated as 'senior orator') is pronounced with a short vowel and is hence phonologically distinct from the word *mātua*, meaning 'parents,' with a long *ā*.

13. Sometimes this name is given in a longer form as *Moe'ono'ono*. Krämer (1902/3, 278) has only the shortened form, *Moe'ono*.

14. The word *Tuiatua* can be diachronically reconstructed as *Tui-a-Atua*, that is, 'King-of-(the) Atua (district),' but the word is now pronounced [tuya-tua], with a short *a* instead of the expected long vowel resulting from the combination of the (genitive) preposition *a* with the first vowel of *Atua*.

15. Of the two aloali'i mentioned in the current version of Falefā's fa'alupega, only Luafalemana is mentioned in Krämer (1902/3, 278). Muagututi'a, who was the son of the King Fonotī, is talked about in Krämer only as "King" and as the father of Tupua. Muagututi'a is however mentioned as an aloali'i in the fa'alupega of Sauano (spelled "Sauago") in *O le Tusi Fa'alupega o Samoa* (1958).

16. Krämer (1902/3, 278) reports instead that Moe'ono is "der Sprecher des Alai'aSā," that is, the spokesperson for the high chief Alai'a-Sā. None of the people I consulted in the village wanted to even entertain the idea that Moe'ono might have switched office from one descent group to another.

17. Bradd Shore's (1982) ethnography of a Samoan murder case and its cultural implications is a detailed study of a conflict that seemed to have partly originated from the ambiguity in the relationship between the matua and the chiefs in the village of Sala'ilua on the island of Savai'i.

18. I am following a convention from linguistics of capitalizing the term *Agent* to underscore its use as a syntactic and semantic category (e.g., Dixon 1979) rather than as a sociological one. The connection between the two is something that I try to argue for in the rest of this book but I did not want to take for granted.

19. Jeannette Mageo (1992, 453) uses the term *respect language* for "good speech." This characterization is also problematic given that 'respectful words' *'upu fa'aaloalo* is the Samoan name for the special lexicon used in certain contexts when talking about matai and other high-status individuals (Duranti 1992a; Milner 1961). As shown by the speakers in the fono and other public events I recorded, one can in fact be very respectful without using the good speech.

3. Hierarchies in the Making

1. See the discussion of the fa'alupega ('ceremonial address') in chapter 2.

2. The only exceptions were the times when I knew that I might be expected to deliver a speech or be in some way directly involved in the proceedings. In those cases I was usually too busy worrying about my own performance to be thinking about recording.

3. My attitude was different when I returned to Falefā in 1981 and 1988. In 1981, supported by the Australian National University, Elinor Ochs and I had access to several hours of Sound Super 8 film that we used to document as many different activities as we could, including parts of small fono, restricted to the matai from one subvillage or to a village committee. In 1988, I dared to video record an entire Monday fono (*fono o le Aso Gafua*). By that time, with electricity installed in the village, several families had video cassette players and all the villagers were avid consumers of commercial as well as homemade videos. Camcorders were becoming a common feature of public ceremonies. I felt then that my presence with the camera for an extended time was less of an imposition on the participants.

4. A different view is represented by Freeman (1983), who took ceremonial addresses quite literally and characterized the phrases contained in them as powerful guardians of local hierarchies:

A fa'alupega, whether it refers to a local polity or district or the whole of Samoa, is thus an institution of quite fundamental importance, for, with the formal reiteration of the relative rank of titles on every significant social occasion, a chiefly hierarchy becomes so firmly established as to make it exceedingly difficult to effect any fundamental change in its order of preference, except, as happened in ancient Samoa, by force of arms. (Freeman 1983, 122)

5. This was the reason, we were told, for the respectful term *faletua*, literally 'back (*tua*) of the house (*fale*)', which is used for a chief 's (as well as any high-status person's) wife—orators' wives are called *tausi*, which literally means 'caretakers'.

6. In this case the high status of center as opposed to periphery (see Shore 1982, 80) is not at work. The center of the back is not for the highest-ranking person among those sitting in the back, as shown by the fact that it is usually, albeit briefly, occupied by those, usually young women, who announce (*folafola*) the food contributions to the to'ona'i or bring the tin bowls for washing hands after the meal.

7. His full title was Lealaisalanoa; Aukusitino was his (Christian) birth name, by which he was at times distinguished from another Salanoa, Salanoa Mago, who was not however a Lealaisalanoa. The fact that other titleholders of the four most important chiefly titles in the village were not usually present at the meetings was explained to me in a number of ways, including the fact that Leutele was sick and living in another village and that other titleholders were busy with jobs somewhere else or did not care to attend.

8. Feeling important or more important than others (*fiamaualuga*) is con-

sidered a negative quality even for important people in Samoa. In this case, sitting "off the center" is an act of humbleness by the two matua, who thereby show distance from their own high status.

9. In Western Samoa, unlike American Samoa, the same matai title can be held by more than one person.

10. The title *Tafili* is from Falevao, and in 1979 there was a man who also held that title and lived in Falevao. Savea's sister, instead, lived in Falefā in the same compound with her brother. Given her title, in the context of a fono, she would normally be considered as representing Falevao.

11. In this specific case, this mention of the "family" could be an allusion to the fact that Moe'ono and Savea are related: Tafili married Moe'ono's brother.

12. The intermittent use of "no" (*leai*) in a formal speech is a rhetorical device used by some speakers to emphasize the point they are making and should not be seen as negation of what has just been said. See also Tevaseu's speech in chapter 3.

13. She will do so by using a respect vocabulary term, *finagalo* 'wish, desire, opinion', which is appropriate in talking about chiefs but less appropriate when talking about one's kin (the particular passage in which this word is used is briefly discussed in Duranti 1984, 1992a).

14. See Ochs 1988 for a discussion of Samoan socialization practices. A similar relationship, called *adε*, between siblings of different sex is discussed among the Kaluli of Papua New Guinea by Schieffelin (1990).

15. In a fono some of the ceremonial roles, gestures, and ritual instruments found in other events are absent: thus, there is no use for the strainer made of hibiscus fiber (*fau*); in its place, a simple cloth is wrapped around the pounded kava, which nowadays may be bought already pulverized at the local store. This alteration eliminates the need for certain protocols, such as the person in charge of shaking the strainer (*tāfau*) (see Duranti 1981a).

16. Literally, *tufa'ava* means 'the one who distributes (*tufa*) kava (*'ava*)'. *Tufa* is a verb that is typically used for describing the act of deciding how to assign different gifts or food items on a given occasion. Ceremonially, it implies the power (*pule*) to decide the distribution of goods, a privilege that was given in ancient Samoa to matai from that section of the village who would act as the vanguard during a battle (see Brown 1908). This fact alone confirms the non-high-status role of the person in charge of distribution, a position that is not held for instance by high chiefs. The actual announcing (*fōlafola*) is done by another orator with a formal speech in which the kava roots and their donors are presented to the gathering of matai. Although common in ceremonies like the installation of titles or various forms of ritual exchanges, this formal presentation of kava roots was not performed in the type of fono discussed here.

17. In this case, as elsewhere unless otherwise stated, "in a fono" means "in a fono in Falefā." By no means do I intend to make general statements here about how fono are organized all over Western Samoa (even less in American Samoa).

18. By 1988, when I returned to Falefā for the third time, Lutu had in fact been given the title of Leutele.

19. I also found that, contrary to what is reported by Freeman (1983), formal greetings were not exchanged again after the meeting. For more discussion of Samoan ceremonial greetings, see Duranti 1992b.

20. For a discussion of different kinds of fono, see Duranti 1981a and Shore 1977.

21. Alai'a-Sā could have spoken either after all the first round of orators or in the fourth position, when the orator from his subvillage, Gaga'emalae, had the right to take the floor. This was said to be possible because the Alai'a-Sā title, as often the case with chiefs (ali'i) from the subvillage of Gaga'emalae, shared certain prerogatives with orators (tulāfale) and thus could speak on behalf of their subvillage on public occasions.

22. At the time when these events were taking place, four men held the title of Alai'a-Sā. This particular holder of the title, a man in his mid- to late sixties, was well known for his lack of conformity to social etiquette, something that of course was very upsetting to the other holders of the same title, including the senior orator Moe'ono, who was one of them (in Western Samoa, more than one person can hold the same title).

23. The relation between Alai'a-Sā's turn and 'Alo's is difficult to assess. If we assume that 'Alo was going to speak after Loa, which is possible given that 'Alo's title is from Sagapolu and an orator from this subvillage (usually, but not always, Moe'ono) always speaks second (see fig. 11), then Alai'a-Sā's speech is an interruption of 'Alo's speech or at least in competition with it. However, since Alai'a-Sā in fact speaks *before* 'Alo takes the floor, it is possible to interpret 'Alo's claim to the floor as a first attempt to stop Alai'a-Sā from speaking and hence taking away the floor from Moe'ono, who would have very likely opened up the discussion and thus presented in some detail the charges against Alai'a-Sā. In this case, Moe'ono will in fact have to wait until his next chance to talk before bringing out the charges. At that point, his attack on Alai'a-Sā will be merciless.

24. Other typical reactions were comments like 'the man is dying to be a speechmaker!' (*fia failāuga ā le tamaloa!*).

4. Politics and Verbal Art

1. The fact that Salmond refers to *take* at one point as one part of a speech, namely, the discussion of the topic (p. 53), and at another point as an entire, topical speech (p. 58), makes me think that perhaps Maori oratory exhibits some of the features of heteroglossia I will discuss in the rest of this chapter as characteristic of Samoan oratory.

2. Sermons, like any other form of public performance, are routinely evaluated in separate, often more private, contexts, when people discuss the preacher's ability to get a point across or his knowledge of the sacred scriptures. To give a feeling for what these discussions are like, I am reproducing here an excerpt from a discussion among three matai waiting for a meeting to start.

Matai in Saleapaga, 1981. Three matai are sitting in High Chief Salanoa Aukusitino's house waiting for other matai to show up: Salanoa Aukusitino (SA), orator F., and chief SM. Since F. and SM are members of the Congregational Christian Church whereas SA is Catholic, the discussion of the preacher's sermon is told as a story to and for SA.

F;   ((to SM)) *ga 'e loku fo'i- ga 'e loku (i) le afiafi*
Did you also (go to) church- did you go to the afternoon service
i le lāuga (a) le ali'i o: faia'oga lea (i Malua Fou)?
to the sermon of the gentleman who is a teacher (at the New Malua [College])?
[

SM; ((LG)) *hehe. ī. ī.*
((laughing)) hehe. Yeah. Yeah.

?;   *sole!*
Man!

SA; *i le ā?*
To what?

?;   *e-*
is-

F;   *le lāuga a le ali'i (fia) faia'oga Malua Fou lea,*
The sermon of the gentleman (who wants to be) a teacher at the New Malua (College),
(1.0)

F;   *ga lāuga i le mākou afiafi.*
(He) gave a sermon at our afternoon (service).
(1.0)

SA; *e ā?*
What (about it)?
(1.0)

F;   *'o le kagaka ali'i e- (. . .)*
The person, sir, is-
'ese fo'i oga uiga o le faife'au
the pastor's actions are really strange
'o lea kagaka lea a'oa'o.
that person who (is a) teacher.
(1.5)

SA; *(?) fai le mākou-*
(?) gave our-
[

F;   *'a lea- (. . .) e le'i umi le lāuga a le ali'i.*
How about (that)- . . . the gentleman's sermon is not long.

F;   *'ae (le) aukū ā le 'upu o le makua a le ali'i.*
But the words of the topic of the gentleman (don't) really have a point.
(1.0)
ga'o ka'u mai ā
(He) just told us
(1.5)

F;   *kāko(u) ō ā 'i le fale (ali'i)-*
we go then to the house (sirs)-
kāko ke maua ai le mapu filemū ma le-
(where) we (can) have some peaceful rest and-
(1.)

ko'afilemū (')o le fale o Ieova.
relief (that's) the Lord's house.
(2.0)
ia'. 'uma le lāug(h)a ((laughing)) *hehehehe.*
So. The sermon is over ((laughing)) hehehehe.
(1.5)

SM;   ((softer)) ia' oga le ka'u mai lā po 'o-
Right. Because (he) didn't tell us whe-
po 'o fea le kogu kū ai fale o Ieova, (?)
where in fact the house of the Lord is, (?)

3. Tupua, the son of Fuimaono and Oilau, was adopted by the king Muagututi'a and made king around A.D. 1700.

4. This expression refers to the kava announcer's subvillage, Sanonu, which is located inland, along the Falefā river. Other times the same part of the village is referred to as *āiga pule* 'family (with) authority' because the people from Sanonu have the right (*pule*) to divide up goods, kava included, during ceremonial encounters (see chap. 2 and note 16 on p. 183).

5. This list is a revised and expanded version of the one presented in Duranti 1984.

6. Thus, Moe'ono, in inviting the chiefs to give their opinion, on April 7, 1979, uses the term *lāuga* in its loose sense of formal speech:

2906   Moe'ono;   fai ea ali'i gi a kou lāuga,
Give then your speech sirs,
2907   po 'o lea ou koe fai aku fo'i.
before I speak again.
[
2908   Salanoa;   ia',
Okay,
2909   fa'a- se'i fai aku ā si a'u kamai makā'upu fa'amolemole.
let- let me please say a few things about the agenda.

On other occasions, Moe'ono would simply use the term *saunoaga* (pronounced /saugoaga/), that is, the respectful term for a chief's speech:

Fono of January 25, 1979.

Moe'ono;   ia' ali'i 'amaia se kou saugoaga a le kou kala.
okay, sirs, give us a speech from your side of the house.

5. The Grammar of Agency in Political Discourse

1. Ochs (1982, 1987) found that there were socially relevant factors in the distribution of the ergative marker *e*: among intimates in informal situations the ergative preposition *e* is left out more often than among non-intimates and in formal interactions. I should also mention here that in Samoan the Agent role

in a transitive clause can also be expressed by a nonemphatic preverbal clitic pronoun such as *'ou* 'I', *'e* 'you', *tā* 'we-dual-inclusive', and so on. In this and the next chapter, I will discuss only cases in which the Agent is expressed by full independent noun phrases (which include full independent pronouns, e.g., *'oe* 'you (singular)').

2. In a few cases, the absolutive noun in postverbal position may be preceded by the particle *'o*.

3. One of the seven cases is an Agent-verb sequence, that is, an utterance without an explicit (but equally understood) object noun phrase. Verb-Agent was a common syntactic type in my data (the second group after verb-Agent-object).

4. In more than 80 percent of the cases I examined (87 out of a total of 105 utterances), the Agent noun phrase follows the verb complex and is marked by the ergative *e*.

5. In other words, I have not only examined cases with all three major constituents expressed, namely, verb, Agent, and object, but also cases with only the verb and the Agent.

6. The total number of ergative Agents in this fono was 39. The difference in the January 25 fono and the April 7 fono may be explained in part by the fact that on April 7 three different items were discussed by the assembly, whereas on January 25 only one was discussed. Each time an agenda item is introduced, there is a high probability of ergative Agents appearing with the statements that define the reasons for the meeting. It is in these statements that we find accusations and complaints about people's actions. As I will discuss later in the chapter, such speech acts are a likely context for the use of ergative Agents.

7. See Appadurai 1990 for an ethnographically grounded discussion of praise toward deities and people of power in another society, Hindu India.

8. In this recognition of a job done, the first orator, Taofiuailoa (or Loa), is referred to with a title, /le Laukogia/ (see note 9), which is further removed from his individual persona. It is, in other words, only as a representative of a larger body or "office" that Loa is given recognition.

9. The term *Lautogia* is a special title given to the orator from the subvillage of Sanonu who introduces the topic of the day (*matā'upu o le fono*) in the first speech (see chap. 4).

10. The pronoun *'oe* 'you' receives particular emphasis here where it doubles the information already conveyed by the preverbal second-person singular clitic pronoun *'ē*. Grammatically speaking, this is an example of what syntacticians call "right-dislocation," although in the case of Samoan, where the full subject noun phrase typically appears after the verb, that is, on the right, and the "copy" pronoun (in this case the clitic *'ē*) must appear before the verb, the notion of dislocation seems inappropriate. It should be added that this is a rather complex construction that should be seen either as a case in which the preposition *'i* 'in' before /le gu'u/ 'the village' is left out or as a case of noun-incorporation, in which /mea leaga/ is the incorporated nominal and /le gu'u/ has become the object (in the absolutive case).

11. Cook (1991) suggested that the presence of a *-Cia* suffix (the vowel *-a* in this case) on the transitive verb in this example is itself a marker of "Agent

Defocusing" (see Chung 1978 and Cook 1988 on the history and functions of this suffix and Duranti 1981a on the higher occurrence of verbs with *-Cia* suffixes in the fono speeches).

12. A particularly telling example of this use of ergative marking is given in the example below, in which the senior orator Moe'ono uses a negative construction with a full ergative Agent in talking about himself:

Fono of April 7, 1979.

808	Moe'ono;	*e lē 'o pāloka.*
		it is not the elections.
809		*pei ā go'u kaulala aku,*
		As I said (to you),
810		*'o le gakula o kagaka ou ke lē fiafia ai. . . .*
		it's people's nature (that) I don't like. . . .
811		*le gakula. . . .*
		the nature. . . .
812		*e le iloa e Moe'ogo se mea. . . .*
		TA NEG know ERG Moe'ono ART thing
		Moe'ono doesn't know anything. . . .
813		*'a lo kākou gu'u lava e 'aumaia, . . .*
		but our very village gets (the news), . . .
814		*'o le ō mai o Keva ma Fagaloa, . . .*
		The going of Teva and (the people from) Fagaloa, . . .
815		*ō iā Iuli, . . .*
		go to Iuli, . . .
816		*ōmai- ō age iā- iā Savea.*
		come- go (there) to- to Savea.

In this case, the rhetorical strength of Moe'ono's speech is given by the fact that he is telling everyone not only that *he* as an individual living in the community didn't know about the secret campaigning going on in the village—here people's "visits" to Iuli (line 815) and Savea (line 816) hint at the secret commerce of votes—but that he as *Moe'ono*, the senior orator, didn't know, while the village did know (line 813). The use of the ergative Agent here establishes Moe'ono as an important actor in the events. While complaining about his exclusion from the political action in his community, Moe'ono Kolio is also rebuilding his public persona as someone who should count because he is "Moe'ono."

13. I was in fact tape recording and I had been writing down information that would not be available on the audiotape (people's names, where they were sitting, who was arriving, who was leaving, and so on). Although the tape recorder was visible, Fuimaono was not in a position to know what I was writing down.

14. The courts in the capital (Apia) are thought of as an "alternative" legal system, one that is strongly associated with the modern Samoan state and with the Western legal system, as opposed to the "tradition" (*aganu'u*), which favors intra- or inter-village settlements. Curiously, the term *tulāfono* has come to acquire the double meaning of 'laws (in general),' including the laws established

by the village fono, and the modern state law and state bureaucracy, which must be avoided whenever a more "local" solution can be invoked.

15. Salanoa Aukusitino was not present on January 25. In his place, another chief, Salanoa Mago, spoke as representative of the chiefly side or 'Āiga (see chap. 2, the discussion of the fa'alupega). Despite the apparent homonymy, Salanoa Mago's title was not a "Lealaisalanoa" but an "Alaisalanoa," and although he was at the time the village *pulenu'u* (a sort of "mayor" or government representative), Salanoa Mago was considered extremely softspoken and rarely participated in the fono I recorded. Such a perception by the people in the village is well reflected in his speech, which contains no instance of ergative Agents.

16. One of the nine cases is a bit peculiar. The ergative agent (/e le Agaga/ 'ERG the Spirit') appears after a predicate, /pau/, that is not usually considered a transitive verb. Another potential case, which I decided to leave out of the final count, was uttered by Salanoa in the blessing of the kava in the second ceremony of the day (line 1966) and, unlike the other cases, is a directive, in which Salanoa asks God to bless the day:

fa'amaguia mai le Akua i- koe makā'upu o le kākou aso!
bless   DX ART Lord in again   topic of ART our-INC day
God bless (us) in- the rest of the agenda of our day!

Given the absence of the ergative marker on the post-verbal Agent (/le Akua/) and the preposition /i/ in the following phrase /i- koe makā'upu o le kākou aso/, there is also a possibility here that Salanoa is treating the transitive verb /fa'amaguia/ as a semi-transitive or "middle verb" (see Chung 1978; Cook 1988), in which case /le Akua/ would not be an ergative Agent and the object (or actually the "middle object" to be distinguished from the object of transitive clauses) would not be the implicit 'us' (partly conveyed by the deictic particle /mai/) but the prepositional phrase that follows /le Akua/. In the latter interpretation, the utterance would mean 'God bless our next topic of the day'.

17. This does not mean that Moe'ono never produced ergative Agents referring to God, but simply that, proportionally, he did it much less than other matai. On the meeting of January 25, for instance, Moe'ono's sixteen ergative Agents (see table 6) included three references to God. The mention of God was usually part of attempts at softening his attack on a particular party.

6. From Political Arenas to Everyday Settings

1. This is the way the participants themselves characterized their actions in one of the recordings I will be analyzing later in this chapter. In the segment below, I (A. in the transcript) had just arrived with my camcorder to record four women who are about to have lunch. The exchange of greetings is at the beginning of the recording. After the exchange of greetings, one of the women, Vg., jokingly refers to her own and the others' future actions as 'gossip' /faikala/.

Women eating.

> A;   *mālō!*
>   Congratulations/hello!
>   *(1.0)*
> ?;   *mālō!*
>   Hello!
>   [
> Vg; *mālō Alesana!*
>   Hello Alesana!
>   *(0.5)*
>   *lea 'o le 'ā fai le mea'ai.*
>   Now (we) are going to eat.
>   *(1.0)*
> A;   *lelei.*
>   Good.
> Vg; *e ā?*
>   What?
>   *(1.0)*
> A;   *fai.*
>   Do (it).
>   *(1.0)*
> → Vg; *ma faikala?*
>   And do some gossip?
>   *(1.0)*
> A;   *ioe.*
>   Yes.
> Vt; ((LG)) *haha//haha!*
> Vg; *ia', lelei.*
>   Okay, good.

2. The word /kolosisi/ (a borrowing from English *cold chisel*) is used here first as a noun and then (right after) as a verb, as indicated by the use of the pronoun /ai/ that follows the second occurrence of /kolosisi/.

3. As I discussed in chapter 5, when a potential Agent is mentioned as part of a genitive construction, its "agency" is reduced or mitigated.

4. This was the case in a fono only when the macro-turn structure of the proceedings (see chap. 3) broke down and quasi-conversational exchanges took place, such as toward the end of a meeting or during a break (see the discussion of examples [39] and [40] in chap. 5).

5. The little girl's use of her mother's name (or title, if she has one) in line 507 instead of the kinship term is the common way of addressing one's kin in Samoa, as is also shown in line 521.

6. This is the verb *va'ai* 'to see, look' with the so-called " -*C(i)a* suffix" (see Cook 1988). In this case, the suffix -*a* does not make the middle verb *va'ai* transitive, but it gives it an emphatic connotation, similar to the English *look at that!*

7. The /fo'i / implies that it is something that both mutually know about.

8. Earlier on, his father had called him (see above). This is taken as talking back to his mother. The same feeling is present in the next turn, when he talks to his father as if finding a reason to justify himself against his mother's wish.

9. This use of the term *ali'i,* literally 'chief' (from Proto-Polynesian *ariki), as an address term is not gender specific and can be used with adults and children alike.

10. This is a variant of the affirmative answer *ioe* 'yes' and not the second person singular pronoun *'oe.*

11. Alternative hearing: /ia' lā 'ua 'ave aku ā e le keige o Moaga/ (*Moana,* like all other proper names in this transcript, is a pseudonym).

12. This is the plural form of the verb *ta'e* 'break, smash' (said of pottery, glass), despite the fact that the understood Agent is the boy mentioned in the prior discourse. A possible explanation for the plural here might be the fact that it is understood as referring to many different parts of the house.

13. The highest chief in the village; see the discussion of the fa'alupega in chapter 2.

14. Thus, for instance, during my first stay, when I was 28, I received all three descriptors. I was at times /kama/ 'boy' (see example [40] in chap. 5), other times /kamaloa/ 'man', and finally even /koea'iga/ 'old man.' On the expression of affect in Samoan, see Ochs 1988.

15. This is a mistake. The right expression is to 'eat' (*'ai*) marijuana and not 'drink' (*inu*). This shows the little familiarity these women have with the activity they are discussing here.

16. This is understood as the singular despite the fact that the absence of the article *le* usually indicates plurality, for example, *le tama* 'the/a boy' versus *tama* 'boys'. In this case, however, the plural form would be different, namely, /kamaiki/ (*tamaiti*).

17. This is the kind of incident that is taken care of by a small committee of matai (*komiti*) rather than by the village fono.

7. Conclusions

1. A further distinction has been recently made by Chafe between "active" and "semi-active" (corresponding to Du Bois's "accessible").

2. An exception to this tendency can be found in line 1915 of example (26) in chapter 5. In that example /le Akua/ 'the Lord' is mentioned in two adjacent utterances and the second time it is expressed by a lexical Agent:

1914   *pau lea kākou si'i le vi'iga i le Akua.*
       The only (thing) let us raise the praise <u>to the Lord</u>.
1915   *'ua faia e le Akua mea kekele,*
       <u>The Lord</u> has done many things,

3. An obvious problem that Du Bois (1987) faced in his study is the low number of clauses with lexical Agents in his corpus, namely, 11 (out of 384).

References

Appadurai, A. Topographies of the Self: Praise and Emotion in Hindu India. In *Language and the Politics of Emotion*, ed. C. A. Lutz and L. Abu-Lughod, 92–112. Cambridge: Cambridge University Press, 1990.

Atkinson, J. M., and P. Drew. *Order in Court: The Organisation of Verbal Interaction in Judicial Settings*. London: Macmillan, 1979.

Bakhtin, M. M. *The Dialogic Imagination*, trans. C. Emerson and M. Holquist. Austin: University of Texas Press, 1981.

Bateson, G. *Steps to an Ecology of Mind*. New York: Ballantine Books, 1972.

Bauman, R. *Verbal Art as Performance*. Rowley, Mass.: Newbury House, 1977.

———. Contextualization, Tradition and the Dialogue of Genres: Icelandic Legends of the *Kraftaskáld*. In *Rethinking Context: Language as an Interactive Phenomenon*, ed. A. Duranti and C. Goodwin, 125–145. Cambridge: Cambridge University Press, 1992.

Bauman, R., and J. Sherzer. *Exploration in the Ethnography of Speaking*. Cambridge: Cambridge University Press, 1974.

———. The Ethnography of Speaking. *Annual Reviews 4* (Palo Alto, Annual Reviews, Inc.), 95–119, 1975.

Besnier, N. Conflict Management, Gossip and Affective Meaning on Nukulaelae. In *Disentangling: Conflict Discourse in the Pacific*, ed. K. Watson-Gegeo and G. White, 290–334. Stanford, Calif.: Stanford University Press, 1990a.

———. Language and Affect. *Annual Review of Anthropology* 19: 419–451, 1990b.

Bloch, M. Introduction. In *Political Language and Oratory in Traditional Society*, ed. M. Bloch, 1–28. London: Academic Press, 1975a.

———. Review of *Explorations in the Ethnography of Speaking*, ed. R. Bauman and J. Sherzer. *Language in Society* 5: 229–234, 1976.

————. *Ritual, History, and Power: Selected Papers in Anthropology*. London: London School of Economics, 1989.

————, ed. *Political Language and Oratory in Traditional Society*. London: Academic Press, 1975b.

Bourdieu, P. *Outline of a Theory of Practice*, trans. R. Nice. Cambridge: Cambridge University Press, 1977.

Brenneis, D. Grog and Gossip in Bhatgaon: Style and Substance in Fiji Indian Conversation. *American Ethnologist* 11: 487–506, 1984.

————. Language and Disputing. *Annual Review of Anthropology* 17: 221–237, 1988.

Brenneis, D. L., and F. R. Myers, eds. *Dangerous Words: Language and Politics in the Pacific*. New York: New York University Press, 1984.

Briggs, C. L. *Learning How to Ask: A Sociolinguistic Appraisal of the Role of the Interview in Social Science Research*. Cambridge: Cambridge University Press, 1986.

————. *Competence in Performance: The Creativity of Tradition in Mexicano Verbal Art*. Philadelphia: University of Pennsylvania Press, 1988.

Brown, G. *George Brown Missionary and Explorer*. London: Hodder and Stoughton, 1908.

Brown, P., and S. C. Levinson. *Politeness: Some Universals in Language Usage*. Cambridge: Cambridge University Press, 1987.

Burling, R. Review of *Political Language and Oratory in Traditional Society*, ed. M. Bloch. *American Anthropologist* 79(3): 698–700, 1977.

Carnap, R. *Introduction to Semantics*. Cambridge, Mass.: Harvard University Press, 1942.

Chafe, W. Givenness, Contrastiveness, Definiteness, Subjects, Topics, and Points of View. In *Subject and Topic*, ed. C. N. Li, 25–56. New York: Academic Press, 1976.

————. The Flow of Thought and the Flow of Language. In *Syntax and Semantics: Vol. 12, Discourse and Syntax*, ed. T. Givon, 159–181. New York: Academic Press, 1979.

————. Cognitive Constraints on Information Flow. In *Coherence and Grounding in Discourse*, ed. R. S. Tomlin. Amsterdam: Benjamins, 1987.

————, ed. *The Pear Stories: Cognitive, Cultural, and Linguistic Aspects of Narrative Production*. Advances in Discourse Processes. Norwood, N.J.: Ablex, 1980.

Chomsky, N. *Aspects of the Theory of Syntax*. Cambridge, Mass.: MIT Press, 1965.

Chung, S. *Case Marking and Grammatical Relations in Polynesian*. Austin: University of Texas Press, 1978.

Cicourel, A. V. The Interpenetration of Communicative Contexts: Examples from Medical Encounters. In *Rethinking Context: Language as an Interactive Phenomenon*, ed. A. Duranti and C. Goodwin, 291–310. Cambridge: Cambridge University Press, 1992.

Clifford, J. *The Predicament of Culture: Twentieth-Century Ethnography, Literature, and Art*. Cambridge, Mass.: Harvard University Press, 1988.

————. Notes on (Field)notes. In *Fieldnotes: The Makings of Anthropology*, ed. R. Sanjek, 47–70. Ithaca, N.Y.: Cornell University Press, 1990.

Clifford, J., and G. E. Marcus, eds. *Writing Culture: The Poetics and Politics of Ethnography.* Berkeley, Los Angeles, London: University of California Press, 1986.

Cole, M. The Zone of Proximal Development: Where Culture and Cognition Create Each Other. In *Culture, Communication, and Cognition: Vygotskian Perspectives,* ed. J. Wertsch, 146–161. Cambridge: Cambridge University Press, 1985.

Comaroff, J. Talking Politics: Oratory and Authority in a Tswana Chiefdom. In *Political Language and Oratory in Traditional Society,* ed. M. Bloch, 141–161. London: Academic Press, 1975.

Comrie, B. Ergativity. In *Syntactic Typology: Studies in the Phenomenology of Language,* ed. W. P. Lehmann, 329–394. Austin: University of Texas Press, 1978.

Cook, K. W. A Cognitive Analysis of Grammatical Relations, Case, and Transitivity in Samoan. Ph.D. diss., University of California, San Diego, 1988.

———. The Samoan *Cia* Suffix as an Indicator of Agent Defocusing. *Pragmatics* 1(2): 145–167, 1991.

Craig, C. G. Jacaltec: Field Work in Guatemala. In *Languages and Their Speakers,* ed. T. Shopen, 3–57. Cambridge, Mass.: Winthrop, 1979.

Dixon, R. W. Ergativity. *Language* 55: 59–138, 1979.

Dreyfus, H. L. *Being-in-the-World: A Commentary on Heidegger's* Being and Time, Division I. Cambridge, Mass.: MIT Press, 1991.

Du Bois, J. The Discourse Basis of Ergativity. *Language* 63: 805–855, 1987.

Duranti, A. *The Samoan Fono: A Sociolinguistic Study.* Pacific Linguistics Monographs, Series B., vol. 80. Canberra: Australian National University, Department of Linguistics, 1981a.

———. Speechmaking and the Organisation of Discourse in a Samoan Fono. *Journal of the Polynesian Society* 90(3): 357–400, 1981b.

———. Samoan Speechmaking Across Social Events: One Genre In and Out of a Fono. *Language in Society* 12: 1–22, 1983.

———. Lauga and Talanoaga: Two Speech Genres in a Samoan Political Event. In *Dangerous Words: Language and Politics in the Pacific,* ed. D. L. Brenneis and F. Myers, 217–237. New York: New York University Press, 1984.

———. Sociocultural Dimensions of Discourse. In *Handbook of Discourse Analysis: Vol. 1, Disciplines of Discourse,* ed. T. A. V. Dijk, 193–230. New York: Academic Press, 1985.

———. Intentions, Language and Social Action in a Samoan Context. *Journal of Pragmatics* 12: 13–33, 1988.

———. Doing Things with Words: Conflict, Understanding and Change in a Samoan Fono. In *Disentangling: Conflict Discourse in Pacific Societies,* ed. K. Watson-Gegeo and G. White, 459–489. Stanford, Calif.: Stanford University Press, 1990a.

———. Code Switching and Conflict Management in Samoan Multiparty Interaction. *Pacific Studies* 14(1): 1–30, 1990b.

———. Language in Context and Language as Context: The Samoan Respect Vocabulary. In *Rethinking Context: Language as an Interactive Phenome-*

non, ed. A. Duranti and C. Goodwin, 77–99. Cambridge: Cambridge University Press, 1992a.

———. Language and Bodies in Social Space: Samoan Ceremonial Greetings. *American Anthropologist* 94: 657–691, 1992b.

Duranti, A., and C. Goodwin, eds. *Rethinking Context: Language as an Interactive Phenomenon.* Cambridge: Cambridge University Press, 1992.

Duranti, A., and E. Ochs. Literacy Instruction in a Samoan Village. In *Acquisition of Literacy: Ethnographic Perspectives,* ed. B. B. Schieffelin and P. Gilmore, 213–232. Norwood, N.J.: Ablex, 1986.

———. Genitive Constructions and Agency in Samoan Discourse. *Studies in Language* 14(1): 1–23, 1990.

Earle, T., ed. *Chiefdoms: Power, Economy, and Ideology.* Cambridge: Cambridge University Press, 1992.

Ervin-Tripp, S. On Sociolinguistic Rules: Alternation and Co-occurrence. In *Directions in Sociolinguistics: The Ethnography of Communication,* ed. J. J. Gumperz and D. Hymes, 213–250. New York: Henry Holt, 1972.

Fillmore, C. The Case for Case. In *Universals of Linguistic Theory,* ed. E. Bach and R. T. Harms, 1–88. New York: Henry Holt, 1968.

———. Verbs of Judging: An Exercise in Semantic Description. In *Studies in Linguistic Semantics,* ed. C. J. Fillmore and D. T. Langendoen, 273–289. New York: Henry Holt, 1971.

———. *An Alternative to Checklist Theories of Meaning.* First Annual Meeting of the Berkeley Linguistic Society, Berkeley, Department of Linguistics, University of California at Berkeley, 1975.

———. The Case for Case Reopened. In *Syntax and Semantics: Vol. 8, Grammatical Relations,* ed. P. Cole, 59–81. New York: Academic Press, 1977.

Firth, R. *We, the Tikopia.* London: Allen and Unwin, 1936.

———. Postures and Gestures of Respect. In *Échanges et communications: mélanges offerts à Claude Lévi-Strauss à l' occasion de son 60éme anniversaire,* ed. J. Pouillon and P. Maranda, 188–209. The Hague: Mouton, 1970.

———. Speechmaking and Authority in Tikopia. In *Political Language and Oratory in Traditional Society,* ed. M. Bloch, 29–63. London: Academic Press, 1975.

Frake, C. O. How to Enter a Yakan House. In *Sociocultural Dimensions of Language Use,* ed. M. Sanchez and B. G. Blount, 25–40. New York: Academic Press, 1975.

Freeman, D. *Margaret Mead and Samoa: The Making and Unmaking of an Anthropological Myth.* Cambridge, Mass.: Harvard University Press, 1983.

Gailey, C. *Kingship to Kingship: Gender Hierarchy and State Formation in the Tongan Islands.* Austin: University of Texas Press, 1987.

Gazdar, G., E. Klein, and G. K. Pullum. *Generalized Phrase Structure Grammar.* Cambridge, Mass.: Harvard University Press, 1985.

Geertz, C. *The Interpretation of Cultures.* New York: Basic Books, 1973.

———. *Local Knowledge: Further Essays in Interpretive Anthropology.* New York: Basic Books, 1983.

Gibson, J. J. *The Ecological Approach to Visual Perception.* Hillsdale, N.J.: Erlbaum, 1986.

Giddens, A. *Central Problems in Social Theory: Action, Structure and Contradiction in Social Analysis.* Berkeley, Los Angeles, London: University of California Press, 1979.

———. *The Constitution of Society: Outline of the Theory of Structuration.* Berkeley, Los Angeles, London: University of California Press, 1984.

Goffman, E. *Frame Analysis: An Essay on the Organization of Experience.* New York: Harper and Row, 1974.

Goldman, I. *Ancient Polynesian Society.* Chicago: University of Chicago Press, 1970.

Goldman, L. *Talk Never Dies.* London: Tavistock, 1983.

Goodwin, M. H. He-Said-She-Said: Formal Cultural Procedures for the Construction of a Gossip Dispute Activity. *American Ethnologist* 7: 674–695, 1980.

———. "Instigating": Storytelling as a Social Process. *American Ethnologist* 9: 799–819, 1982a.

———. Processes of Dispute Management Among Urban Black Children. *American Ethnologist* 9: 76–96, 1982b.

———. *He-Said-She-Said: Talk as Social Organization among Black Children.* Bloomington: Indiana University Press, 1990.

Grice, P. H. Logic and Conversation. In *Syntax and Semantics,* vol. 3: Speech Acts, ed. P. Cole and J. L. Morgan, 41–58. New York: Academic Press, 1975.

Grimshaw, A. *Conflict Talk.* Cambridge: Cambridge University Press, 1990.

Gumperz, J. J. Introduction. In *Directions in Sociolinguistics: The Ethnography of Communication,* by J. J. Gumperz and D. Hymes. New York: Holt, Rinehart and Winston, 1–25, 1972.

Gumperz, J. J., and D. Hymes. *The Ethnography of Communication.* Special Issue of *American Anthropologist,* 1964.

———. *Directions in Sociolinguistics: The Ethnography of Communication.* New York: Holt, Rinehart and Winston, 1972.

Hägerstrand, T. Space, Time and Human Conditions. In *Dynamic Allocation of Urban Space.* Farnborough: Saxon House, 1975.

Hanks, W. F. *Referential Practice: Language and Lived Space among the Maya.* Chicago: University of Chicago Press, 1990.

Haviland, J. B. *Gossip, Reputation, and Knowledge in Zinacantan.* Chicago: University of Chicago Press, 1977.

———. "Con Buenos Chiles": Talk, Targets and Teasing in Zinacantan. *Text* 6(3): 249–282, 1986.

———. "That Was the Last Time I Seen Them, and No More": Voices Through Time in Australian Aboriginal Autobiography. *American Ethnologist* 18(2): 331–361, 1991.

Heidegger, M. *Being and Time.* New York: Harper and Row, 1962.

———. *The Basic Problems of Phenomenology,* rev. ed. Bloomington: Indiana University Press, 1982/1988.

Henry, B. F. *History of Samoa.* Apia: Commercial Printers, 1979.

Hogbin, H. I. *Law and Order in Polynesia.* New York: Harcourt, Brace, 1934.

Hojer, H. Anthropological Linguistics. In *Trends in European and American Linguistics 1930–1960,* ed. C. Mohrmann, A. Sommerfelt, and J. Whatmough, 110–125. Utrecht and Antwerp: Spectrum, 1961.

Hopper, P., and S. A. Thompson. Transitivity in Grammar and Discourse. *Language* 56: 251–299, 1980.

Hovdhaugen, E. *The Chronology of Three Samoan Sound Changes.* Papers from the Fourth International Conference on Austronesian Linguistics, Pacific Linguistics, 1986.

Howard, A., and J. Kirkpatrick. Social Organization. In *Developments in Polynesian Ethnology,* ed. A. Howard and R. Borofsky, 47–94. Honolulu: University of Hawaii Press, 1989.

Hymes, D. On Communicative Competence. In *Sociolinguistics,* ed. J. B. Pride and J. Holmes, 269–285. Harmondsworth, Middlesex: Penguin, 1972a.

———. Models of the Interaction of Language and Social Life. In *Directions in Sociolinguistics: The Ethnography of Communication,* ed. J. J. Gumperz and D. Hymes, 35–71. New York: Holt, Rinehart and Winston, 1972b.

———. *Foundations in Sociolinguistics: An Ethnographic Approach.* Philadelphia: University of Pennsylvania Press, 1974a.

———. Ways of Speaking. In *Explorations in the Ethnography of Speaking,* ed. R. Bauman and J. Sherzer, 433–451. Cambridge: Cambridge University Press, 1974b.

———. Breakthrough into Performance. In *Folklore: Performance and Communication,* ed. D. Ben-Amos and K. S. Goldstein, 11–74. The Hague: Mouton, 1975.

Irvine, J. T. Formality and Informality in Communicative Events. *American Anthropologist* 81: 773–790, 1979.

Johnson, A., and O. R. Johnson. Quality into Quantity: On the Measurement Potential of Ethnographic Fieldnotes. In *Fieldnotes: The Makings of Anthropology,* ed. R. Sanjek, 161–186. Ithaca, N.Y.: Cornell University Press, 1990.

Keenan, E. L. Semantic Correlates of the Ergative/Absolutive Distinction. *Linguistics* 22: 197–223, 1984.

Keenan, E. O. A Sliding Sense of Obligatoriness: The Poly-Structure of Malagasy. *Language in Society* 2: 225–243, 1973.

———. Conversation and Oratory in Vakinankaratra, Madagascar. Ph.D. diss., University of Pennsylvania, 1974.

———. Questions of Immediate Concern. In *Questions and Politeness,* ed. E. N. Goody, 44–55. Cambridge: Cambridge University Press, 1978.

Keenan, E. O., and B. B. Schieffelin. Topic as a Discourse Notion: A Study of Topic in the Conversations of Children and Adults. In *Subject and Topic,* ed. C. N. Li, 335–384. New York: Academic Press, 1976.

Keesing, F., and M. Keesing. *Elite Communication in Samoa.* Palo Alto, Calif: Stanford University Press, 1956.

Kertzer, D. I. *Ritual, Politics, Power.* New Haven, Conn.: Yale University Press, 1988.

Krämer, A. *Die Samoa-Inseln.* Stuttgart: Schwertzerbartsche, 1902/3.

Kristeva, J. The Bounded Text. In *Contemporary Literary Criticism,* ed. R. C. Davis, 448–466. New York: Longman, 1986.

Kuipers, J. C. *Power in Performance: The Creation of Textual Authority in Weyewa Ritual Speech.* Philadelphia: University of Pennsylvania Press, 1990.

Labov, W. *Sociolinguistic Patterns.* Philadelphia: University of Pennsylvania Press, 1972a.

———. *Language in the Inner City: Studies in the Black English Vernacular.* Philadelphia: University of Pennsylvania Press, 1972b.

Lave, J., and E. Wenger. *Situated Learning: Legitimate Peripheral Participation.* Cambridge: Cambridge University Press, 1991.

Lawrence, D., and S. Low. The Built Environment and Spatial Form. *Annual Review of Anthropology* 19: 453–505, 1990.

Leach, E. The Influence of Cultural Context on Non-Verbal Communication in Man. In *Non-Verbal Communication,* ed. R. Hinde, 315–347. Cambridge: Cambridge University Press, 1972.

Leech, G. N. *Principles of Pragmatics.* London: Longman, 1983.

Levinson, S. C. *Pragmatics.* Cambridge: Cambridge University Press, 1983.

Lindstrom, L. Context Contests: Debatable Truth Statements on Tanna (Vanuatu). In *Rethinking Context: Language as an Interactive Phenomenon,* ed. A. Duranti and C. Goodwin, 101–124. Cambridge: Cambridge University Press, 1992.

Lyons, J. *Semantics.* 2 vols. Cambridge: Cambridge University Press, 1977.

Macaulay, R. Polyphonic Monologues: Quoted Direct Speech in Oral Narratives. *IPrA Papers in Pragmatics* 1(2): 1–34, 1987.

Mageo, J. M. Male Transvestism and Cultural Change in Samoa. *American Anthropologist* 19(3): 443–459, 1992.

Malinowski, B. *Coral Gardens and Their Magic.* 2 vols. London: Allen and Urwin, 1935.

Mata'afa, T. F. *Lauga: Samoan Oratory.* M. A. thesis, University of Auckland, New Zealand, 1985.

Mead, M. *Social Organization of Manu'a.* Honolulu: Bishop Museum Press, 1930.

———. The Samoans. In *Cooperation and Competition among Primitive Peoples,* ed. M. Mead, 282–312. Boston: Beacon Press, 1937.

Milner, G. B. The Samoan Vocabulary of Respect. *Journal of the Royal Anthropological Institute* 91: 296–317, 1961.

———. *Samoan Dictionary: Samoan-English English-Samoan.* London: Oxford University Press, 1966.

Moerman, M. *Talking Culture: Ethnography and Conversation Analysis.* Philadelphia: University of Pennsylvania Press, 1988.

Morris, C. W. Foundations of the Theory of Signs. In *International Encyclopedia of Unified Science,* 77–138. Chicago: University of Chicago Press, 1938.

Mosel, U., and E. Hovdhaugen. *Samoan Reference Grammar.* Oslo: Scandinavian University Press, 1992.

Myers, F., and D. L. Brenneis. Introduction: Language and Politics in the Pacific. In *Dangerous Words: Language and Politics in the Pacific,* ed. D. L. Brenneis and F. Myers, 1–29. New York: New York University Press, 1984.

Ochs, E. Transcription as Theory. In *Developmental Pragmatics,* ed. E. Ochs and B. B. Schieffelin, 43–72. New York: Academic Press, 1979.

———. Ergativity and Word Order in Samoan Child Language. *Language* 58(3): 646–671, 1982.

———. Variation and Error: A Sociolinguistic Study of Language Acquisition in Samoa. In *The Crosslinguistic Study of Language Acquisition,* ed. D. I. Slobin, 783–838. Hillsdale, N.J.: Erlbaum, 1986.

———. The Impact of Stratification and Socialization on Men's and Women's Speech in Western Samoa. In *Language, Gender and Sex in Comparative Perspective,* ed. S. U. Philips, S. Steele, and C. Tanz, 50–70. Cambridge: Cambridge University Press, 1987.

———. *Culture and Language Development: Language Acquisition and Language Socialization in a Samoan Village.* Cambridge: Cambridge University Press, 1988.

Ochs, E., C. Taylor, D. Rudolph, and R. Smith. Story-telling as a Theory-building Activity. *Discourse Processes* 15(1): 37–72, 1992.

Ochs, E., R. Smith, and C. Taylor. Dinner Narratives as Detective Stories. *Cultural Dynamics* 2: 238–257, 1989.

O le Tusi Fa'alupega o Samoa [Book of Samoan Ceremonial Addresses]. Apia: Malua Printing Press, 1958.

Pader, E. Inside Spatial Relations. *Arch. & Comport./Arch. Behav.* 4: 251–267, 1988.

Paine, R., ed. *Politically Speaking: Cross-Cultural Studies of Rhetoric.* Philadelphia: Institute for the Study of Human Issues, 1981.

Pawley, A. K. Samoan Morphosyntax. *Anthropological Linguistics* 8: 1–63, 1966.

Peters, A. M., and S. T. Boggs. Interactional Routines as Cultural Influences upon Language Acquisition. In *Language Socialization across Cultures,* ed. B. B. Schieffelin and E. Ochs, 80–96. Cambridge: Cambridge University Press, 1986.

Philips, S. *The Invisible Culture: Communication in Classroom and Community on the Warm Springs Indian Reservation.* New York: Longman, 1983.

———. Contextual Variation in Courtroom Language Use: Noun Phrases Referring to Crimes. *International Journal of the Sociology of Language* 49: 29–50, 1984.

Pitt, D. *Tradition and Economic Progress in Samoa.* Oxford: Clarendon Press, 1969.

Radford, A. *Transformational Grammar: A First Course.* Cambridge: Cambridge University Press, 1988.

Sacks, H., E. A. Schegloff, and G. Jefferson. A Simplest Systematics for the Organization of Turn-Taking for Conversation. *Language* 50: 696–735, 1974.

Sahlins, M. *Culture and Practical Reason.* Chicago: University of Chicago Press, 1976.

Salmond, A. Mana Makes the Man: A Look at Maori Oratory and Politics. In

Political Language and Oratory in Traditional Society, ed. M. Bloch, 45–63. London: Academic Press, 1975.

Samarin, W. J. *Field Linguistics.* New York: Henry Holt, 1967.

Sanjek, Roger, ed. *Fieldnotes: The Makings of Anthropology.* Ithaca, N.Y.: Cornell University Press, 1990.

Schegloff, E. A., G. Jefferson, and H. Sacks. The Preference for Self-Correction in the Organization of Repair in Conversation. *Language* 53: 361–382, 1977.

Schegloff, E. A., and H. Sacks. Opening Up Closings. *Semiotica* 8: 289–327, 1973.

Schenkein, J. *Studies in the Organization of Conversational Interaction.* New York: Academic Press, 1978.

Schieffelin, B. B. Teasing and Shaming in Kaluli Children's Interactions. In *Language Socialization Across Cultures*, ed. B. B. Schieffelin and E. Ochs, 165–181. Cambridge: Cambridge University Press, 1986.

———. *The Give and Take of Everyday Life: Language Socialization of Kaluli Children.* Cambridge: Cambridge University Press, 1990.

Schieffelin, B. B., and E. Ochs, eds. *Language Socialization Across Cultures.* Cambridge: Cambridge University Press, 1986.

Schultz, D. E. *Samoan Proverbial Expressions (Alaga'upu fa'a-Samoa).* Auckland: Polynesian Press, 1953.

Searle, J. The Classification of Illocutionary Acts. *Language in Society* 5(1): 1–23, 1976.

Searle, J. R., and D. Vanderveken. *Foundations of Illocutionary Logic.* Cambridge: Cambridge University Press, 1985.

Sharff, S. *The Elements of Cinema: Toward a Theory of Cinesthetic Impact.* New York: Columbia University Press, 1982.

Sherzer, J. *Kuna Ways of Speaking: An Ethnographic Perspective.* Austin: University of Texas Press, 1983.

Shore, B. *A Samoan Theory of Action: Social Control and Social Order in a Polynesian Paradox.* Chicago: University of Chicago Press, 1977.

———. *Sala'ilua: A Samoan Mystery.* New York: Columbia University Press, 1982.

———. Mana and Tapu. In *Development in Polynesian Ethnology*, ed. A. Howard and R. Borofsky, 137–173. Honolulu: University of Hawaii Press, 1989.

Silverstein, M. Hierarchy of Features of Ergativity. In *Grammatical Categories in Australian Languages*, ed. R. M. W. Dixon, 112–171. Canberra: Australian Institute of Aboriginal Studies, 1976.

———. The Functional Stratification of Language and Ontogenesis. In *Culture, Communication and Cognition: Vygotskian Perspectives*, ed. J. V. Wertsch, 205–235. Cambridge: Cambridge University Press, 1985a.

———. The Culture of Language in Chinookan Narrative Texts; or, On Saying that . . . in Chinookan. In *Grammar Inside and Outside the Clause*, ed. J. Nichols and A. Woodbury, 132–171. Cambridge: Cambridge University Press, 1985b.

Slackman, E., and K. Nelson. Acquisition of an Unfamiliar Script in Story Form by Young Children. *Child Development* 55(2): 329–340, 1984.

Tedlock, D. *The Spoken Word and the Work of Interpretation.* Philadelphia: University of Pennsylvania Press, 1983.

Tu'i, T. F. M. *Lāuga: Samoan Oratory.* Suva: University of the South Pacific, 1987.

Turner, V. *Dramas, Fields and Metaphors: Symbolic Action in Human Society.* Ithaca, N.Y.: Cornell University Press, 1974.

Valeri, V. *Kingship and Sacrifice.* Chicago: University of Chicago Press, 1985.

Verschueren, J., ed. *Pragmatics at Issue. Selected Papers of the International Pragmatics Conference, Antwerp, August 17–22, 1987.* Vol. I. Amsterdam: Benjamins, 1991.

Vološinov, V. N. *Marxism and the Philosophy of Language,* trans. L. Matejka and I. R. Titunik. New York: Seminar Press, 1973.

Vygotsky, L. S. *Mind in Society: The Development of Higher Psychological Processes.* Cambridge, Mass.: Harvard University Press, 1978.

Watson-Gegeo, K., and D. Gegeo. Calling Out and Repeating Routines in the Language Socialization of Basotho Children. In *Language Socialization Across Cultures,* ed. B. Schieffelin and E. Ochs, 17–50. Cambridge: Cambridge University Press, 1986.

Watson-Gegeo, K., and G. White, eds. *Disentangling: Conflict Discourse in Pacific Societies.* Stanford, Calif.: Stanford University Press, 1990.

Whorf, B. *Language, Thought, and Reality: Selected Writings of Benjamin Lee Whorf,* ed. J. B. Carroll. Cambridge, Mass.: M.I.T. Press, 1956.

Wittgenstein, L. *Philosophical Investigations,* trans. G. E. M. Anscombe. New York: Macmillan, 1953.

Index

Designer: U.C. Press staff
Compositor: Impressions, a division of Edwards Brothers, Inc.
Text: 10/13 ITC Galliard
Display: ITC Galliard
Printer: Edwards Brothers, Inc.
Binder: Edwards Brothers, Inc.